Organic

A Journalist's Quest to Discover the Truth behind Food Labeling

PETER LAUFER, PHD

LYONS PRESS
Guilford, Connecticut

An imprint of Globe Pequot Press

To buy books in quantity for corporate use
or incentives, call **(800) 962-0973**
or e-mail **premiums@GlobePequot.com.**

Lyons Press is an imprint of Globe Pequot Press.

Project editor: Meredith Dias
Layout: Adam Caporiccio

Library of Congress Cataloging-in-Publication Data is available on file.

ISBN 978-0-7627-9071-5

Printed in the United States of America

10 9 8 7 6 5 4 3 2 1

With love to

Sheila

Who triggered my appetite for this work

with approximately 14,235 meals (and counting)

Contents

Contents

Ninety percent of the diseases known to man are caused by cheap foodstuffs. You are what you eat.
—*from a* Bridgeport *(CT)* Telegram *advertisement for beef, perhaps where the cliché was coined, 1923*

In the abstract you can complain about Big Brother and how this is a program run amok, but when you actually look at the details, I think we've struck the right balance.
—*Barack Obama, defending hitherto secret government monitoring of citizens' telephone and Internet use, 2013*

There is not a crime, there is not a dodge, there is not a trick, there is not a swindle, there is not a vice which does not live by secrecy.
—*Joseph Pulitzer, from his mission statement for the Columbia University College of Journalism, 1903*

ORGANIC?

Those of us fortunate enough not to be worried about where our next meal is coming from nonetheless often act obsessed about food. We check how many calories are packed into this and how much fat (and what type) is in that. We're morbidly obese because we eat too much, and we're Karen Carpenter anorexic because we're worried we look too fat in those pants. We scarf up the latest fads when they promise us instant energy and long life, from nasty-tasting tough kale to magic potions of spirulina. We line up at overpriced restaurants just because some trendy reviewer showcases the eateries even while tables sit empty across the street at joints with great food. We stare dazzled at chef competitions as so-called celebrity cooks show us how to make complex dishes we'll never try to replicate in our own kitchens. We switch whimsically from strict vegan diets to debauched snout-to-tail pig feasts. And more and more, across America and around the globe, we seek organic groceries. Whatever the heck "organic" means.

I invite you, dear reader, to come with me as I chase a couple of food products produced in the Third World from my local grocery store shelves back to their point of origin, and to join me as I investigate whether we shoppers and cooks and eaters are being deceived by the seductive word "organic."

Growing awareness regarding the quality, value, and safety of the food supply is fueling surging growth in the organic food industry.

Giant retailers offer supermarket sections labeled "organic," filled with products claiming organic status. In addition to confusion and inconsistencies with formal definitions of the word "organic" as it pertains to food, globalization means that distributors are bringing products to the marketplace from locales far from home, locales rife with political and business corruption.

To check the validity of food labeled organic that is grown and processed in places with histories that make this claim suspect, I embarked on a project: to trace beans and nuts from my modest kitchen back toward where they were grown and processed. This book is not a trashing of the Third World nor a condemnation of organics. I believe an organic food diet is ideal and know that the First World is also rife with corruption. I report in these pages the story of a food distributor from my own Oregon county sentenced to federal prison for committing food-labeling fraud. Skepticism is appropriate throughout the food distribution system.

This story is a quest. I want to know what this buzzword "organic" really means outside of the privileged culinary environs where I live, especially when it is slapped on a growing number of foodstuffs— along with price tags substantially higher than the same banana or can of beans or bag of walnuts marked with what's becoming a disparaging term: "conventional"—or just "banana" or "beans" or "walnuts."

It seems obvious, but it's worth saying: We all eat. Perhaps that explains the continuing and growing success of books about food, especially those books that help us understand what we eat and why. However, the food-oriented bookshelf does not yet deal with the pivotal and crucial issue of provenance. We rarely ascertain the origins of most organic foods we consume. That provenance is suspect at best and tainted at worst. It's time to advance the debate from "Is organic better?" to "Is what's sold as organic really organic?" We need to question the organic guarantees the marketplace promises consumers who pay premium prices for organic food, question the integrity of the organic food chain, and question the morality of sourcing high-priced organic food in locales where farmworkers and food producers labor in abusive conditions. If we are what we eat, we need to know what we're eating and how it came to our dinner plates.

Annual organic food and drink sales just in the United States grew from one billion dollars in the early 1990s to about twenty-seven billion dollars in the subsequent twenty years, according to the USDA. When there's money to be made, the scam artists are never far behind.

NUTS AND BEANS

My wife, Sheila, brought home a bag of walnuts from Trader Joe's labeled "organic," and they tasted rancid. No big deal. These things happen. I was about to take them back across town to return them to the store, but first I decided to read the label. Walnuts they were for sure, and they were organic, claimed the label. It was the small print that caught my eye: organic and a product of [dramatic pause] *Kazakhstan.*

Call me a skeptic and a cynic, but my journalist's radar kicked in about here. As I was driving back to the store, I thought about the authoritarian regime in power in Kazakhstan, the struggling farmers over there, and the culture of bribery and corruption that lingers in most former Soviet republics. I wondered if there was anything organic about the spoiled nuts besides the word "organic" on the cellophane bag.

Of course Trader Joe's gave me my money back. The collegiate-looking clerk and I joked about the credibility of the Kazakhstan organic food industry. I went home with a replacement bag of conventionally grown California-sourced walnuts and pretty much forgot the episode.

Fast-forward a few months, and Sheila is looking at the label of a can of organic black beans she has brought home from the Whole Foods competitor here in the college town of Eugene: Market of Choice. The brand is Natural Directions, and Sheila's worry is BPA. She's endeavoring to keep Bisphenol A out of our household, concerned that the plastic lining in cans is a health hazard. She's on the phone with a representative of Natural Directions who says that in order to know the type of can, it is necessary to know the origin of the product. On the top of the can is stamped "Product of Bolivia."

I immediately think of the walnuts. The scenario is the same. A package design created to lure consumers such as me and Sheila to grab it off the shelves—that code word "organic" attracting us like a flashing neon sign. And then the unlikely country of origin, Bolivia—as incredible as Kazakhstan. Bolivia, rife with corruption because of its massive cocaine trade. Bolivia, one of the poorest countries in the Western Hemisphere. It stretches my credulity to believe the organic claim here as well.

I write this from my home in Oregon, famous for its organic food industry. Oregon is home to Oregon Tilth, one of the oldest, largest, and (at least in the old organic days) strictest organic certification programs in America, and a model for other similar regulators. Oregon is also home to fifty-five-year-old Harold Chase, sentenced to more than two years in a federal prison for selling more than four million pounds of conventionally grown corn to a wholesaler. His crime? He claimed the corn was organic, raised the price, and doubled his money.

As we concerned consumers struggle to make informed purchasing decisions about what's for dinner, whom can we trust regarding the provenance of our food? As much as we may try, for most of us it is impractical to trace each item on our menus.

A hysterical, famous scene in the IFC sketch comedy *Portlandia* comes to mind: A couple is quizzing their waitress about the chicken they are considering ordering, and she pulls out a file, providing them with his name—Colin—and his pedigree. They are not satisfied and leave the restaurant to check out his farm home to make certain that he was properly raised.

Nonetheless, with Wal-Mart filling its grocery aisles with food labeled organic, with Trader Joe's offering us nuts from Kazakhstan and Natural Directions claiming to import beans from Bolivia, I felt motivated to conduct a test: trace those walnuts back to their Kazakhstan grower and those legumes back to their Bolivian bean field. So I did. But this book is no mere travelogue. My goal is to reverse-engineer the history of the nuts and beans—and our overall organic menu. What occurs from the time of planting through harvest on to processing, packaging, transport, and finally the delivery to the point of sale? How did those words get on this bag and that can?

Are these globalized nuts and beans (and by extension other global food products) what we want to spend our money on and put in our stomachs? Who certifies them as organic? Can we trust that stamp of approval? And even if we can, how do we feel about the conditions for workers along the route the food takes to our plates? Are these nuts and beans examples of global greenwashing, hidden behind that splashy word on the label?

The third element of the quest I make in this book takes place close to my Eugene home. Is the fraudster Harold Chase an anomaly, or are we at risk here at home of spending premium prices for foodstuffs made in America that we believe are organic but that are, in fact, something else?

What is the origin of this food I'm eating? Can I trust the label? What does the label mean? Is it just an example of slick advertising?

I left the comfort of my sleepy little college town on a journalistic and gastronomical odyssey to trace the walnuts and beans from my local store shelves back to the trees and vines from whence they supposedly came.

After more than a year on the road, scores of interviews, and stacks of research, I found the answers and added more questions.

Chapter One

TRAITOR JOE

Back in 2010, when I first moved to Eugene, Oregon, advertisements for a show at the Lane County Historical Museum were impossible for me to ignore. In the same fluid and familiar typefaces that called me to San Francisco concerts back in the 1960s at the Avalon Ballroom and the Fillmore, the museum posters hawked "Tie Dye and Tofu: How Mainstream Eugene Became a Counterculture Haven." A Volkswagen bus, not unlike the ones I had owned over the years, was a focal point of the exhibit, its radio blaring Janis Joplin and Jimi Hendrix. Other icons of the times were displayed—from faded blue jeans to "underground" newspapers—relics that I did not need to buy a ticket to experience. Not only did I live through the period, much of the stuff in the museum was what my wife and I still make use of at home.

"Tie Dye and Tofu" documented the genesis of the Oregon back-to-the-land movement and the origins of what were then alternative food brands. Companies like the Springfield Creamery were marketing products impossible to find in the supermarkets of the day, like Nancy's Organic Yogurt. Organic foodstuffs were sold in funky, locally owned so-called health food stores in Lane County and across America. One of those stores was in Austin, Texas, and called itself Whole Foods.

Today, of course, food labeled organic is available everywhere. Trader Joe's stocks it; even Wal-Mart does. Organic food is a multibillion-dollar industry. Multibillion as in about twenty-seven billion dollars a year—just in the United States (although that's less than 4 percent of the total US grocery dollars spent).[1]

My kitchen is a prime example.

The tea I drink is the French St. Dalfour brand, flavored with mango. I like the taste, the packaging, and the price (a relative bargain for organic). Each box is filled with twenty-five tea bags sealed in their individual foil envelopes for freshness. (What is the unnecessary upstream and downstream waste generated by those pouches?) I am seduced by the label. I figure tea plantations—located far from most consumers—must be susceptible to all sorts of nasty fertilizers, herbicides, fungicides, and insecticides. The word "organic" seems like insurance. The package promises that the product is inspected by the Institut für Marktökologie Institut D'Ecocommerce of Switzerland (sounds impressive—Switzerland is so clean!) and certified organic by Oregon Tilth.

The oatmeal I eat is Old Wessex Ltd. Brand Irish Style. It is certified organic by Quality Assurance International in San Diego. There is a bottle of Tunisian olive oil in the cabinet along with the oatmeal. The organic claim on its label is endorsed by Ecocert. Nearby is a half-full box of Doctor Kracker organic crackers, a promise certified by the Texas Department of Agriculture. The Texas promise is also featured on a box of Arrowhead Mills organic Rice and Shine hot cereal. A jar of organic Adriatic Fig Spread—produced for Whole Foods by Hermes International in Croatia—carries a certification by IMO Switzerland, likely the abbreviation of the institute on the tea box. A plastic box of United with Earth brand Medjool dates ("juicy fresh"—an odd selling point for a dried food product) is certified organic by the abbreviation CCOF.

A tin of Flying Bird brand cinnamon is labeled "certified organic" with no indication of who certified it, under what conditions, or to what specifications. "Organic," of course, means a lot of things. That's the problem.

In the refrigerator is a jar of Lundberg Farms brown rice syrup called "Eco-Farmed" and "Non GMO Project verified." An Organic Valley carton promises that the large brown eggs in it were laid by "organic hens" eating a "100% organic vegetarian diet," certified by Oregon Tilth. The Spectrum Naturals toasted sesame oil is touted organic and boasts the USDA Organic badge on the label, but offers no suggestion of what third party is acting the role of watchdog over the claim.

There are two ears of corn in the vegetable bin with a strip of plastic tape around them guaranteeing they were "organically grown," and also offering no source for the claim. The ketchup, along with the vegetable broth and the Greek yogurt, all sport the stylized Q trademark of Quality Assurance International.

Trader Joe's Is None of My Business

My local Trader Joe's is just across the Willamette River from my office on the University of Oregon campus. "I go there because I feel like they edit their products," reports one of my journalism students, a comment more about TJ's image than anything. I confess to being entertained by the danceable rock 'n' roll music blaring in the store and lured by the bargain prices, along with some products I've not been able to find elsewhere. The popcorn cooked in olive oil is an example. It's addictive. According to the label, it, too, is organic. Like the Guiltless brand baked (not fried!) organic corn chips I stuff myself with, the organic popcorn I devour makes me feel as if my diet is healthy.

Biting into a rancid walnut is an unpleasant experience. But when I brought the bag of uneaten Kazakh nuts back to my Trader Joe's, the familiar smile of the store's "crew" was on the manager's face. The employees appear happy with their work. Before I left the store with the fresh bag of California walnuts, I asked the manager why the "grown in Kazakhstan" walnuts were no longer on the shelf. He told me to query headquarters via the store's website, and that's what I went home and did.

A reply came in short order and with typical Trader Joe's cuteness, or casualness—depending on your point of view.

"This automated response confirms that your email has successfully been sent to Trader Joe's," I was told.

We value your comments and will do our best to get back to you as soon as humanly possible. (That's because a few humans are busily reading and responding to ALL of the great customer feedback.) If this is a matter that requires immediate attention, please contact your local Trader Joe's to speak to one of our crew members live. It's the fastest way to get a response, plus, they just might tell you a good joke.

Of course it was a crew member who told me to check with the website in the first place. The note ended with "Mahalo," a Hawaiian thank-you from the island-themed subsidiary of the German grocery giant that owns Trader Joe's.

A few days later Kerry in customer relations sent me a more personal response.

"I do apologize for the disappointing experience you had," she/ he wrote, "and I am so glad that you took advantage of our Product Guarantee Refund." Kerry explained that Kazakh nuts were in the store because the walnut demand was greater than the American-grown supply. "We buy all the Organic California Walnuts we can get. Once we've sold through all of those, then we move to ones from the rest of the world, including the Republic of Kazakhstan." But regarding my specific question about quality control—who guarantees that nuts from Kazakhstan are organic—Kerry reverted to vague corporate-speak:

Please know, at Trader Joe's, food safety is of the utmost importance. Apart from our own stringent QA requirements on all products— organic and conventional—(we will not offer an item that we, ourselves, at Trader Joe's would not buy and enjoy!), our international suppliers are held to the same high Organic Certifications and FDA safety standards as U.S. suppliers. We also contract with U.S.-based, third-party certification companies to make absolutely sure that our international and domestic supplier's food safety procedures are top-notch. We work with reputable vendors who abide by all governmental guidelines, and we are always in contact with the specific suppliers who understand these guidelines (our buyers even make on-site visits throughout the world).

I hope this helps!
Kind regards,
Kerry

There was no bricks-and-mortar address for Kerry, no telephone number, and no e-mail address other than the nebulous webRelations@traderjoes.com.

I went one more round with Kerry. I told her/him that as a journalist I was studying the source of organic foods and that I wanted to join one of the buyers on a site visit to some of the Trader Joe's product providers. I asked her/him to arrange a trip for me.

I wasn't surprised that I never heard from Kerry (perhaps she/he was a computer-generated avatar?) again.

O MARY, CONCEIVED WITHOUT SIN, PRAY FOR US pleads the legend over the doorway to the Immaculate Conception Church on Shamrock Avenue. Across the street are the fading gas pumps of an old, out-of-commission Flying A service station, the price on one pump showing its age: thirty-three cents a gallon. A block down Shamrock is a private Victorian house, sitting behind a white picket fence. I'm in Monrovia, California, in the neighborhood of the corporate headquarters for Trader Joe's, which sits at 800 Shamrock Avenue, across the street from Immaculate Conception.

The morning fog is lifting from the Southern California skies but not from the opaque company philosophy of Trader Joe's, evidenced by the anonymity of its offices. Nothing identifies the bland one-story building—with the American flag floating in a slight breeze over the parking lot—other than the address, nothing except the harsh NO TRESPASSING signs at the entrance to the parking lot: "Violators will be prosecuted to the full extent of the law." And probing journalists are also unwelcome. "Thank you for reaching out to Trader Joe's," wrote Alison Mochizuki from the office of the Trader Joe's CEO, Dan Bane, when I suggested a meeting. "Unfortunately, we have to pass on the opportunity as we don't participate in research or book projects. Thank you again and I wish you all the best." Bane is famous in the business world for being unavailable for questions and comments about his business.

For a *Fortune* magazine story about Trader Joe's, reporter Beth Kowitt speculated that the company's "obsessively secretive management [style] may be because Trader Joe's business tactics are often very much at odds with its image as the funky shop around the corner that sources its wares from local farms and food artisans." Kowitt acknowledges that while some items may be local, other Trader Joe's private-label products are made by food conglomerates such as PepsiCo (TJ's pita chips, for example). The magazine quoted from a copy of the Trader Joe's agreement that it reported the store's vendors must sign to do business with the grocer. "Vendor shall not publicize its business relationship with TJ's in any manner,"[2] it reads.

In a book about his experiences working at a Trader Joe's in Kansas City, Mark Gardiner quotes CEO Bane from the company's Member Handbook: "The mission of Trader Joe's is to give our customers the best food and beverage values that they can find anywhere and to provide them with the information required for making informed buying decisions."

Exactly who in Kazakhstan claims to be growing organic walnuts—and why on earth I should believe the claim—apparently isn't considered information I need to make an informed buying decision. Another quote Gardiner attributes to Bane from the handbook tells employees, "We view ourselves as the purchasing agent of food and beverages for intelligent, educated, inquisitive individuals."[3] Unless, of course, those "inquisitive individuals" wonder where those walnuts were grown, under what conditions, and by whom.

Just a few blocks west of the main Trader Joe's offices, on Huntington Boulevard in a typically banal Southern California strip mall (false-fronted stores and endless parking), I wander into a welcoming Trader Joe's market (Bed Bath & Beyond is a neighbor, as is Marshalls). The bouncing music machine is blasting "Winter Wonderland" to prepare me for Christmas. I grab my usual Trader Joe's supplies: a tub of hummus and a bag of those Pepsi-made "reduced guilt" pita chips to go with it, the Trader Joe's brand Spicy Lentil Wrap with its Spicy Tahini Sauce, the habit-forming organic popcorn with olive oil, and a plastic bottle filled with the pricier, organic carrot juice. My e-mail encounter with Kerry makes me wonder if Joe just pours the same juice into bottles with different labels. Before I leave the store I check out the organic walnuts as I usually do whenever I stop in at a TJs. I'm looking for another package of those Kazakh nuts. But the ones for sale here in Monrovia are labeled California, so I leave them on the shelf.

Back in Oregon, University of Oregon graduate teaching fellow Charles Deitz, who is helping me with some research for this book, hangs out in the parking lot of the Coburg Road Trader Joe's. His job is to stop a random bunch of shoppers and pepper them with questions about what's in their grocery bags and why.

"Do you buy food labeled organic?" he asks Dee.

"Yeah," she tells him, saying she hopes that "they have fewer pesticides in them or on them." But she's skeptical about label claims. "Some stuff that says organic on it, I know it isn't all certified organic. There's not a lot of truth to labels."

When he asks her if she favors American products as she looks for organic groceries, she expresses ambivalence. "I think I would trust US organics more than another country, although I buy organic things from Mexico." She considers the questions for another moment and adds, "Who knows? Maybe other countries have better organic standards than we do." She acknowledges the power of global merchandising regarding details about the ingredients of what she eats. "I don't know how you would ever, as a consumer, know."

Deitz hails Kelly, who tells him she buys what she likes and ignores labels. If food is marked organic, she figures that is supposed to mean that it's "raised naturally, without chemicals and bug sprays and fertilizers."

Marsha is busy knocking her fist on watermelons, seeking a ripe one, when Deitz approaches her.

She says that she does buy organic, when she has the choice to. But she's not label literate, as is made clear when she admits, "I thought there was some kind of parent organization that gives them a seal of approval of some sort, but I don't think it's a federal thing that decides—although I don't know."

Steve loads purchases marked organic into his old pickup truck because of his girlfriend's influence. "She specifies it," he says. "I prefer to buy organic when I can. Anything that grows above the ground we try to get organic. But we're not eating entirely organic. Root vegetables are not as important to us." But proximity is. "I like to get food from close to home whenever possible, to support local businesses." Not that he would necessarily avoid nuts from Kazakhstan or beans from Bolivia. "We put a certain amount of trust in Trader Joe's to buy quality produce, to make sure that it's organic.

It's based on trust. You shop with people you trust and you hope that you don't have to watch every product every time you come in the store. The word 'organic' should be enough. But it's also very reassuring if it says 'certified by Oregon Tilth.'"

"Not if they're terrifically more expensive than the conventional," Maureen says about how she decides if organics fill her cart. "I suspect it's better for me. I know you can't wash the pesticides off berries and cherries, and some other things you eat raw." Organic means no pesticides, according to Maureen, "and probably something about the quality of the soil." And who decides? "I think there is some kind of board or commission that makes the decision."

Another fellow is loading his pickup when Deitz approaches him. "Do you buy food labeled organic?" Deitz asks.

"Yes I do," the older man answers.

"Why do you trust the labels?"

The answer is simple: "I don't."

"And if a product is labeled organic and it's from Kazakhstan or Bolivia, is that a claim that makes you suspicious?"

"Yes it is."

"What's your name?" Deitz asks. We're trying to keep the man-on-the-street interviews organized with at least first names.

"None of your business," says the curmudgeon as he dismisses Charles Deitz with the same brusqueness Trader Joe's uses for pointed consumer inquiries.

Defining Organic

Trader Joe's, Wal-Mart, and other mainstream chain grocers, along with the ubiquitous Whole Foods, are cashing in on consumer vogues and fears by purveying foods labeled organic—and selling them at premium prices.

In order to put this quest into perspective, I make a list of some basic questions that I need answered: How do standards for growing, processing, and labeling foods as organic differ in the face of contradictory laws, varying certification programs, and consumer expectations? Who polices the food industry's use of the term "organic?" Why is it that a United States Department of Agriculture sticker proclaiming food organic does not, in fact, mean that it is 100 percent organic?

I muse about the actual provenance of "organic" walnuts from Kazakhstan or "organic" black beans from Bolivia, based on my experiences as a journalist working in the former Soviet bloc and in South America. I read comments from anonymous fellow Trader Joe's customers about the store's organic claims, customers who post their opinions on various food-oriented websites. From the bubbly "TJ's is the place to see and be seen like Chili's and Applebee's," to the skeptical "TJ's should reveal more about the origins of its food," these conversations show the folkloric niche the store has created for itself in American culture.

BUY UGLY, IT'S ORGANIC, read the sign at the Bethesda Co-op produce department in Cabin John, Maryland. We lived just down the street from the co-op back in the 1980s, when I was an NBC News correspondent based in Washington. We bought the ugly. Then, as now, we usually paid more for the ugly (although organic gets prettier as farming techniques become more sophisticated). The organic sign meant to us that the apples and pears, the zucchini and tomatoes, were grown without chemical herbicides, pesticides, and fertilizers on farms free of such additives for enough years that the soil was unadulterated as well. We trusted the co-op and never asked where our food originated. I'm not sure why we trusted their signs. Maybe it was the times. The place looked wholesome and we wanted to believe. I still do: I think that produce they sold us in the 1980s likely was from family farms in Maryland and Virginia, and that the wrinkled vegetables and bruised fruit were untainted by poisons.

The blemishes added credibility, as did the earnest look on the jeans-clad clerks' faces and the political statements on their T-shirts. One of our sons worked there stocking shelves. We were members.

But my organic walnuts and organic beans clearly deviate from those from the early days at the Bethesda Co-op. In the years since we first shopped at the co-op, the word "organic" has become unavoidable, almost cliché. As an indicator of what's in the food we eat, its meaning is a moving target. Take, for example, the US Department of Agriculture's definition. If you eat something sporting the USDA Organic button, it merely means that at least 95 percent of all the ingredients in it meet the government's standard for organic.

It's the same 95 percent rule with European Union government regulations. Official organic on both sides of the Atlantic means ingredients free of chemical herbicides and pesticides, ingredients free of genetically modified Frankenfoodstuffs, ingredients not irradiated, ingredients not laden with chemical preservatives. Except for that remaining 5 percent. And what mysteries hide in that 5 percent?

Other labels are confusing, and more likely designed to be misleading. What's not local in the jet age? How free is the range? "Natural" means whatever you and I want it to mean, although the USDA does regulate legal use of the term when it's applied to meat and eggs.* What doesn't come from nature, including—as the DuPont chemical company used to boast—better living through chemistry?

---

* Meat and eggs labeled "natural" must be "minimally processed" according to the USDA (a vague constraint) and "contain no artificial ingredients."

Chapter Two

Branding the Organic Industry

Another down-home grocery from my past was the good old Good Earth in Marin County, California. The original hole-in-the-wall shop is now a sparkling organic food palace. Up a winding road from the storefront where I first shopped at Good Earth back in the late 1960s, Janet DiGiovanna and Danny Rubenstein welcome me into their expansive living room—a spectacular site with floor-to-ceiling windows that make it feel as if we are hovering over Mount Tamalpais as we sit on white leather couches. The day is blustery, and as the sweeping view changes from gray and rainy to bright blue skies with puffs of white clouds, it becomes difficult for me to keep my eyes on the two of them, despite their sobering stories from their years as marketing advisors to the organic food industry—since its "hippie days," as they call the '60s.

Janet and Danny sport a client list that reads like a Whole Foods shopping list: Tazo and Numi teas, Odwalla, Driscoll's Berries, Naked Juice, POM Wonderful. In fact, Whole Foods is on that list, too. The couple agree to brief me about organic food labeling from their perspective as consultants to industry. They specialize in advising businesses thriving because the word "organic" adorns their packaging. The two exude fervor for food, but it's a passion that's mixed with disdain for what they perceive are compromised industry ethics. They reminisce about a business they remember that was led by entrepreneurs more interested in healthy diets than fat wallets.

I am meeting with Janet and Danny to both learn from their experiences and take advantage of their considerable Rolodex. Between offering me names of the critical organic players, Janet and Danny do not shy from providing commentary on the industry they helped build, commentary delivered almost faster than I can take notes. They remind me of a couple of stand-up comics—except that the lines I am hearing are no joke.

"Your hypothesis that there is a lot of greed and bullshit in the organic industry is true," they tell me. "It's a shame that organic no longer means what it used to mean." Those good old days they are reminiscing about were several generations ago, back in the 1960s and 1970s, when the bohemian/hippie/anti–Vietnam War/pick-your-subculture Baby Boomer–fueled counterculture pored over the *Whole Earth Catalog* and *Mother Earth News,* dreaming of— and often creating—alternative lifestyles fed by something other than Cheez Whiz and Wonder Bread. Those were the days when California Certified Organic Farmers (known on the labels in your kitchen as CCOF) and Oregon Tilth* were founded.

These early certifiers were not-for-profit organizations (Oregon Tilth still is; CCOF spun off its certification unit into the for-profit world), but today you're much more likely to see the stylized letter *Q* on the label of packaged foodstuffs marked organic. Entrepreneurs who figured out early that there is big money to be made putting a "Seal of Approval" on organic products founded Quality Assurance International. QAI is a for-profit operation, what Janet and Danny describe to me as "the first kink in the armor" of that first wave of organic food evangelists, who were originally purists on a mission.

"Americans do not have a clue about what constitutes organic food," they say. "There's a lot of confusion and misunderstanding. Ask someone what organic means. They think it means no herbicides

---

* The word "tilth," in its most basic definition, means simply cultivated land, as in tilled land. But it also refers to the condition of the land.

and pesticides were used." Those two criteria are just part of the story. If you want to be confident about what you're putting in your mouth, they argue, "From dirt to table, there must be a paper trail."

Janet and Danny spew out examples of the complexities that should worry us. What if a smelting plant is next door to pristine land? What if water used for irrigation is contaminated with lead? They point to produce from Mexico with particular concern. "Follow the water," they suggest, a variation on the "follow the money" advice given to Woodward and Bernstein, perhaps history's most famous intrepid reporters. What is the integrity of the water used on crops grown in Mexico and certified organic? Who is testing the water and for what? Is the water being tested?

The questions continue after harvest, after the produce leaves the farm—where it might, in fact, be organically grown. But then crops like the black beans in my Natural Directions can are processed. What cleaning products are used on the processing equipment? What flavorings and other processing agents are added?

Janet, Danny, and I look out at the sweeping view and the blustery day. "The natural products industry is owned by corporate America," they both sigh. And it is with another resigned sigh that they indict the globalized organic trade. "China is the biggest fraud regarding organics that you can imagine."

My notebook is full of names, including a trio Janet and Danny identify as the "gold standard" of the industry—the good guys. Apple and pear farmer Gene Kahn, the pioneer who founded Muir Glen, Cascadian Farms, and Fantastic Foods—and sold them all to General Mills. Gary Hirshberg, the founder of Stonyfield Farms—now owned by Dannon, the international yogurt concern. Andy Berliner and his wife, Rachel, who named their TV-dinner company after their daughter Amy.

But as we say good-bye, Janet and Danny caution me. "People really don't know what is pure. This is a business based on trust. There are a lot of ugly stories." Organic standards suffer, they insist, from errors and neglect and greed. They cite USDA organic standards as a prime example of the degraded and compromised organic food world, a sector that's grown so fast and big it's been co-opted by corporate America and its massive lobbying machine.

Immer Zum Besten Preis!

When I lived in Berlin, before my family found our own apartment, we stayed with a friend whose flat was just around the corner from an Aldi market. It always was an adventure shopping at the Aldi because the stock changed from day to day. If we found a product we really liked, we learned to buy lots of it. It might not be available the next day.

That neighborhood Aldi, near Bundesplatz, was decidedly down-market. The foodstuffs were stacked in their original shipping cartons, the cardboard boxes sliced open just enough to show off the labels so shoppers would know what was inside. There were no compelling displays, just products jamming the narrow aisles. At the exit the lines for the checkout clerks were notoriously long. The clerks themselves were more often surly than not, flinging purchases past the cash register as they calculated prices; we shoppers were expected to pay and pack our food into our own bags faster than the clerk could fling the next customer's stuff toward our pile. It was a stress-filled shopping experience, ridiculous from the point of view of a spoiled American consumer accustomed to being catered to by retailers. Ridiculous and irritating.

But it was also cheap. Aldi promises *immer zum besten Preis—* always the best price—and Aldi delivers cheap prices. Brothers Karl and Theo Albrecht founded the German grocery chain in 1961 ("Aldi" is derived from Albrecht Discount). The brothers split the company into Aldi Nord and Aldi Sud; Aldi Nord owns Trader Joe's. Aldi, like Trader Joe's, is famous for corporate secrecy, yet its recent history revealed what for some customers is a much more horrific tale than the questionable origin of its walnuts: selling horsemeat marked as beef.

The horsemeat scandal of 2013—horsemeat in frozen lasagna, horsemeat in hamburgers sold by sprawling European chain supermarkets such as Tesco and Lidl, in addition to Aldi—was a labeling scandal. Blame was pushed up the food chain. Not that there's anything wrong with eating horsemeat if you're a meat eater. Unless, of course, you exercise discretion when you choose which meat you eat. The horsemeat scandal reminded consumers around the world that labels are suspect.

"This is a very shocking story, it is completely unacceptable," was the response from the British prime minister David Cameron, who correctly pointed out, "This isn't really about food safety, it's about effective food labeling, it's about proper retail practice. And people will be very angry to find out they have been eating horse when they thought they were eating beef."[4]

As the horsemeat scandal galloped across Europe, Aldi pulled frozen meals marked "beef lasagna" and "spaghetti Bolognese" off its shelves. The company announced that test results confirmed that the meat in those TV dinners was dosed with horsemeat—as much as 100 percent. Aldi's weary public relations staff announced that the supermarket was "angry and let down" by its lasagna and spaghetti supplier, the French processed-food giant Comigel. Aldi's official corporate response was, "If the label says beef, our customers expect it to be beef." Comigel passed the buck (stallion?) to its beef supplier, Spanghero. Comigel said it contracted for French beef from Spanghero, but after the scandal broke Comigel said Spanghero changed its story. The meat wasn't French; it came from Romania.[5]

If Aldi was conned by its suppliers into accepting horsemeat from Romania marked as beef, how much faith in the stock on the shelves ought the customers who shop at its subsidiary, Trader Joe's, have? An editorial in the Spanish newspaper *El País* headlined "More Than Mere Fraud" extends that question along the entire food chain. "The detection of horsemeat in products labeled as beef has revealed a fraudulent practice so widespread as to indicate grave shortcomings in the system of monitoring the food that is sold to the public," reported the paper, which then went on to press for a severe government response. "The fact that the label on packaging does not correspond to its real content is a fraudulent practice that must be prosecuted and punished."

Nothing wrong with eating horses, said *El País*. "It is the extent of the fraud that alerts us to the disturbing vulnerability of the food supply system. The stages involved in the production, packaging and distribution of a hamburger or a packet of meatballs is so complex, extensive and generally subcontracted that its monitoring is becoming ever more difficult. It has not even been possible," complained the paper, "to determine where the meat came from in some cases."[6]

The unknown-to-customers origin of the tainted hamburgers and meatballs is matched by TJ's walnuts. Trader Joe's does all it can to prevent its customers from knowing who grew those nuts and where. There are of plenty of places to look in Kazakhstan—it's a gigantic country, as big as Western Europe. With just a plastic bag that claims "Product of Kazakhstan," and no proof and no trail—along with the opaque corporate culture at Trader Joe's regarding the sources of its products—connecting the nuts to their orchard may be impossible.

Organic Barcelona

I'm considering the integrity of the world's food supply over a copy of *El País* at a Barcelona cafe; the day is warm enough to drink my *té verde* at an outdoor table. The Global Food Safety Conference brings me to Spain—the organizers promise "a unique annual event that will bring together over 1000 leading food safety professionals from more than 60 countries around the world to advance food safety globally," a statement that makes me figure it's a conference worth prowling around, given my current investigation.

But today is Sunday, so I'm taking advantage of the Latin lifestyle, lingering over the newspaper, enjoying the cityscape, and watching the street scene. The bright Mediterranean sun feels and looks so good, I snap a picture of the table still life: the glass of tea casting a shadow on my paper. I've stopped a few blocks off La Rambla to escape the tourists on that famous tree-lined walk. The atmosphere here on the Carrer d'en Robador is relaxed and local—at least at this relatively early hour. Clothes hang to dry from the balconies of the apartment houses that line the narrow street, and as noon approaches I notice more and more women pacing the sidewalks—one in a short-short skirt, for example, worn with high-heeled knee-high boots and fishnet stockings. Storefronts near where she walks and waits for her customers offer "Afro-Latino" hairdressing, tandoori, and couscous (Bob Marley's "Stir It Up" wafts out of the couscous place), and there is a *carnisseria islamica* selling halal meat. At a corner grocery the graffiti warns, "*Hoy no curra nadie,*" or "No one works today"—referring not to this day of rest but to the prolonged Spanish economic crisis. In fact, I see several out-of-business shops.

I'm drinking green tea on Carrer d'en Robador, waiting for Restaurant +Organic to open so that I can check out the lunch at the place most often recommended by my Barcelona guidebooks for those of us who skip *la carne* at mealtime. "We use organic products, micro-filtered water and lots of love," promises the restaurant's leaflet. It's well after noon when I show up, but I am the first customer of the day for this late-eating city. "Too early?" I ask the waitress. "*Un poco temprano,*" she says, but agrees to let me stay and eat. The cook is wearing a T-shirt emblazoned with "Organic is Orgasmic." Lunch for me is a buffet of spinach and carrot soup and a salad (endive and tomato with olives) and potatoes cooked with onions. Delicious.

I ask the manager about what I am eating.

"Everything is organic," he assures me.

"How do you know?" I ask.

"It's certified by the Catalan government," he says, and he expresses confidence in the growers and processors who supply +Organic. The music player is switched on and a guitar-laden, schmaltzy rendition of "Can't Take My Eyes Off You" blasts through the high-ceiled empty food hall, a couple passionately singing in Spanish. As I hear the line "You're just too good to be true" over and over, it sounds to me like it should be the theme song for my journey.

I wash down my meal with a glass of fresh carrot juice. But a visit to *el baño* before I leave +Organic suggests that the plus sign in the restaurant's name might be a subtle indicator that the menu makes exceptions. I pass a glass-door refrigerator with shelves full of that ubiquitous American import yet to offer an organic variant: Coca-Cola.

Buy something organic in Barcelona that's a Catalan product, and it's likely to carry not only the European Union organic seal (a green background with a stylized leaf outlined by the European Union stars) but also the seal of the Catalan Council of Organic Production—the government entity that certifies local organics.

In a working-class neighborhood far from Gaudí's soaring Sagrada Família cathedral and the souvenir hawkers on La Rambla, I arrive at the Health Ministry for a meeting with Isidre Martínez, the man who oversees certification of organic food in Catalonia. His office demeanor is casual: an open-necked corduroy shirt, a mop of curly hair, and an easy smile.

"Zero risk is not possible around the world at this moment," Martínez says about the credibility of organic food imported into

Spain. "There are mistakes and there are criminals everywhere. Always." But that's not his only concern—and he believes fraud in the organic food chain is not rampant. Even if he's convinced a product from India or China meets all health and safety standards for organic foodstuffs, to make Martínez happy it must also pass his holistic standards.

Martínez has been studying organic food production since his student days, and his entire working life has been devoted to the field. Unlike in Oregon, the controlling authority that certifies Catalonian farms and producers as organic is a public body. As is the case back home, farms and producers must pay a fee to the certifier for the service. But Martínez is convinced that since the government does the certifying there is no potential for conflict of interest because there is no competition between certifiers. "We made this choice to avoid conflicts of interest," he says. The extra Catalonian seal on organic food produced and certified in Catalonia alerts consumers that the product is subject to what Martínez says is even more rigorous testing than required by European standards *and* that it originates in Catalonia. "If the consumer has some doubt, they can call the control authority and ask their questions."

Those questions can include: Where the heck did these beans and walnuts come from? Martínez says the Catalan government will provide the names and locales of purveyors to its citizens, citizens he's convinced—given the choice—pick Catalan organics over imports. In fact, his office has surveyed organic consumers asking if they would prefer an organic product from elsewhere or a conventional product made in Catalonia. "Sixty percent of the consumers asked want to choose the Catalan product."

"Even though it is not organic?" I ask because I want to make sure I heard him correctly. I think about markets back in Oregon with produce sections full of presumed organic fruits and vegetables from around the world.

"Yes," he says about the survey results, "because ecological, as we call organic, is a concept that is wider than rules for production." Organic concepts can be applied to commerce, and farm-to-market proximity is an integral element of his organic food definition. "Most of the organic consumers are people who have an ecological behavior and they prefer a local product."

I inquire, "Is that nationalistic behavior?" Catalonia is an autonomous part of Spain and identifies itself as a nationality.[7] Martínez and I are talking at a time when Catalan nationalist politicians are moving the region toward greater independence from Madrid. Catalan flags fly from balconies throughout Barcelona.

"I don't think it's nationalistic," he says, rejecting that theory as too limiting. "It's for ecological reasons."

"Don't bring asparagus from Peru to Barcelona on a polluting airplane?"

"It's a mad thing," he says about long-distance produce. But Spain enjoys year-round agriculture; there's a cornucopia of fresh local produce available in December around Catalonia. Try that at Christmastime in Duluth or Lansing or Rochester. "Ecology is a stronger reason than politics." That's what motivates Martínez to avoid grocery stores for his produce and buy directly from farmers. "I favor people who are producing locally on small farms around Barcelona. I choose organic because they are not using chemicals. And of course with products like tomatoes, for the taste."

Who Inspects the Inspectors?

The next day I collect my convention badge and join the throng at the Global Food Safety stakeholders meeting. Global food traders invest mightily in keeping us from getting ill when we eat their wares. Nothing worse for the food business than customers sick and dying from what they ate. I wander around the booths on the exhibition floor until I find the NSF exhibit. NSF International ("Live Safer" is its motto) is the mother ship of Quality Assurance International. According to the official company history, NSF was founded in the University of Michigan's School of Public Health as the National Sanitation Foundation. Renamed in 1989, NSF International bought the for-profit QAI in 2004.

When I chat up NSF representative Dan Fone at the convention booth, he acts thrilled with the idea of helping me trace my beans and nuts back to their sources. We talk Barcelona, food, organics, and Ducks—as in my university's football team.

"I think it would be great to have this independent look," Fone says about my traceback project. "They're not called trust marks for nothing." "Trust mark" is the term of art (not science) for the ubiquitous seals that now litter package design, from sustainable this to fair-trade that. We exchange business cards, and I give Fone one of the souvenir pens I carry around to help contacts remember their encounter with me. It's bright yellow with a tiny duck head on the top. Push the duck head and the pen quacks.

But within a month my e-mail exchanges with Greta Houlahan, the communications manager for NSF (and hence QAI), add fuel to my initial skepticism about the safeguards in place regarding the validity of foodstuffs certified organic.

The first note in the trail is from Fone to Jaclyn Bowen. Bowen is the general manager of QAI, where—according to company literature—she "focuses on verifying compliance with the USDA National Organic Program regulations."

"Jackie," writes Fone,

> Can I introduce you to Peter Laufer at the U. of Oregon (go Ducks!). Peter is looking at a research project tracing a couple of Q marked products from the shelves of Trader Joe's back along the supply chain to the grove/orchard where they were grown. Would you be kind enough to reach out to him next week to discuss further?

So far, so good. And routine.

I respond with a thank-you to Dan, copied to Jackie (we're all informal Americans here), and a straightforward confirmation: "Jackie, I look forward to connecting with you next week."

Jackie writes back immediately. "Peter, I head out on vacation late afternoon on Monday. Do you have an availability that morning? Looking forward to speaking with you."

"Come to Barcelona for your vacation, Jackie," I muse. "The rain stopped. It is a gorgeous evening, and it is almost time for *tapas* and *vino tinto.*" I then suggest some times that would work for an initial telephone meeting.

She politely tells me that she is going to Australia, and then she hands me off to Houlahan, the professional communications manager, with the understandable excuse of last-minute work she needs to attend to before her interlude Down Under.

The next note comes from Houlahan.

"Hello Peter," she writes. "It's very nice to meet you. Can you tell me a little more about your research project on organic traceability to see if we can help? Thanks in advance." She offers both her direct office phone number and her cell.

"Good morning, Greta," I write back.

Thanks for the note. I am following a bag of walnuts and a can of beans from the shelves of two grocery stores where I shop here in Oregon back through the supply chain to their sources in the orchard and the field. Is there a time when it would be convenient to talk and I can explain the project in whatever detail you would like, and we can discuss how you may be able to help? I look forward to that. Thanks in advance,

Peter

Next Houlahan and I engage in a delightful phone conversation, during which I tell her in detail what I want to do and why: find out where those nuts and beans came from, and why I should trust that they weren't dusted with DDT on a farm in South America or a field in Central Asia, far from the scrutiny of us trusting consumers and our advocates. And I don't hear from her again until I send another e-mail. She answers promptly.

Hi Peter,

I'm really sorry, but Trader Joe's and Natural Directions can't participate in the project. I also have reached out to another company but to date have not received a response. If/when I hear back, we will let you know. Good luck with your project.

All the best,

Greta

A corporate Dear John letter. I am surprised. This is the same Greta who, on the NSF website, solicits journalists on the page titled "Story Ideas" with this attempt at seduction: "If you're looking for a great news story on issues related to public health and safety, chances are you'll find it here. NSF International," she continues, "The Public Health & Safety Company™ has compiled the following story ideas to provide key tips to help every one to Live Safer®." Why are those two proprietary symbols slapped on such generic phrases, I wonder. The list of "great news story" ideas includes bottled water, dietary supplements, food safety, green living, hand washing, and pool safety. Not on the list is the great news story that's become a subplot of my search for the origin of my black beans and walnuts: the lack of transparency in the organic food supply chain.

"Can't participate" implies a force exists that dictates Trader Joe's, Natural Directions', and QAI's relations with their customers (and journalists). I find the word "can't" curious given the tangled relationship of the USDA, certification companies such as QAI and their clients, along with the Trader Joe's and Natural Directions of the world. The USDA authorizes QAI to certify that organic products meet the USDA National Organic Program standards (standards already diluted from what purists consider organic). Certification company representatives sit on the USDA board that sets those standards. The potential for conflict of interest regarding the value of the USDA Organic seal starts at that point. It's reminiscent of Vice President Dick Cheney meeting (in secret) with oil company executives to work out the George W. Bush administration's energy policies.

But perhaps even more problematic is the fact that the companies the certifiers certify pay fees to the certifiers for the certification. Conflict of interest? Nope, says the industry. Not at all, says the USDA. But QAI, for example, certifies Natural Directions and Trader Joe's products, and the vast majority of the organic food in my Eugene refrigerator and cupboards, and now QAI is telling me—in my position as consumer, academic researcher, and journalist—that Natural Directions and Trader Joe's "can't" participate in my request to trace the work QAI does to certify food as organic.

I write back to Houlahan.

In answer to my question, "Why is it that Natural Directions and Trader Joe's cannot participate?" she answers simply, "I'm sorry Trader Joe's and Natural Directions didn't specify why they couldn't participate."

I respond immediately.

Thanks, Greta. But what I do not understand is how Trader Joe's and Natural Directions can make the decision. Isn't it NSF/QAI who is operating the certification? Isn't it your company's call? Thanks, as always.

The next note from Houlahan explains the rationale behind the refusal, but does not negate the conflict of interest:

Trader Joe's and Natural Directions would have to provide you with their supply chain information since that's considered confidential business information. I hope that helps clarify.

In other words, trust us at QAI. We'll make sure that the companies that pay us to certify them organic are selling you pristine walnuts and untainted black beans. Trust us, but we cannot allow an outsider to know what we do and how, because it might result in the consumer knowing where those beans and nuts originate. I don't accept the premise.

If the Drug Enforcement Administration wasn't worried that I would wreck their efforts at cocaine interdiction when I joined them to report on a raid in the jungles of Bolivia, I'm convinced there's a process for protecting the coordinates of the field where Natural Directions sources its beans. If keeping the location secret is crucial for Natural Directions, put a blindfold on me at the La Paz bus station and don't take it off until we're in the anonymous bean field. Or make me sign a nondisclosure agreement. Or study my years of history reporting sensitive stories without revealing my sources. There are all sorts of devices for allowing journalists and academics access to proprietary information without jeopardizing its secrecy.

I write:

Shouldn't we be able to find a strategy whereby I can observe the farm-to-fork certification process that QAI is in charge of for the black beans and the walnuts without compromising Trader Joe's or Natural Directions understandably confidential business information? Perhaps we can brainstorm about that.

Fat chance.

"Hi Peter," she writes next (and she obviously hopes for the last time),

I'm really sorry, but we cannot find a company that can participate in your project. We wish you the best on your book and safe travels.

Sorry? I doubt it. Just hoping never to hear from me again.

I am puzzled, Greta. How can the public trust the QAI seal if the certification process is not transparent—if an independent observer is precluded from witnessing your work? Please help me understand this.

Go away, she writes back. Well, not in those words, of course.

I understand and want to help you, but I can't in this case. The certified company needs to provide you with the supply information.

And next she cited the law that sanctifies the QAI subterfuge:

A certifier is not allowed to disclose this type of information without permission from the handler or producer per section 205.501 a(10) of USDA NOP [National Organic Program] regulations. For more information, you may want to reach out to the NOP and/or the OTA.

The OTA, in this organic alphabet soup, is the Organic Trade Association. I have already spoken to Miles McEvoy, head of the USDA NOP (more from him later), who told me that his budget allows him to field only *one* inspector at the most for every one billion dollars of trade in the United States of "organic" products. Yes, billion with a "B." And that's one as in one.

"Thanks, Greta," I respond.

I appreciate your counsel. I have met with Miles McEvoy at the NOP. It seems to me that the consumer may be at risk of suffering from a dearth of information about the products they're considering for purchase. May I ask you to arrange an interview for me with whomever at NSF or QAI is the responsible party for the credibility of the QAI seal? That would, I believe, be a helpful next step.

Get out of my face, buddy, she screams.
No, that's not quite correct.

Hi Peter,
This is not something QAI can discuss in more detail. You can contact the Organic Trade Association for more information that's available to consumers. You may want to reach out to companies with products that are certified organic.

Of course. The Organic Trade Association is the industry lobby, not to be confused with the Organic Consumers Association, a membership organization created as a critical reaction to the USDA's organic regulations and "the Wal-Martization of the economy," as their literature worries. "Buy local, organic, and fair made" is the Organic Consumers Association slogan.[8] The Organic Trade Association identifies its mission as one "to promote and protect organic trade to benefit the environment, farmers, the public and the economy."[9] But again Houlahan has not answered the question, and corporate representatives not answering basic questions posed in the public interest is an unacceptable response to me. So I try again.

I explain to Houlahan that QAI's silence speaks volumes. I make a formal request that she arrange an interview with a QAI executive who can explain QAI's role in the organics sector economy. I make it clear to her that of course I am checking in with the Organic Trade Association and with companies that QAI (and others) certifies, and that I have already met with McEvoy at the USDA. I certainly don't need a Journalism 101 course from a public relations maven.

Since QAI controls a majority of the American organic certification market, learning its point of view is crucial for an understanding of the processes, I argue.

After that note is ignored, I make still another request to Houlahan for a meeting with a QAI executive. Her last e-mail message to me dispenses with the usual "Hi Peter" salutation and the "good luck with your book" before her signature. In fact, there is no signature. It reads merely, "I'm sorry but we can't be of further assistance."

Chapter Three

JUST RETIRED AND READY TO TALK

Even if she dutifully serves her QAI corporate masters' short-term goals, Greta Houlahan does nothing to assuage this reality: The organic certification system is fraught with conflicts of interest and the opportunity to abuse consumer confidence. Despite her diligence, a few days after our final e-mail exchange I find myself enjoying a hearty conversation with a fellow still listed on the corporate propaganda as senior vice president of Quality Assurance International, specializing in "operations, government regulatory affairs and international business development." Joe Smillie, says the corporate biography, is a founder and past president of the Organic Trade Association, was the certification industry representative on the USDA National Organic Standards Board, and is an author. (And surprise: We used to share a publisher—the Vermont-based Chelsea Green Publishing, "bringing the politics and practice of sustainable living to the world.")

I find Smillie—with no help from QAI—at home in Vermont, just a couple of weeks after he retired.

"From active duty, yeah," he tells me.

"Why?" I ask. "All indications are you're a spry and relatively young man."

"Oh, I'm sixty-six. And I'm . . ." he laughs, "tired of it."

"Really?" Smillie is so intertwined with the organic food business that it's hard for me to imagine him disengaging.

"I never intended to be a government bureaucrat," he says. Then surprisingly, "When we lit up the pipe in 1967, that wasn't the idea."

"We were both there," I offer, thinking back to my own 1967, skipping classes at Tamalpais High School to head over Mount Tamalpais to Stinson Beach—not bothering to inform him that "the pipe" was not part of my 1960s routine.

"I was a back-to-the-lander," he tells me. He seems, in these first days of retirement, keen on reliving those times. Why would I break the spell? "The *Whole Earth Catalog* was my bible."

Later I dig up an old copy of the *Whole Earth Catalog* and flip to the "Farming Philosophy" section. There Wendell Barry notes:

The scientific respectability of organic methods has been obscured for us both by those who have insisted upon making a cult of the obvious and by the affluence and glamor of technological agriculture—the agriculture of chemicals and corporations."[10]

The classic text's editor, Stewart Brand, introduces the "Land Use" chapter with an order to readers. "Because 'land use' too often means 'use up,' there's considerable repair to do," he wrote in 1980. "Usually it's a choice between soil and oil. Choose soil. It takes longer to make oil (about 40 million years longer). Oil was alive. Soil is alive."[11]

I browse through the "Farming" section. I read about the newspaper *Acres, U.S.A.* (now a magazine)—touted as a chronicle of farms and farmers transforming their fields into organic farms—I look at a summary of the services of Agriculture Extension offices, and I check out the availability of used farm equipment. "We are as gods and might as well get good at it," the *Catalog* announces as its purpose. Smillie was paying attention back in his pipe days.

"I did all that stuff," he says about the *Whole Earth Catalog* lifestyle. "And then gradually one thing led to another, and I helped create the whole certification system and the regulations. I basically became a bureaucrat. That was okay. It needed to be done. I did it, and it's done. I have a grandson now and I've got other things to do."

"But you weren't a government agent. You were working on the private side of the organic food world."

Smillie's response exemplifies the incestuous relationships in the organic certification business as he points out precisely what I'm becoming convinced is wrong: The inspectors are paid by those they inspect. "We were approved by the USDA, and we were verifying compliance to the US regulations. That makes you a bureaucrat whether Uncle Sam pays your check or your company pays your check. You're basically a bureaucrat." He could have added: or whether your company pays your check *with income earned from fees it charges to the company it's certifying.*

Without any prompting, the next thing out of Smillie's mouth seems a non sequitur. "I got into a fair bit of trouble in a *Washington Post* interview in which I told the truth and got crucified for it. It really pointed out to me that, you know, it's just a nasty game out there." He laughs and I puzzle over the reference.

I agree with him about it being a nasty game, although I haven't seen the *Post* article.

"Oh, don't look it up; it makes me look terrible," he says. Smillie is a jolly-sounding guy, easy to talk with. I am enjoying his company. And even as he's telling me not to look up the *Post* story, he's making it sound intriguing and guiding me to it. (He reminds me of Brer Rabbit pleading, "Oh, please don't throw me in the briar patch!")

"It's one of those classic 'take it out of context' stories," Smillie complains. "They quoted me saying a couple of things, which I did say, but when you take them out of context, they don't sound quite right. I'm telling you this because I want to make sure that this interview isn't that type, that this is more academic and not that type of attack article."

No worries, I assure him.

"She phoned,"—referring to the *Post* reporter—"and we had quite a long conversation, and I told her all the stuff about organics. I thought she honestly wanted to know the whole story. She'd already basically written the article and just wanted to get some damaging quotes. And she managed to string me along long enough so that she got them. She talked about organic as supposedly pure food, and I said, 'It's not pure food. What are you talking about?' I said, 'We live on this planet. This planet is polluted. And there's nothing pure about it. Water moves everywhere. Air moves everywhere.' I said, 'If you're looking for pure food you might have to get it from a greenhouse on Pluto.' And of course that's what's got quoted." He laughs. I laugh. And of course I go looking for the *Post* article, which pops up on my laptop with one search click.

The article by Kimberly Kindy and Lyndsey Layton is detailed, and it draws attention to the nonorganic ingredients the USDA (with advice from its Standards Board—which includes industry members) allows in foods that carry what the reporters correctly identify as the "coveted green-and-white USDA Organic seal."[12]

The article offers examples: Wood starch in grated cheese as an anticlumping agent and nonorganic hops approved for beer that's labeled organic. The reporters credit successful industry lobbying for the waivers. When the *Post* story was published in 2009, 245 nonorganic substances were approved by the USDA's National

Organic Standards Board for food stamped with the USDA Organic seal (a number that dropped to 203 by late 2013*).

By law 5 percent of a USDA certified organic food product can be nonorganic, but any nonorganic components must be on the approved list. (If the food is labeled 100 percent organic, it must be 100 percent organic—no exceptions allowed.) Items approved for that 5 percent are not supposed to be a health hazard, just neutral processing agents or additives with supposedly beneficial properties, like vitamins—or, in the case of the beer, some of the hops. It is hard to defend labeling beer as organic if the hops are otherwise. It just seems arbitrary to take the hops out of the equation. Hops means beer! It defies logic to make it legal to call beer organic if the hops are otherwise.

"Is you is or is you ain't my baby," sang Louis Jordan. "Is you is or is you ain't organic," I cry into my beer.

The article notes that Smillie's company, QAI, certifies 65 percent of the organic food boasting the USDA seal. Smillie tells the newspaper that it's unrealistic for consumers to seek an absolutist attitude from regulators toward organic food products, and that such a policy would restrict the sector's growth. "People are really hung up on regulations," the *Post* quotes him. "I say, 'Let's find a way to bend that one, because it's not important.' What are we selling? Are we selling health food? No. Consumers, they expect organic food to be growing in a greenhouse on Pluto. Hello? We live in a polluted world. It isn't pure. We are doing the best we can."

Smillie shouldn't expect that his compromises will be ignored by reporters. He enjoys resorting to hyperbole, and his Pluto example

---

* To calculate this number researcher Willemien Calitz tallied the allowed synthetic substances listed in the four different categories of what the USDA National Organic Program calls the National List of Allowed and Prohibited Substances. These categories are 1) nonorganically produced agricultural products allowed as ingredients in or on processed products labeled as organic, 2) nonagricultural nonorganic substances allowed as ingredients in or on processed products labeled as organic or as made with organic, 3) synthetic substances allowed for use in organic livestock production, and 4) synthetic substances allowed for use in organic crop production. Calitz counted the substances that were cross-referenced in different categories only once, and came up with the number 203.

offers an ideal opportunity to call into question something at the heart of my quest: the meaning of the USDA Organic seal.

An Inherent Conflict of Interest

Joe Smillie's candor is refreshing, so I ask him the question that so baffles me: Why should consumers have faith in the certification process since the certifiers are paid by those they certify?

"There's a long and complicated answer to that," he tells me, but he doesn't hesitate to tackle it. "I don't think the payment of the certifiers by their clients has anything to do with credibility," and he credits his company for adding integrity to the system. One formula for certification charges is based on percentage: The bigger a company's sales volume, the higher the certification fee, "and that's just wrong. That would lead to the kind of mistrust that's implicit in your question. One great step forward was made by QAI, and it is a reason why QAI is so prominent. Basically QAI charges a flat fee. Its job is to enforce the regulations. So just because they're paying you doesn't mean that they're paying for certification. They're paying for verification. And that's what they get. If you decertify or don't grant certification to a company, you still get paid. Now, admittedly, you won't get paid the next year if they don't get certified because they may not reapply for certification."

"If they don't come into compliance," I add, "then you've lost a customer."

"Correct. That's part of the game. But if you look at the numbers, most companies that apply for certification get certified. Very few companies that apply for certification don't eventually achieve certification." He's referring to companies that seek to adhere to the USDA standards. "We're not talking about fraud."

But there are crooks in the organic food world, just as there are in the rest of the world. Smillie and I talk about Harold Chase peddling conventional corn in Oregon as organic and serving federal prison time for the crime. We talk about a 2011 Italy case: tons of conventional grain from Bulgaria and Romania passed off as organic—authorities charged both government officials and traders with a crime that contaminated the organic food supply chain across Europe. I ask him if he worries that the fast-growing organic sector is attracting bad guys. How much fraud might be perpetrated that no one is discovering?

He first claims not to know, that it's an impossible thing to answer. But he adds, "I don't think as much as people fear. But there will be some, for sure." He's quick to offer what he calls "an alternative case," another opportunity to blame the messenger—us journalists. "There was a news channel in Washington that was going to do an exposé of organics." He tells me the station targeted a Whole Foods–branded product called California Stir Fry Mix, and all the ingredients in it were from China. "They made a big stink about it being fraudulent because it was called California Stir Fry. We were involved because we certify the Whole Foods private brand. Calling it 'California Stir Fry' was bad marketing, but it wasn't fraud. They weren't saying the vegetables were from California."

According to Smillie, the television station tested the vegetables "and they all turned out clean. They went into Whole Foods and they grabbed everything they could find that came from China and tested it all. Almost all of it tested clean except some ginger. They found a breakdown residue of a chemical product—I can't remember the name right now, but it's one used on potatoes, a really nasty, nasty pesticide." He tells me that the USDA did a thorough investigation and that QAI cooperated with checks back to the fields in China. "We could not find any fraud or any improper behavior. It was a chemical residue that can last many, many years. The ginger picked up this residue." Nonetheless, he complains, "the TV program didn't come out and say, 'Hey, the certification system actually works.' They didn't get the story they wanted, so they dropped it. They aired the accusations, then they didn't air anything of the follow-up."

"That sounds like just lousy journalism," I say. But that's just one case, and it lacks some important details—like the name of the TV station. Smillie says he can't recall. As do so many who discover their names in the press, Joe Smillie finds it easy to blame the messenger.

I steer him back toward my concerns. What is the definition of organic food? Why should I trust a label that claims what's inside the package is organic? And what about those walnuts and beans? What about Kazakhstan and Bolivia?

"In my ideal world," Smillie says, going back to his boilerplate, "the baseline is organic. It's not a plus or a minus; it's a base. You've got to be organic, and then you can make additional claims on nutrient density, on food miles, on carbon sequestration, on fair trade, on social responsibility, on community benefits. All of those things are interesting and valuable and each has its own metric, right?"

I agree. I understand the idealistic versus realistic concept.

"You can't ask organic to do all of these things. The mule cannot carry that much of a load. That was a debate that we had early in the organic industry. Many of the people wanted fair trade and social responsibility to be included in the organic standards. We made a wise decision at that time to say no. We can't solve the problems of the world with organic agricultural regulations. There are different metrics for all these other benefits."

If you wish to be a purist, you can make a list for yourself and decide if your philosophy of life allows you to eat asparagus in Oregon out of season, asparagus that is flown north from Peru in jets overheating Earth, asparagus that is, perhaps, cultivated by farm laborers working in unhealthy conditions, workers making inadequate wages and living in nasty slums. And asparagus that is— to use the Oregon vernacular—spendy.

"Some things are more important to you than others," Smillie says. He advocates using available technology so that smartphone-equipped shoppers can read a QR (quick response) bar code and immediately know the pedigree of a product. But all those other factors regarding its provenance—the miles it traveled to the grocery store, the working conditions on the farm and in the factory—should not, Smillie believes, influence whether food is called organic. "Nothing is perfect."

But Smillie says he is convinced, from his years around the world conducting inspections, that the system is sound, that it serves the needs of consumers who seek food free of poisonous pesticides and herbicides, harmful additives and preservatives.

"Anybody can commit fraud. Whether you inspect them unannounced or five times a year, if they're really committed to it, anybody can commit fraud." He sees the marketplace as the best regulator. "The number one way to discover fraud is competition. The competition blows the whistle. They know what's going on, whether it's adzuki beans from China or dried apricots from Turkey, they know that trade. If somebody's putting out stuff at a much lower price and inferior quality, they're going to blow the whistle. Number two is your famous disgruntled employee. That's how most fraud is discovered, by those two mechanisms."

Quality Assurance International and its competitors in the certification business, Smillie tells me, are not detectives looking for abuse. "What people don't understand is that basically when you do an inspection, you're not there looking for fraud. You're not trying to kick the garbage can or look for bags of chemicals or conventional prunes in the fruit juice mix. You're there to show that their system is organic and works."

He nevertheless offers a story of how surveying an organic farm with a practiced eye can result in finding the cheats.

"I remember doing a farm inspection at this one place. The crops looked good, and the fields were free of weeds, and I said to the manager, 'Jesus, this is a really clean field. It's really an incredible job on weeds. How do you do such a good job?' He said, 'Oh, I really cultivate a lot.' I said, 'Let's go look at your cultivators.' 'Oh, well,' he said, 'they're really far away.' 'Well let's go,' I said. We go, and the cultivators are rusty and I said, 'Hmm.' I looked at the guy and I said, 'Jeez, for someone who does a lot of cultivation, these are pretty rusty.' He said, 'Well, yeah, it's been a good year.' He was cheating. And I caught him. But that's pretty rare." Smillie is a natural storyteller.

"The way you catch them," he says of cheats, "is you see how their system works."

Again he points to the market as the best policeman.

"They have too much at stake to cheat," he says. It remains his working theory for most of the organic food industry.

Walnuts from Organicstan

I brief Smillie about my saga of beans and nuts marked Bolivia and Kazakhstan that has led to my quest.

Smillie emits a cynical-sounding laugh.

"And that's exactly the kind of laugh we exchanged," I say about my encounter with the Trader Joe's clerk when I returned the walnuts. "We laughed about the likelihood—in a place as awash with corruption as Kazakhstan—that these nuts could meet organic standards." Next I tell him about the black beans from Bolivia and how skeptical I am—especially after spending time in Bolivia chasing cocaine and seeing the corruption there—that the organic claim on the bean can is credible.

"I did some initial poking around and couldn't find any evidence that there's any kind of organic sector in beans or walnuts in Bolivia or Kazakhstan." I tell Smillie that I've been fantasizing that maybe there's some eccentric Brit named Nigel leaning up against a Kazakh walnut tree and he's got fifty acres of organic walnuts flourishing, and this was his dream life and the orchard is pristine. But then my daydream turns bleak and I think maybe there's some old bureaucrat from the Communist days guarding his pesticide- and herbicide-ridden orchard with an old AK-47, and he's got bags of DDT leaning up against the trees, and he's forging organic certification paperwork. I ask Smillie if those nuts and beans labels would raise questions for him. I tell him about my idea to trace the stuff back to the source.

He says if it were quinoa or coffee from Bolivia, it wouldn't trigger suspicion. "I didn't know they did beans." But he insists I ought to be able to learn the origin of the nuts, the beans, and whatever else I find on my grocery store shelf. "By law there has to be trail back. I'm not sure if you would have access, but the USDA certainly would have access to that entire trail and to all of the paperwork that would go back to Bolivia. And Kazakhstan."

Smillie outlines the international certification process for me and explains how the USDA accredits companies like QAI to peddle inspections that certify food to the USDA National Organic Standards. "Does that mean QAI had boots on the ground in Kazakhstan?" he offers. "The answer is not necessarily at all. Trader Joe's gets a lot of organic product certified by a lot of different agencies and if they had to, by law, put who it was certified by on each package and if their supplier of walnuts changed because they got a better price in Kazakhstan, they'd have to change their packaging. So to avoid that entire problematic and very disruptive process, Trader Joe's gets certified by us as a 'trader,' and they have to have a legitimate USDA certificate from whoever they bought the walnuts from."

In other words, QAI outsources its inspections in faraway places like Kazakhstan to still another certifier, one that is on an approved USDA list of worldwide USDA-accredited certifiers who supposedly meet USDA requirements for checking the veracity of growers, producers, and shippers claiming to meet American organic standards. In theory, that certifier inspected the walnuts, or at least the walnuts' paper trail. But neither Trader Joe's nor QAI needs know anything about the day-to-day operations of the walnut orchard in order to slap a USDA Organic label on those rancid nuts I bought in Eugene.

Nonetheless, again in theory, both Trader Joe's and QAI ought to be able to determine where those walnuts were grown, even if Trader Joe's is buying them from a wholesaler located far from the orchard. Or maybe not. The wholesaler could have sourced the walnut inventory from a Kazakh silo stuffed with walnuts from any number of individual growers. Again—in theory—there would be paperwork to study from each of the farms. But if the documentation from one of the farms was suspect, of course it would be impossible to differentiate the walnuts piled in the silo and pick out those of concern. In order to vet the entire batch, all the growers contributing to the silo would need to be investigated.

No big deal, says Smillie. It's the reality now that organic food is big business.

I tell him about Kazakhstan's dreadful post-Soviet-era history of corruption—the discredited government officials, the assaults on press freedom, and the abandoned EuropeAid project to develop an organic sector for Kazakh agriculture.

We chat for a few moments about *Borat,* Sacha Baron Cohen's film about a bumbling Kazakh journalist. There's a scene in the movie where Borat sings what is supposedly Kazakhstan's national anthem: "Kazakh industry best in world / We invented toffee and trouser belt / Kazakhstan's prostitutes cleanest in the region / Except of course for Turkmenistan's." The anthem parody achieved further fame in 2012 when Kazakh sharpshooter Mariya Dmitriyenko won a gold medal in the Arab Shooting Championship held in Kuwait. As she received her award, organizers of the event played a recording apparently sourced from the Internet—Borat's version of the Kazakh anthem. A good sport, Dmitriyenko kept her hand over her heart as the faux anthem marched on with its martial beat and bizarre lyrics, "Kazakhstan, Kazakhstan you very nice place / From the plains of Tarashek to the northern fence of Jewtown / Come grasp the mighty penis of our leader / From junction with the testes to the tip of its face."[13]

41

If the staff at an international sporting event cannot differentiate between Borat's anthem and the official version, is it unreasonable to question organic labels from Kazakhstan? (The Kazakhstan Parliament responded to the anthem insult: Get caught in the country "desecrating" the anthem these days, and the penalty is a year in prison.[14])

I tell Smillie that his colleagues at QAI refuse to help me find the source of the walnuts (or the black beans), claiming they need authorization from Trader Joe's (and Natural Directions), and that both companies refused, citing proprietary business interests.

"That's pretty normal," he says. "People don't want to disclose their sources because they think they've got a commercial advantage on their competitors."

I'm not convinced. "If that's normal, how is it possible that protecting business secrets is of greater import than providing the kind of transparency that would give credibility to a claim that sounds as far-fetched to me as organic walnuts from Kazakhstan?"

"It's a balance of interests," he explains patiently. But then he suggests a possible alternative route toward the nut orchards and bean fields. "Make a formal complaint to the USDA. They will jump in and determine which interest is paramount here. They can demand from us at any second that we track this and do an investigation on it." He's only a few weeks into his retirement, so the corporate "we" is understandable. "That's in their power, and it's in your power to file a formal complaint. You don't have any solid information to say that these things aren't organic, but you have reasonable suspicions. You think it's highly specious. That's what we always, always recommend: go to the USDA."

Which I do.

The Organic Taliban

But first I want to take advantage of Joe Smillie for a few more thoughts about organic food and compromise, about labeling and consumer literacy. According to the USDA National Organic Program regulations, processed foods with as little as 70 percent organic content may be labeled "made with organic ingredients" even if the product does not meet the 95 percent organic threshold that allows a producer to slap the USDA Organic seal on the package. Which of those ingredients are organic must be cited, and those ingredients must meet USDA standards. Smillie likes the compromise and offers an example to explain why.

"Corn chips have about 23 percent oil," he tells me. Reason enough to switch to carrots for the hummus dip, that figure makes me think. "That's what they run. If you're in a corn chip factory, you can bring in organic corn and thread it through the machine, deep fry it in oil, and come out with a product. To change the oil bath and switch oils is monumental work. It's not just the cost—the increased cost of organic oil—but it's actually switching the bath, which is a huge operation. [Given] the fact that organic oil is really expensive and that changing over from conventional to organic oil is a really laborious operation, producers decided to make corn chips—most of them—with organic corn, but the oil isn't organic. It allows them to buy organic corn and support organic corn growers, but put out a product that's reasonable in price for the Twinkie and the corn dog lovers of the world." We both laugh at his reference to shoppers who abandon organics for favorites. "And still sell a product that is checked and proven to be over 70 percent organic."

"I wonder how many consumers understand the nuances of the rules." I'm thinking about a lunch I shared with friends in Georgetown, just across DC from the monumental Agriculture Department headquarters. "You think shoppers believe that it's all organic?"

I tell Smillie about a journalist friend of mine and his wife, a psychologist. I figure her training ought to include an understanding of what Vance Packard identified back in the 1950s as "the hidden persuaders" in his book with the same title. "Motivational analysts," Packard wrote, "are learning to offer us considerably more than the actual item involved." The author points to soap and skin cream as an example. Soap is cheap, but it only cleans. Skin cream is expensive, but it promises beauty.[15]

My friend and his wife do most of their grocery shopping at the Wisconsin Avenue Whole Foods. When I told them about my quest for the source of my "organic" nuts and beans, she expressed shock that there could be any question about what she piles in her shopping cart. She told me she just figured Whole Foods inspected every organic product before putting it in their store.

Smillie reiterated that he supports not just the 70 percent rule. He embraces the fact that a product can show off the USDA Organic seal if at least 95 percent of it qualifies as organic, by USDA definition. (That other 5 percent, as noted earlier, may include any substances on the long USDA list titled—appropriately—the National Organic Program List of Allowed and Prohibited Substances.[16])

"The list of allowable ingredients in the 5 percent is very closely examined and determined," says Smillie. The National Organic Standards Board (Again, Smillie is a former member who represented the organic food industry) reviews petitions to add or subtract from the list, petitions ruled on by the National Organic Program administrator. "I think they just recently disallowed carrageenan, which is criminal. The purists in the organic movement are becoming like the Taliban."

I suggest this comparison is a bit strong.

But he laughs and reiterates his characterization. "Carrageenan was a very reasonable ingredient, and somehow they militated against it and now you're not allowed to use carrageenan, which is a biopolymer from the kelp plant. It's not organic, but goodness gracious, it should be allowed."

The "Organic Taliban" would include the Cornucopia Institute ("Promoting economic justice for family scale farming"), which lobbied against the carrageenan waiver, citing research that "links the controversial food ingredient to gastrointestinal inflammation, including higher rates of colon cancer, in laboratory animals."[17] In 2013 the National Organic Standards Board did recommend that carrageenan be prohibited in food labeled organic, but the recommendation was denied. The board expressed concern about the safety of consuming carrageenan, but since the Food and Drug Administration considers carrageenan a safe food additive, it stayed on the approved list.[18]

Cornucopia calls the carrageenan decision a prime example of inappropriate and overwhelming corporate influences skewing National Organic Standards Board choices. It insists that USDA stewardship on what organic means "is illegal and has inappropriately favored corporate agribusiness over the interests of ethical businesses, farmers and consumers." Cornucopia issued a scathing report detailing the backgrounds of board members with what the organization identified as clear conflicts of interest. It pointed to board member Carmela Beck, for example, who filled a board chair reserved for a farmer and was identified by Cornucopia as "a full-time employee at Driscoll's, which markets both conventional and organic berries. Beck manages the organic certification for Driscoll's farmers and suppliers, and does not own or operate an organic farm."[19]

Another of Smillie's Organic Taliban would be Eden Foods founder Michael Potter, who, after the carrageenan vote, spat, "The board is stacked. Either they don't have a clue or their interest in making money is more important than their interest in maintaining the integrity of organics."[20] Eden Foods was founded as a co-op in late-1960s Ann Arbor, Michigan, and is a well-respected major player in the organic world. Once Sheila learned that the can of Natural Directions black beans were BPA suspect, she turned to Eden and its well-publicized BPA-free packaging as a substitute. Eden's Potter told the *New York Times* that the USDA Organic label is a fraud, and Eden refuses to display it on it products, from cans of beans and tomatoes to boxes of soy milk and pasta.

Third-party certifiers inspect Eden Foods' operation, and the company announces with pride that its product line "meets and exceeds requirements for the USDA organic seal, but we do not use it because it does not reflect Eden standards, in spirit or in practice." Eden cites "hundreds of chemicals and 'allowables' permitted in the USDA National Organic Program that Eden avoids. With USDA," laments Eden, "organic certification requirements vary a lot, all the way to nonexistent. Accountability is rare, especially for imported food."[21] Those words about the USDA organic certification process clearly resonate with me as I chase my walnuts and black beans: *Accountability is rare, especially for imported food.*

At a 2013 National Organic Standards Board meeting in Portland, the Oregon Tilth farm program manager Richard Carr argued that the antibiotic tetracycline should remain on the list of allowable substances until a practical organic substance is developed to replace it. There's nothing other than tetracycline to fight apple blight, he claimed. Cornucopia Institute lobbyist Mary Mann testified otherwise. "I'd like to see organics be part of the solution and not part of the problem," she told the board. "Consumers Union polling data show that I am not the only one who believes apples or pears treated with antibiotics should not be sold as organic." Mann referred to the parents in her extended Oregon family. "When something says 'organic baby food,' and that's what they're putting in their baby, they want to know that 100 percent of that pear juice or that pear puree is organic."

The Organic Taliban won that battle. Following public comments in Portland, the board rejected the appeal by growers to continue the use of the antibiotic on apples labeled organic; it had been allowed in an effort to fight fire blight, a bacterial pathogen.[22]

Before we say good-bye, I ask Smillie if the organic sector is going to take over the grocery business or if it's a passing fad.

"Ten years ago you could ask that question," he says. We're talking in 2013. "It was a legitimate question ten years ago. No, it's a trend. If we don't shoot ourselves in the foot or the head because we're changing the rules of the game and things get too complicated. An overly simplistic purist attitude that organic food has to be pure is dangerous. It's really hard to produce pure food. A lot of people are trying to make organics totally pure, and by doing so they throw the baby out with the bathwater. A lot of people hate the fact that organics are in Wal-Mart. I disagree. I think it's great. Some poor family that would never be exposed to organics buys it and they like it and the kids say, 'Oh, this is good, Mom, buy this stuff.' All of a sudden you've got some kids having some organic baby food that otherwise wouldn't get it if it wasn't carried by Wal-Mart."

His closing sermon surges.

"Am I hard on the purists? Yeah. I've been battling the purists from day one. My idea is that organic food shouldn't be Yuppie Puppy Chow. It should be available to everyone. I don't have problems with operations like General Mills getting into organics. I think it's a good thing. I certified a lot of these companies. People always say, 'Well, don't the big companies bend the rules?' and no, they don't. They actually want stricter rules so that they have a bigger price differential between their conventional food and their organic food. The purists, by trying to tighten the organic regulations, are making it hard on the small grower. And if General Mills says, 'You know what, this organic regulatory thing is just too crazy; we got too many crazy exposé writers trying to condemn organics and put it down. We just can't take chances with organics anymore; let's pull out of it,' well, who suffers? The farmers who would have supplied them with their organic goods—organic raw materials—go out of business. What good does that do? That's my argument."

Vermont-based reporter Ken Picard once asked Smillie how an organic food inspector and certifier does his job. "Almost Zenlike," Picard called Smillie's answer. "If you're looking for something, you won't find it," Smillie told Picard. "But if you're not looking for something, you see *everything*."[23]

That analysis seems to fit my quest. I started out looking for organic beans in Bolivia and organic walnuts in Kazakhstan. I have yet to find them (and doubt more and more that they exist, as my search for them continues). But what I was not looking for—and what I fear I may well be seeing—is a fast-growing globalized organic food sector of the economy that at worst is fraud ridden and at best suffers from compromises that make every package of food certified organic suspect.

Chapter Four

THE MAN BEHIND USDA ORGANIC

The United States Department of Agriculture building on the Washington Mall is a mammoth landmark—covering two full city blocks. Built in the 1930s, its architecture is called Depression Modern by the government, a so-called "starved classicism" that borrows from the ancients while announcing grand pragmatic purpose.[24] It's time to meet the bureaucrat at Agriculture who is in charge of the National Organic Program, the guy who—figuratively, of course—puts the USDA Organic seal on our pricey groceries.

I arrive there on a frigid late-winter day; the wind is fierce, biting into my West Coast self. As I wait in line outside to pass through the airportlike security, I'm more interested in getting into the warm building than worried that the schoolkids ahead of me may intend to do harm to American agriculture. A uniformed guard with a Smokey Bear ranger hat, big curls of fake eyelashes, and a big gun to match finally gives me the A-OK. After noting a sign that informs me it is National Nutrition Month, I begin the long march down seemingly endless corridors to the headquarters of the USDA National Organic Program.

Miles McEvoy came to the USDA following twenty years at a similar job in Washington State. He welcomes me into his simple office suite, empty because his secretary is not working. With his wire-rimmed glasses framing earnest-looking eyes, his close-cropped hair, and lanky frame, McEvoy reminds me of a Boy Scout leader. "That sounds really fun," he says with enthusiasm when I tell him of my beans and nuts quest.

"It ought to be great fun," I agree, and then offer a glimpse of what I've been imagining I'll find at the end of the walnut trail. "There's either some guy named Nigel from England who decided to buy acreage in Kazakhstan and he's got this idyllic, organic farm there, which he watches over while leaning self-satisfied against one of his pristine trees, or I'm going to find some hustler with a bag of DDT and a stack of fake organic labels leaning against the tree. Those are my two images."

He seems surprised by Nigel, but still happy hear about my trek to primary sources. "Your story is my passion, I guess. What I really enjoy about this work is that as auditors we track the product from receiving through shipping, from the farm all the way to the market or from the market all the way back to the farm. It's a fascinating story of how that happens on both a local level and a global level. I'm glad you're doing this story."

We're off to a good start. The US government (unlike Denmark's) does not, as noted, inspect and certify food labeled organic. "We oversee the folks that are doing that. We make sure systems are in place so that inspections are done with high integrity and verify what the label claims." His office oversees and audits the certifying outfits like Oregon Tilth and Ecocert and Quality Assurance International. In order to qualify as a USDA certifier, a company like QAI must satisfy McEvoy that its inspections meet USDA requirements.

Those requirements include "preventing conflicts of interest" by engaging in internal reviews, employing qualified inspectors, and overseeing the personnel who do the fieldwork. The USDA is not just looking out for the American consumer, it's taking care of business. Certifiers, McEvoy explains, "must be confidential in terms of business-related information, but also disclose information that must be publicly available."

I bring him back to the beginning of his litany and ask how we consumers can feel confident when certifiers are paid by those they inspect. Especially since some certifiers base their fees on a percentage of the total sales of the products they inspect, the system seems like such an obvious case of the fox guarding the (free-range) henhouse. He cites what he calls industry norms. "That's probably the most common way that most regulatory programs are set up, through some kind of user fees. The ones that are paying for the inspection are paying some kind of inspector to come in and verify it. That's a very common model worldwide." Conflicts of interest, he insists, are not inherent in such a model.

"What is really, really important," he contends, "is that those organizations that are doing the inspections and certifying products have systems in place to ensure that they are not unduly influenced by being paid for doing the work." *Unduly?* That's a worrisome modifier. But McEvoy insists that self-interest kicks in and acts as a control agent. "The incentive for them to not be unduly influenced is that if they are unduly influenced, then they're going to lose their USDA accreditation and lose their ability to do the work at all."

Right. But who is keeping track of the certifiers, making sure that their clients don't "unduly" influence *them?*

Don't worry, McEvoy comforts me, claiming the "integrity is very much there." Where does that integrity come from? Pride and a generation of dedication to a lifestyle, he says, because "the people involved are generally very committed to organic agriculture and making sure that the standards are being met." That makes sense when the players are graduates of the *Whole Earth Catalog.* But in this globalized economy, with Wal-Mart filling its aisles with "organic" this and that, are consumers expected to believe that the buyers from Bentonville, Arkansas, stop to check on the veracity of the QAI seal on a box of breakfast cereal? And what about the different histories of Oregon Tilth and Quality Assurance International? Oregon

Tilth's roots do go back to the 1960s' and 1970s' back-to-the-land movements; QAI is a corporate animal.

"Well, sure," McEvoy agrees, "there's a cultural difference. They're different organizations. They came from different places, but now they're regulated, and very tightly regulated, mostly by the US, but by the EU as well. A lot of people are looking at what they're doing."

Our talk is not combative, even when I ask if his own USDA office is susceptible to conflicts of interest since it charges certifiers for the audits they must pass to be licensed by the government to do business.

"Nobody's stuffing twenty-dollar bills in your pocket?"

"No," he laughs. "It wouldn't make a difference anyway."

Miles McEvoy exudes confidence; it's delightful to talk with him because of his enthusiasm for the industry he oversees—even at points where I fail to appreciate the compromises the USDA makes, government-industry deals that constitute the National Organic Program.

I tell him what he knows well: "You guys are attacked all the time for the National Organic Standards. Your critics claim that the standards aren't adequate, that you allow for additives and nonorganic ingredients that compromise the philosophy of organic food movements."

"Right," he agrees readily.

"How do you rationalize the point of no return? What's okay to allow in a package that still claims the status of USDA Organic?" I'm not asking him for a product-by-product rationalization or explanation. I want to understand conceptually and philosophically why it's okay to slap on a government seal claiming "organic" when it's not 100 percent so. "How can you sit here in Washington and say, 'I'm taking care of organic for America,' when there's this other stuff in the box?"

In response he recounts the history of the US organic policy, how the National Organic Standards Board—made up of so-called stakeholders: organic farmers, environmentalists, consumers, handlers, certifiers, scientists—recommend the definitions of "organic" for USDA labeling purposes. "From our perspective, we're just implementing the standards that the organic community, expressed through this National Organic Standards Board, has recommended."

Some stakeholders believe the standards should be stricter, while others want them looser, and the standards change over time. That's the beauty of the USDA system, says McEvoy. "It's actually the envy of the world. In Europe they have a much less transparent process in terms of how they develop the organic standards and there's a lot of complaints that there's not enough access by the organic community in terms of the development of the standards. If you compare the standards of Europe and the US, the US has much stronger standards in terms of organics, and so our process is, I guess, working in terms of making sure that the standards are very strict."

He cites antibiotics as an example, saying they're prohibited in USDA-approved organic livestock in the United States and only restricted in the European Union. Pesticide restrictions are tighter, he says, in the United States than across the Atlantic.

Nonetheless, products proudly displaying the USDA Organic seal may contain "agricultural ingredients that, if they're not available in an organic form, can be sourced nonorganically." These, McEvoy explains patiently, "tend to be mostly colors and a fairly small list of herbs and spices. But the agricultural ingredients in an organic product that displays the seal basically have to be organic."

I ask him about the sanctity of the environment where crops considered organic grow. "What about the dirt? What about the water?"

"It wouldn't make any sense to require testing of water if you were in a pristine area of Ecuador," he says, "where there's no upstream contamination."

"As long as there isn't a gold mine upstream."

"Right, it's all going to be site-specific. Some of the beauty of the National Organic Standards is it protects natural resources, improving and maintaining soil and water quality."

McEvoy starts preaching his organic gospel to me, insisting that the National Organic Standards protect soil, water, and crops against contamination. He claims that the rules force farmers to consider how their neighbors work the land, and he cites pesticide drift as an example. If a conventional farm is next door to an organic one, the organic grower may be required to create a buffer zone between his crops and the ones across the fence line if the conventional farm is doused with pesticides from a crop duster.

An Official Trackback Story

I ask Miles McEvoy if he's ever reverse-engineered organic foodstuffs, gone out in the field himself and tracked a product back to its origin. "Sure," he says.

"Tell me a great story," I urge, "of going back to a source and finding a Nigel—either surveying his pristine organic crop or spraying his illicit DDT."

He thinks back to his Washington State days and a shipment of organic fruit to Europe. "I'm not sure if it was the UK or the Netherlands that found residues of diphenylamine, DPA, on the fruit. We had to evaluate where it was coming from, and it was partially coming from the fruit bins. Apples are put into wooden bins and for conventional fruit, if it's going into long-term storage, those bins are then put through a drench, which includes the DPA that reduces scald during storage. What was happening was that those bins that had been drenched were then used the next year for organic fruit. The diphenylamine is a low-molecular-weight substance that was in the wood and would volatize. Low levels of it would then be present on the organic fruit."

The investigation led to changed business practices for the organic apples.

"They either used plastic bins that were washed or they used dedicated organic bins that were never drenched. That, more or less, eliminated the DPA. DPA would occasionally still show up because it actually occurs naturally in a few agricultural products and so, at very low levels, sometimes you can detect it. It also was occasionally found when there wasn't adequate separation on the packing line. There was an organic packing line and a conventional packing line. When you find residues you must determine why those residues are there. Are they there because of a misuse, because somebody actually used the DPA on the organic apples, or is it there because those measures to prevent commingling or contamination were not adequate?"

Not a very sexy story, but an example of the kinds of problems that can occur when producers and processors mix the conventional and the organic.

I ask him, from his vast experience, what he thinks I'm going to find in Bolivia and Kazakhstan.

His is an optimist's answer. "You'll find organic farms at the end of the line that will be incredibly interesting with an interesting community of people who are involved in producing those organic products for export."

"Of appropriate standards?"

"Yeah, absolutely. And I hope that's what it is. But it's not like it's a perfect system that's 100 percent across the board. We find problems. We helped put three people in jail this last year; one guy was from Oregon, buying conventional corn and selling it as organic, Harold Chase."

I congratulate him on helping catch Chase.

"We had two fertilizer dealers in California who were selling fertilizer, liquid fertilizer, and spiking it with synthetic urea or ammonium sulfate, synthetic nitrogen sources, and selling it to organic farmers. Part of our job is to enforce as appropriate."

"But only three cases all of last year?" I find the number tiny, given the extent of the organic food trade. One of the fertilizer hustlers was Canadian Peter Townsley, who, as acting president of California Liquid Fertilizer, sold six million dollars' worth of fertilizer the company called Biolizer XN and labeled organic. In fact, Biolizer contained banned synthetics. Townsley pleaded guilty and was sentenced to 364 days in jail, hit with a $125,000 fine, and ordered deported to Canada after he served his jail time.

Still another organic fraud case was initiated by the Texas Department of Agriculture against Basilio Coronado and his Sel-Cor Bean and Pea Company headquartered in Brownsville. Coronado falsified Sel-Cor paperwork and sold conventional milo and beans as organic. His sentence was two years in prison, another three of supervised release, and a hefty half a million dollars in restitution.

"Those cases took a number of years to prosecute," McEvoy says, "and those are very significant levels of fraud. Last year [2012] we handled or closed 279 complaints and those are a wide variety of complaints." Most of the complaints he characterizes as minor. "They were about operations making organic claims without certification. It doesn't mean it's not organic; it means that they're trying to avoid the certification process." Some companies lose their certification because of sloppy paperwork or because they fail to pay required fees to the USDA. McEvoy is proud to report that his office levied $120,000 worth of fines in 2012 for various violations—but since the US organic sector is worth over two dozen billion dollars a year, either the industry is angelic or it's suffering barely a slap on the wrist.

One USDA Inspector per One Billion Dollars

It's illegal, McEvoy tells me, to market something that says "organic" that does not meet the criteria—even if you aren't putting a fraudulent USDA seal on it.

"I can't sell something and call it Peter's Organic Food on the label?" I ask.

"Unless it's certified. There are some exemptions and exclusions. So a small farm that's under five thousand dollars in sales a year does not have to get certified."

"Like at the farmers' market at Eugene, if a guy is just selling corn out of the back of his truck, he can call it organic?"

"If he has more than five thousand dollars in sales, he has to be certified. It doesn't take much to get up to five thousand dollars in sales, so that's where we get a lot of complaints, because you have certified organic farms that are competing against people that are not being certified."

"But what we hear from some small growers is, 'We can't afford the process, so we're just going to tell you it's organic because we can't pay to get it certified.'"

McEvoy says the USDA is working on a plan to make certification easier and more affordable for the little guys. Until and unless changes are made, "they can't call it organic."

But inspectors are not out looking for little violators. McEvoy works with a skeletal staff. His office is modest—it's a delightful office, comfortable, decorated with a map of the United States and a picture of the globe. An air conditioner is hanging in the push-up-and-down window that is covered by Venetian blinds. We're sitting in a couple of basic government-issue chairs. On an end table are a few agriculture tchotchkes: models of a cow and a pig, a toy harvester.

"Yeah, the National Organic Program is small," he acknowledges. "What do we figure? One person for every billion dollars in sales."

I'm shocked. The USDA figures that annual sales of organic food total about twenty-seven billion dollars (and make up less than 4 percent of America's grocery bills), and Miles McEvoy's staff numbers about twenty-seven? Sounds like easy pickings out there for fraudsters.

He agrees with me that this is a sobering number and that of course he could use more staff and resources.

"What was on the dinner table at your house last night?" I ask Miles McEvoy.

"We had chicken and peas and salad."

"Free range?" I think of *Portlandia*'s chicken, Colin. "Where did you buy the chicken and the peas and the salad fixings?"

"Local grocery stores."

"So was the chicken fresh off the Sysco truck, or was it a free-ranging organic Rocky?"

"I don't know," he acknowledges. "I think my wife picked up something pretty quickly on the chicken part, but mostly we buy organic." The wife is on the staff of a food cooperative. They are fellow travelers. "Organic is the way we've eaten for a very long time. The majority of our food is organic." And they grow some of their own.

I tell him how my wife Sheila is hard-core about these things, whereas I'm happy to buy a regular cantaloupe for half the price.

"Yeah," he agrees. We're talking like a couple of guys at a bar. "My wife is kind of hard-core, too." In addition to favoring the yield from their family garden, McEvoy tells me that he tries to buy produce directly from nearby organic farms. "I know the farmers and I know what they do. I support what they do."

McEvoy expresses overwhelming confidence in foods that exhibit his USDA Organic seal—even if they originate far from home. "It's very, very rare that we find outright fraud where people are buying conventional and selling it as organic."

"The Harold Chases are the anomalies?"

"They're the anomalies, right. But it does happen. You know, there's money to be made. And where there's money to be made, there are people who will try to get away with fraud."

Chapter Five

OLD-WORLD ORGANIC

It's Easter Sunday and I am in Vienna, looking out at the snowfall and the thermometer hanging from the facade of the W. Neuber's Enkel building. Zero degrees it reads: freezing. It is the second week of spring and a continuation of the coldest winter in 130 years, according to a journalist friend here. I am in Austria to witness the growth of organic farming, the rigorous engagement of government in the process that certifies food as organic, and the enthusiastic *wellkommen* to things organic—*bio*, to use the local terminology—at Austrian dinner tables. Not that the Austrian consumer lives without contradictions.

I meet with an American academic at Café Ritter, a traditional Viennese coffeehouse. A waiter in black and white regalia brings a glass of water to accompany the espresso served in china at the table. The academic muses to me over our leisurely drink about how bizarre he finds it to witness Austrians smoking cigarettes while rhapsodizing about their organic diets. And smoking they are in the Ritter as we talk—smoking, well dressed, and reading newspapers attached to classic wooden newspaper sticks.

As is the case in Catalonia, proximity is a crucial criterion for Austrian *bio* products. Austrians are taught to pay attention to the origin of what they eat, and to give preference to Austrian products, by the overt advertising campaigns of supermarket chains and the subtler inferences of xenophobic nationalism. I meet a local journalist at another coffeehouse near my flat, the Hummel—a place laden with Austrian specialities—who laughs about the locavore habits of his neighbors. "Proximity," he scoffs. "That's the argument of my girlfriend, but others say, 'Buy Austrian so you don't give money to the French!'"

Over a beer at the Café Drechsler, a colleague who now lives in Oregon but was born and raised in Austria insists that the extra cost of organic products sits well with the Austrian character. Viennese believe, he tells me, that they should expect to pay high prices if they wish to purchase high-quality goods. He tells me that the American idea of bargain hunting doesn't suggest to Austrians a good deal; it suggests poor quality. The Drechsler family founded the place in 1919, and the spendy menu prices suggest Austrians find the offerings of a decent quality.

Sheila, who is traveling through Europe with me, and I move into a flat in Josefstadt, Vienna's 8th District, on Tigergasse. My shopping street is Josefstädterstraße, where we grab enough survival groceries for the next day or so at Spar—choosing organic (often at a premium price) whenever possible. The olive oil is labeled from Greece, *kaltextrahiert*—"cold pressed," notes Sheila, impressed. The oil is Spar's private label *Natur-pur* (the hyphen is a stylized daisy) and carries the *bio* seal of the Austrian government's AMA—Agrarmarkt Austria—the entity that oversees basic organic certification. The vinegar is also *Natur-pur* and balsamic. We find *bio-produkte* cherry tomatoes, a bag of five lemons, long and skinny sweet red peppers from Israel, a Spanish cucumber, half-price Spanish strawberries (they're quite ripe), a *bio salatmix* ("washed, cut and ready"), and Austrian potatoes—all with the Spar *Natur-pur* label and the government's seal of approval. I grab a box of sencha green tea.

Sheila wants eggs and we find a carton of ten, with a note printed on the box and signed by Joachim Massani, the quality control manager at Spar, guaranteeing that the eggs are organic. We buy organic smoked tofu and note that unlike a bunch of other products at Spar, this brand—*Natürlich für Uns*—does not promise on its label that the soybeans it was made from were not GMO. Trudging back through the snow to the flat, we stop at Gradwohls bakery—which advertises its organic *Brot der woche*: the bread of the week this week is carrot and nut.

Bio Fish

A couple of days later, Saturday, we need more groceries. The blue law here in Austria regarding shopping hours, the *ladenschlußgesetz* (literally the "store-close law"), means that we need to stock up. Markets shut down from Saturday afternoon until Monday morning. For an American used to twenty-four-hour consumerism, the *ladenschlußgesetz* is insane, but plenty of my Austrian friends and colleagues embrace the enforced Sunday of rest.

I head up to the Brunnenmarkt, an open-air bazaar just on the other side of the elevated train tracks from my flat. The difference between the two neighborhoods is radical. My relatively posh 8th District shops and the serious-acting clientele exchanging their soft-spoken *Grüß Gott* and *auf Wiedersehen* greetings change in a few blocks to Istanbul-on-the-Danube. Polyglot hawkers yell out their sale prices. Heaping piles of bright red bell peppers, bags of oranges, off-white cauliflower, and long green zucchini compete for space with cases of animal parts—from heads and hearts to the more traditional cuts familiar to American shoppers. I see nothing labeled *bio*. I head for a stand marked Fisch Paradies—fish paradise—and look at the offerings on ice. The fishmonger asks me what I want as I look at half a salmon and its Technicolor-red flesh.

"Where does the salmon come from?" I ask him, dreaming of the wild sockeye and cojo back home in Oregon.

"Norway," he says.

"Is it farmed?" I ask. It's an idle question. All Atlantic commercial salmon is farmed.[25]

He shrugs, noncommittal.

"Come on," I say. "If it's from Norway, it's farmed. Right?"

"Yeah, it's farmed," he agrees.

I ask him if it's good.

"I don't know. I just sell it."

We're smiling. The banter is as much of the draw at the Brunnenmarkt for me as are the bargains compared with the prices on my side of the tracks.

I go one more round with him. "Does it taste good?"

"You tell me after you eat it," he says.

I buy two steaks and tell him I'll be back with a report next week. (They were nasty: They smelled too fishy when I pulled them from the package to cook them, and once on the dinner table, their chewy flesh competed with gristle and slime.) After buying a bag of oranges, I round a corner on Yppenplatz to buy a tulip for Sheila and see a stand marked Biofisch. There I am with a pound of salmon that was fed who knows what while it swam in who knows what kind of water, and I find an organic fish outlet. Whatever organic fish is. The Biofisch company offers smoked fish and fresh fish: salmon and trout, carp and pike. A smiling clerk with a curly back beard is smoking a stub of a cigarette while cutting up smoked fish samples. He tells me about the pristine conditions where the Biofisch fish are raised, a few hours' drive from Vienna, north near the Czech border. He tells me what they eat (grains and oils) and how they're trucked down to the Brunnenmarkt live, kept in vast tubs at a warehouse until it's time to sell them for dinners. This place merits further exploration—both for my dinner plate and my organic quest.

A few weeks later, at the Biofisch warehouse I meet with the company's founder, Marc Mösmer. The first thing I want to know is what makes his fish organic. The answer is everything: the eggs, the water they hatch in, the feed the fish eat as they grow. "What you feed is what you eat," he says with a fish farmer's variation on the you-are-what-you-eat theme. European Union regulations require that at least two-thirds of the life of a fish sold as organic must be lived in an officially organic environment. "You can't ever say a fish is 100 percent organic. But it's nearly nothing," Mösmer says about the nonorganic characteristics of a fish harvested from his farm. His fish, Mösmer says with pride, are a better catch than the same species swimming in the wild outside the borders of his farm. "I take care of them. My fish get what they need. I feed the fish. In the wild they have to look for it and take care of themselves."

A fish farmer since his early teens, Mösmer appears content, sitting at his desk, farmed fish swimming anonymously in his tanks there in the heart of the city. When I ask him how he rounds them up for the journey in the tanker trucks south to Vienna, his answer reminds me of the time I asked an ice maker in the Nevada desert his business model. He deadpanned, "We freeze water, Peter."

With that same naïveté I was imagining that Mösmer and his crew must fish for the fish. "I drain the water and then I take them with a net," he says. He keeps the live fish in his city aquariums until the day they're sold—just a few hours from the dinner table. "That is what fish should be. It's hard work. It's expensive. But it's the best quality."

A few days before Mösmer and I talk fish in his office, I sampled his product—a delicious grilled trout, tasty as anything wild from the waters of my Pacific Northwest. Mösmer is not surprised by my rave review. What surprises him is the dearth of knowledge expressed by the organic certifiers who come to inspect his operation. "Most of them don't know anything about fish farming," he says with dismissal. They ask him questions, but he's convinced they don't understand the answers. They just check the appropriate boxes on their questionnaires.

"It's the same with chickens and tomatoes," he figures. "They should have a school where they learn about organic farming. They're only checking the papers." Since they don't understand how a fish farm works, "sometimes they don't look at what they're asking about or they don't ask the right questions." Not that customers can pick up the slack by poking around the farm for themselves. "Ha," he says. "The consumers don't know anything." At least the certifiers—especially those who make repeated trips to Biofisch—know something about basic organic concepts and regulations. "The consumer doesn't know anything about fish farming. Why should he?" Why, indeed. Unless we're curious about the origins of our food, shouldn't we expect that we can trust producers and the government officials who inspect them? Or is that as naïve as my question to the ice maker?

On the other side of the Atlantic (an ocean home to farms of salmon, much of it colored with red dye to look wilder for the marketplace), the USDA is floundering about, trying to figure out what aquaculture means to its National Organic Program. As of 2013 no farmed fish were authorized to display the USDA Organic seal. In addition, the National Organic Standards Board was wrestling with the nonorganic stuff America will allow farmed fish to ingest—what vitamins, how much chlorine, the contents of fish feed binders.

Transparency—along with tasty fish—is the Biofisch stock-in-trade. "I'm not producing for an anonymous market," says Mösmer. He invites his regular customers to come up to the farm and experience what he calls the "harvest." There they can connect with what he calls the "soul" of his business, and that soul, he's convinced, is missing from big factory fish farms. "This is not really certifiable," he says about his organic soul food. He ticks off things forbidden for organic fish farming—chemical fertilizers, antibiotics—things that the factory fish farmers may well avoid. "But he needs a soul for it," Mösmer believes, in order to raise an optimal farmed fish. "If you look at the big organic shrimp industry in Ecuador, they put a lot of small farmers out of business. They have thousands of hectares, and they are producing organic. But it's only on paper that it's organic, not in the soul," he says in a soft and resigned voice.

"What does that mean for the product?" I ask.

"There is some link between the soul and the product," he says, his eyes looking out into the middle distance.

"What is that link?"

"Ha," he says again, now smiling at me. "You can't certify it." But then he's serious, insisting, "It is a part of the quality. It is part of the quality that you are connected with your land or with your water or with your animals. But it's not certifiable," he says again. "It's not possible to certify."

"Is it tangible? Can you taste it?" I ask.

"Naw," he says, as if the answer is obvious. "It's what fate is giving you. It's more than taste; it's more than a nutrient."

"It's what binds us as people," I suggest.

"It's what binds us as people or it binds us to nature."

We've transcended grilled trout dinners, and we're sitting in his office—tanks of fish swimming in circles in the adjacent warehouse—drifting into metaphysics.

"I don't know the words for it," he concludes and invites me to take a look at his holding tanks. There I see arctic char and sea trout—healthy specimens.

I wonder aloud if the fish are happy.

"If you look at them very quietly and come in very slowly," Mösmer says with a sense of respect for his flock, "you see that they have a kind of flow, an orientation." Pumps keep the water circulating, and the fish circle against the stream. "This is their nature and they feel it. . . . They're as happy as they can be here," he concludes.

I snap a photograph, and the flash disrupts the organized circling fish. They scatter only to regroup as a spiraling school seconds later. We leave them, apparently happy, at least until they're grilled—slathered with olive oil, dusted with dill, and topped with sliced lemon.

On the Farm

Adamah BioHof is a family business that also sells at the Brunnenmarkt. They operate an organic farm in Marchfeld, just half a dozen miles east from the Vienna border. Adamah sells directly to its consumers at the farm, via subscriptions to boxes of produce prepared for regular drop-off spots in the city and at other Vienna city markets like the Brunnenmarkt.

"Oh, no! You are hippies!" Elmar Fischer's grandparents-in-law gasped when they learned that his wife's parents wanted to convert the family farm to an organic spread.

It's still early in the Austrian growing season. Carrot and tomato starts are flourishing in the greenhouses. A field of fast-growing radishes is getting close to harvest time. Fischer and his wife now oversee a thriving multimillion-dollar food machine. Her parents were organic pioneers.

"Guess how old I am," the smiling and fit-looking Elmar offers as a challenge while we walk his fields. He's convinced—and he's correct—that he looks younger than his thirty-nine years, a fact that he credits to eating food free of pesticides and herbicides, even while acknowledging his graying hair.

"Organic standards start with the soil," he tells me. He squats, scoops up a handful of dirt, and reverently places it back on the earth. "The next step is well-bred organic seeds."

At the time we're talking, the Austrian agriculture minister, Nikolaus Berlakovich, is trying to weather a scandal. He initially opposed a proposed European Union ban on three crop pesticides linked to bee colony collapse. The furor caused by his conventional-agriculture-friendly announcements about the neonicotinoid insecticides was exacerbated when he told Austrians not only that the poisons were safe but also that the amount authorized by the government for use by corn growers is classified information, protected by the country's state secrets act. Within a few weeks Minister Berlakovich (his title translates quaintly to "Minister of Life"), mindful of the upcoming elections and the public rancor, stumbled through an interview on an Austrian public television newscast.

"I understand the agitation," Berlakovich said. "Bees are important for agriculture, and we have programs to support bees and beekeepers. Yet at the same time—and I'd like to ask for some understanding—this concerns the existence of farmers." Farmers need the neonicotinoid insecticides, he told the TV audience, "especially small-scale farmers, the Austrian seed producers and the Austrian vegetable growers. Livelihoods depend on it. We need to balance all of that."

"You are now considered by the public to be the Minister of Poison," interrupted the ORF interviewer. "Is it even possible to win this match in the public sphere?"

"I'm aware that this is an emotional debate," Berlakovich responded. "I'm all for reconciling different interests: protecting the bees—we need bees for agriculture, for the ecosystem—but at the same time protecting the livelihoods of farmers. I will ask for more research in general that looks into the causes of the death of bees because it might be that varroa mites are responsible or mobile phone frequencies or many more things. There's death of bees all around the world and reasons differ."[26]

"He loves money more than agriculture," mocks farmer Fischer as we stroll about his organic acreage. "Maybe he can eat the money."

Organic farming respects the environment, Fischer says. He ticks off where that respect is owed: the soil, the plants, people, and animals. "Why should I spray poison on a plant I will eat three weeks later?" he asks rhetorically. He points to the radishes, the plants thriving under cloth that keeps predators off while the vegetables grow large enough to resist damage until they're harvested. The farm uses mechanical means to keep weeds under control. Tractors scrape the earth between rows of vegetables; stoop laborers from Romania and Slovakia and Poland pull weeds sprouting between crop plants.

"Why not employ Austrians? I'm always asked that," Fischer tells me, a variation of what I've heard so often about Mexican workers in American fields. His answer reminds me of Joe Elliot, a Kentucky tobacco farmer I profiled in my book *Wetback Nation*. Elliot favored Mexican workers over locals he tried to employ. "We had Whiteys out of Owensboro," Elliot said, "and there wasn't any of 'em could drive a stick shift. Grown men." Far from Kentucky, Elmar Fischer can relate to that problem. "The Austrians," he tells me, "are not used to having dirty fingernails."

Fischer, as did Elliot, says he pays fair wages for the tough stoop work. This tranquil farmer, seemingly content with his work-life balance, shows rare irritation when he adds, "And this is what hurts: The people in the supermarkets say about organic vegetables, 'This is so expensive!'"

Part of that expense goes to third-party certifiers, a price Fischer believes is a necessary cost of doing business. He considers European Union standards the first step toward a more rigorous definition of organic and believes that future iterations of the law must be more rigorous. "We need to take care about crop rotation," he says, citing what he suggests, with a laugh, may be the second of one hundred steps. Rotating crops can dissuade pests with specific appetites from permanent residence. He offers another example: "Fair trade needs to be a standard. How you treat your employees." Indeed, as my quest continues, I find that a growing number of producers (and consumers) want working conditions added to the criteria that define organic food.

But to meet the current European, American, and Japanese government standards, Fischer contracts with Austria Bio Garantie, which calls itself "Austria's leading inspection body" and "Your partner for certification of organic products!" He knows small-scale organic farmers who consider the certification process too expensive a burden. But the Adamah farm, he says, believes it is important to support both standards and third-party inspections. "It was a very hard fight for the generation before me to bring certification into the food chain. This was the first time the contents of food were controlled." But only for those producers who wanted a common standard for their organic products.

Despite his support for the certification system, he can't help but play devil's advocate. "Why isn't the skull and crossbones, like on cans of poison, required on conventional food labels? Why do we [organic farmers] have to pay for certification?"

Good question, answers an organic coffee grower from the other side of the globe, in Costa Rica.

Chapter Six

UNCERTIFIED AND SELF-CERTIFIED: A SOJOURN TO COSTA RICA

We sit at a table out in front of his house, the expat coffee grower and the parachuting journalist. Dark glasses shroud Ernie Carman's eyes. Recent surgery has him confined to his house and patio; he's a captive audience for questions. The weather is Costa Rica perfect: sunny and warm here on his twelve-hectare plantation in the heart of Orosi Valley coffee country. We're a couple of hours' spectacular drive from San José through lush mountains, past cascading waterfalls, and overlooking the vast verdant valley. I watch the hummingbirds hover.

Carman calls his coffee organic and yet doesn't bother paying a third-party certifier to stamp it organic with an official seal. I ask him who and what proves his coffee is organic.

"Well, that's a good question," he begins.

Journalism alarm bells ring in my head when an interviewee answers a question by first complimenting it. Most of the time—especially with trained public figures—it's a stall tactic to buy more time or a diversion used to depart radically from the question and insert rehearsed talking points.

But sitting there with Carman, enjoying the peace and quiet of his coffee *finca,* I brush this feeling away. He seems to really consider the crux of this book, to learn what constitutes organic, a good question. It's something he's thought through; he and his wife, Linda, started growing coffee in 1990, and they've been producing coffee that they consider organic since 1992.

"We sometimes have it certified, and sometimes we don't." I'm sipping a cup of espresso he just brewed for me. Certified or not, it's tasty. Smooth, too. And considering I rarely drink anything stronger than green tea, it's opening my eyes wide. "Generally, certifications I don't like," he claims, his syntax turned inside out by a generation of speaking Spanish.

"You don't like them because?"

"They're expensive and they're a lot of work. In the coffee business the guy who benefits from certification is the roaster, not the farmer."

There's a little more money for a grower if the coffee is certified organic, Carman says, but a lot more money for the retailer who roasts organic coffee beans.

"It's bullshit" is his overall analysis of organic certification rules and rigors as they apply to the coffee business. As an example, he suggests that a typical one-pound bag of coffee is worth an extra dollar and a half to a roaster if it's certified organic. "What does the roaster have to do for the certification?" he asks me.

"*Nada,*" I figure, since organic coffee must be certified for the *grower.*

But I'm not quite right. "He has to certify his roaster," Carman says.

I'm surprised. "The roaster? The machine?"

Carman tells me that roasters are asked by inspectors to explain what else besides coffee the equipment is used for and how the roasting machine is cleaned before the organic beans are dumped into it. "If you roast coffee in one of those things, how much residue could possibly be in there? Some of the certification guidelines are sort of ridiculous. I mean, they're just too nitpicky and they're not practical." Of that dollar and a half extra the roaster adds to the price of a bag of organic coffee that's certified, Carman says the farmer gets only twenty or thirty cents more than for a pound that isn't.

If the judgment and ruling of a certifier are not the determining factors, I steer him back to my original question: What does he believe constitutes organic?

"We follow all of the organic guidelines: no chemical fertilizers, no fungicides, no pesticides, no herbicides. We do soil conservation. The basic stuff." Carman knows this basic stuff because, he says, his was the first Costa Rican coffee farm certified by the local certifier Eco-LOGICA. That was in the late 1990s, and he offered his coffee farm to Eco-LOGICA as a test case; the certifier was new to the business. Certification now would cost him three thousand dollars a year, Carman tells me, and it's a price tag his family farm simply cannot rationalize. Since he mills coffee *and* roasts coffee, he would be forced to pay extra for certification of the milling and roasting of his farm product.

Carman is aghast at how much the certifiers earn—a couple hundred dollars a day, he says, big bucks for most Costa Rican workers—and how superficial he figures the inspections must be based on how many farms he understands that some inspectors check: two dozen or more a day.

"I thought, Jesus, this is stupid. It means that certification doesn't necessarily mean anything." He tells me he questions whether the inspectors even manage to walk through a farm with such a heavy caseload, let alone inspect the fields and paperwork. "I'd always thought that an inspection was fairly straightforward, and that everybody is sort of honest and all that stuff. So that was a real eye-opener, and it really made me less and less inclined to do the certification."

Back in San José at the Agriculture Ministry, I met with Mauricio Chacón, the Costa Rican government overseer of those field inspections Carman thinks "don't necessarily mean anything." Dressed in jeans and a Western-style open-necked shirt, Chacón welcomes me to his desk at the ministry; I feel overdressed in my summer suit (no tie) as I consider the *pura vida* business casual— the office is alive with other bureaucrats in blue jeans mode. Chacón studies some figures he has punched up on his computer.

"We have 2,159 organic producers throughout Costa Rica," he reports to me, "but out of those 2,159, only 30 are individual producers. The rest are part of a group and under a grouped verification system." What that means is that the paperwork for the individual farms is in a central repository so certifiers can go to one office and review the records of several farms in one sitting. "The verification agency pays random visits to the producers." This system allows the inspectors to certify those couple of dozen farms a day that Carman puzzles over— they only get their boots dirty at what they consider a representative sample from about two thousand farms nationwide.

"These spot checks seem liable for an easy *mordida* [bribe]," I suggest. "Aren't the field trips ripe territory for corruption?"

"I think that as in any human activity, there always is that chance," Chacón says. But he believes the system the Agriculture Ministry has in place—third-party certifiers licensed by the ministry auditing paperwork that is first checked by farm group managers—deters fraud, especially since the possibility of on-site inspections lingers.

"That doesn't mean, of course, that the system is infallible," he says, but the fact that both the European Union and Canada accept the Costa Rican organic seal as legitimate adds to its credibility.

"What about conflicts of interest?" I ask. "The farmers pay for the inspections. If the inspector is too tough on a farmer, the certifier may lose the client."

He is a realist. "That could happen," he says, "but it is more common that the producer complains to us about the excess force exerted by the certifying agencies—and that their inspectors are excessively rigorous.

That doesn't mean bribes are impossible." But he thinks competition helps keep Costa Rican certifiers living the *pura vida*—the lifestyle the country advertises to the world: the pure life ("pure" of course open to interpretation). "There are four certifying agencies. If a producer doesn't feel comfortable with one of them, he can always change it for another. That kills the possibility of one inspector asking for a bribe from a monopoly. There is less of a chance for bribes with four agencies certifying." Chacón says he's not encountered even one bribery case in the Costa Rican organic food sector.

Most of Ernie Carman's Café Cristina coffee is shipped north; he sells it in the States to customers who trust the beans as organic even though the bags offer no guarantee. "The guy who roasts it for us is not certified. So it makes absolutely no sense to certify the rest of it because you still can't sell it, legally, labeled as organic coffee if the roaster isn't certified."

"But it's organic coffee?" I ask him, sipping my second cup.

"Yeah," he promises. "Our clients know where the coffee comes from. Most of them have been here. If they like the coffee, they buy it. I explain to people what the deal is. It's just too much money, you know?"

Nothing on the Café Cristina labels indicates that what's inside was grown according to the accepted standards for organic agriculture. Marketing is managed by word of mouth and tourist visits to the farm; the *finca* has been a featured landmark in the *Lonely Planet Costa Rica* guide for years. "A two-hour tour of their *microbeneficio*," exudes the guidebook, "is a fantastic introduction to the processes of organic coffee growing, harvesting and roasting."[27]

While we talk, one of Carman's local workers sits at the table with us, patiently going through pile after pile of coffee beans, separating the beans by hand from whatever pebbles and other debris may be mixed in with them.

Coffee vs. Cocaine

Carman is another storyteller. After I mention to him my skepticism regarding my black beans odyssey, he tells me that several years back he made a trip to Bolivia to offer his expertise to coffee growers there. "The government was trying to get people to grow coffee instead of cocaine." He's talking about a US government foreign aid project, a project that failed to impress him as a viable alternative to the cocaine business. What did impress him was a fast trade in bogus paperwork.

"I saw organic certificates," he says, slapping his hand to pantomime a back-alley business deal. "Five hundred dollars. Here, you want to use it on your shipment? Five hundred dollars. These things were just passed around to whoever needed it."

I'm surprised by how routine he makes the fraud sound. But perhaps I shouldn't be shocked. That same sort of business is conducted in the United States with fake green cards for immigrants. As long as there's demand for hard-to-obtain official documents, there's money to be made faking them and of course that means counterfeiters are on the job.

Carman says he didn't see any illegal trading in certificates, but heard about the hustle and saw one of the fakes. There's no question that such fraud exists. The USDA National Organic Program keeps a list updated on its website of growers and shippers who lose their certification for reasons that include faked records. In mid-2013, for example, the USDA pointed to a Berlin company called the Germania Group as marketing chia seeds with a fraudulent certificate. A few months later the Inner Mongolia Tianfu Food Company in China was targeted for selling tomato paste, mushrooms, bamboo shoots, and water chestnuts with false papers, while a false certificate was found in use at Monaz Manufacturing and Supply Services in

Malaysia for wheat and spelt. Other companies on the list busted for using fake paperwork hail from India, South Africa, and Honduras.[28] Still other food suppliers lose their legitimate organic certification because they fail to pay fees or don't comply with NOP requirements or neglect orders to update the strategic general plans for their operations. Sloppy record-keeping can cost a company certification, as can failure to respond to warnings from inspectors.

"I don't like to totally undermine the system," Carman says. He acts concerned that he's been too harsh in his criticism of the certification process. "I realize it's sort of a necessary evil because of lack of trust. At least if you buy coffee that says it's certified, *maybe* it is." He shrugs. "So that's good."

The expat life clearly appeals to Ernie Carman. He's relaxed as we talk, joking about the coffee business, and he lives in what—at least to my starry eyes—is a paradise: majestic mountains, waterfalls, and, except for the songbirds, peace and quiet. I ask him if he makes a living from the coffee.

Not from the farm, he tells me. "For fifteen years we just sold the fruit. When the prices were bad, Linda had a job teaching school and I had a business importing machines so that we could maintain the farm and live here, because it's kind of a nice lifestyle." He laughs at his understatement. "We had those two jobs to maintain the farm. Now we joke that I run the mill and she runs the roasting operation so that we can maintain the farm. If you look at the farm separately, it doesn't maintain itself. It's very expensive to grow coffee here now, and our organic yield is not as high as I'd like to see it." The cash is not in the milling either, he says, but without milling the crop there's nothing to roast. Carman picks up his raw product and offers a lesson in basic coffee production.

"These are ripe fruits, and the first step in the process is to take the seeds out of the fruits." He pulls out one of the green fruits of the coffee plant. "It's like pitting cherries." Indeed, the fruit looks about the size of a cherry. "Except we throw away the cherries and keep the pits." He hands the bean to me. "If you feel these things, they are slimy. You have to take the slime off, which is either done mechanically or by fermentation."

Later Carman takes me on a tour of his mill, a Rube Goldberg maze of machinery that he put together from scavenged pieces originally intended for tasks that have nothing to do with coffee. One repurposed device was designed by its original manufacturer to heat chicken coops. A propane burner is mounted adjacent to a fan. Heated air is blown toward coffee that's drying in a rotating tub, the tub spinning slowly at about one revolution per minute.

"The coffee's dried to the parchment stage." Carman shows me a bean with a paperlike covering on it. It looks like the covering that's on a freshly shelled peanut. Once the crop reaches the parchment stage, it's stable. "And then you can store the coffee. It's no longer a perishable product. The fruit is very perishable. It has to be processed the day it's picked. Once you get the pulp off—the slime off—and you dry it, then you can keep it for a year, if you keep it dry." That is what is referred to as wet milling. The dry mill process consists of taking that parchment off and sorting it, by density. "You get coffee that looks like that." He points over to a woman laboriously cleaning the beans. "That's the final stage."

"It's called green coffee because it's not roasted. But the coffee from this area is not green, it's this color," he says, pulling a sample out of the pile. "Sort of a blue-gray color." After the foreign debris is removed from the beans, they're ready for the roaster.

Why Not Label the Poisoned Food?

I refrain from asking for a third cup of coffee. After years of limiting my morning wake-up drinks to relatively weak green tea, I fear what three cups of Costa Rican espresso might do to my laid-back facade. Our talk returns to the laws governing organic foodstuffs. "Most people have no idea where any of their food comes from," Carman complains. "What if we turned this around? If what we organic farmers are doing is supposed to be good and what the other guys are doing is supposed to be bad, why don't they have to get certified and we do?"

It's an intriguing twist on the call I've heard from other organic farmers to level the growing field and demand that conventional farmers report what insecticides and fungicides, herbicides, and other stuff is applied on and added to the food we eat. After all, it all does seem backward. Why is the onus on those exerting extra efforts and expense producing food without poisons to certify their products as organic? Why not instead make those who dismiss the rigors of organic production with sprays and additives engage in full disclosure of such practices on their labels? "Make them tell everybody what all the crap is that they put on their farms. Do you really want to eat Roundup? Why don't we make that a regulation instead of my having to say what I *don't* put on my farm?"

"And what's the answer to that question?"

He doesn't hesitate. "Money." As an example he points to the 2012 California ballot proposition requiring food with GMO content be so identified. When that referendum was defeated after a vast influx of agribusiness money blanketed the state with anti–Proposition 37 propaganda, we saw money was at least an interim answer.

Café Cristina is a regular stopover on the Costa Rica ecotourist trail, and Carman is poised not just to show off his *finca* but also to give enthused *touristas* an earful about a Costa Rica that's at odds with its famous *pura vida* slogan. He tells stories about illegal pesticides and herbicides dumped in vast quantities on Costa Rican crops that are anything but pure life. Even the legal levels of pesticides used in the country are sobering: as of 2011, far more than other Central American countries, and more chemicals per hectare than any country in the world.[29] Carman claims there's no sewage treatment plant for San José, that the capital city's raw waste is dumped in its river. He's correct, although plans are in progress to begin treating the effluent in 2015.[30] Yet the tourists keep coming to his farm, taking the tour and buying his coffee.

Community-Supported Organics at the San José Farmers' Market

When we meet for a late dinner at a San José Italian restaurant, Favian Scorza digs into the food with the kind of energy and enthusiasm she exhibits talking about the organic farmers' market she manages downtown. She's pragmatic and hungry and knows there's nothing organic—according to her definition—about the food on her plate. She fills up on the pasta with tomato sauce without a care about where the wheat and tomatoes originated. Eating this dinner, at the end of a long day, is a time to compromise for a young woman who looks like a poster child for the lifestyle she espouses: a fresh-scrubbed pretty face framed by flowing dark-brown hair.

"When you're working with organics, you're producing food for the community, for yourself, and for the environment. For me, you cannot work in organics and not give a portion of your food to the life that is around you." That means no "'cides," Scorza says about the compounds that end with that Latin-root suffix that means "killer." "Life is the absence of all these agrichemicals and agritoxics."

I try to pin her down on a definition for organic.

"You can have a big monoculture farm, with no pesticides," she says. "USDA can certify it organic. But for me, it doesn't satisfy. If that farm wants to sell at our market, I will say no because they are trying to adopt conventional agriculture into organics but keeping the same conventional practices, and they're not sustainable. Yes, they can have a stamp that says 'pesticide free,' but it's not real organic because of the model they are using. It's not a cycle of life."

When the Feria Verde market was founded, vendors were not required to be vetted as organic by one of the third-party certifiers recognized by the Costa Rican government. "We'd been on their farms," she says about the uncertified growers selling at the market. "We knew their practices and we knew they were organic." The cooperative market—it's a partnership of consumers and producers—first opened in 2010, and Scorza's customers asked the same question I ask: How could they be sure the products on offer were organic?

She would sit with those skeptical customers, drink coffee, and tell them that she visited the farms. "Just trust my word," she told them, and many—because of the on-the-scene details she brought to arguments—did just that. But as Scorza learned more about the organic food world, she realized that there are hustlers claiming conventional produce as organic. Organic produce sold at the market commands a premium price. "We were forced to get certified," she tells me. In order to differentiate the honest brokers from the scam artists, she had no choice.

The certification fees were daunting for the small family farms that sell at the market. With the Costa Rican government watching their experiment, Scorza says farmers who sell at her market and her customers were trained to conduct certification inspections themselves. "It is trust based," she says about the alternative certifying scheme known as the Participatory Guarantee System (PGS). "We all know each other," as opposed to the purely business relationship that often results from contracting with a traditional third-party inspection company. The PGS inspectors call themselves verifiers and—unlike employees of the traditional certification companies—they earn no salary. "We believe if money is involved, it could change the soul of the system." Fees charged to growers are limited to basic travel expenses for the verifiers. "It's trust," she says again. "People who know you inspect your farm because we all want access to good food."

The International Federation of Organic Agriculture Movements (IFOAM) backs the PGS concept and notes that Participatory Guarantee Systems "certify producers based on the active participation of stakeholders and are built on a foundation of trust, social networks and knowledge exchange." The IFOAM's motto is "Leading, uniting and assisting the Organic Movement since 1972," and its role is to "encourage and support the development of PGS as an alternative and complementary tool to third-party certification." The organization encourages governments like Costa Rica's to recognize the Feria Verde and other grassroots Participatory Guarantee Systems.[31]

At the Costa Rican Agriculture Ministry, Mauricio Chacón recognizes the value of the PGS to struggling organic farmers, but he insists participants prove it works. "They have to define a rigorous and secure tracking mechanism to guarantee they comply with organic norms." The Agriculture Ministry sees the growing organic food sector as a draw for tourists and tries to help connect organic food producers with hotels and restaurants. Ecotours with organic meal service make an attractive marketing ploy for the type of travelers who buy organic food back home.

Some five hundred customers visit the Feria Verde each Saturday morning, not just to buy fresh and local food, but also to socialize. Expect to be serenaded by the likes of a didgeridoo and drums trio while you stuff your organic cotton shopping bag with fruits and vegetables. Casual clothing is on offer. Children romp in the adjacent playground. The atmosphere is festive, but because of the market's premium prices, it's elitist. Scorza concedes this fact but argues, "We must start supporting organic agriculture with people who can afford it." Consider lifestyle choices, she suggests. "If a kilo of blackberries costs three dollars, some people tell us it's expensive. But I'm thinking how much a Coca-Cola costs you and it doesn't give you any nutrients." Scorza sighs, "We human beings are really cheap regarding food. We're cheap!"

At the Feria Verde, Breyner Paniagua (quite the last name: "bread and water"), a vendor since the market opened, told the local English-language newspaper *Tico Times* that he and his colleagues work hard to bring pesticide-free produce to their customers. "We are involved in conscientious agriculture" is his mission statement as he peddles arugula, romaine lettuce, and kale.[32] The Participatory Guarantee System is a natural outgrowth of that conscientious agriculture, and it's an alternative on trial in *El Norte.*

In the States an alternative seal to the USDA Organic is the one designed by Certified Naturally Grown—featuring a stylized barn, sweeping fields, and a joyful-looking sky. Certified Naturally Grown is a US-based Participatory Guarantee System. It's marketed to farmers as an opportunity to promote their organic produce without the expense and bureaucracy of USDA certification. In order to earn a Certified Naturally Grown stamp of approval, farmers must meet all the USDA National Organic Standards, and a few more. The hitch is that they cannot call the yield from their fields "organic" if they sell more than five thousand dollars' worth of it a year. But the inspections—usually carried out by other farmers—cost a fraction of an inspection for USDA certification, and the paperwork farmers must disclose to inspectors is minimal compared with what the USDA requires.

"The annual peer-review inspections ensure the program's integrity," explains the Certified Naturally Grown policy solicitation to potential participants. "The local nature of the peer-review model is a benefit too, since nearby farmer-inspectors are much more likely to know what's happening on your farm throughout the season than a third-party inspector who visits once a year for a pre-arranged inspection. Peer-support networks that develop often help ward off challenges that might tempt someone to cheat if it gets out of hand. Peer-inspectors who participate in CNG have a stake in protecting the program's integrity." Participatory Guarantee Systems are an intriguing alternative to USDA Organic.

In the context of my frustrating quest to trace back the origin of my beans and nuts, and especially after experiencing the closed-mouth arrogance of the certifier with the largest market share in the business, Quality Assurance International, one aspect of the Certified Naturally Grown option is particularly appealing. "Another difference," CNG says about its approach versus the USDA's, "is that Certified Naturally Grown's certification process is transparent and open to the public—you will find every farmer's complete certification application online, as well as scanned copies of Inspection Summaries and Declarations."[33]

What a difference. Greta Houlahan at QAI essentially told me to buzz off about my nuts and beans. But CNG guarantees a certification process "transparent and open to the public." Certified Naturally Grown executive director Alice Varon says more than seven hundred farms across forty-seven states opt for the CNG badge. "Certified Naturally Grown is tailored for direct-market farmers producing food without any synthetic chemicals specifically for their local communities," says Varon. "It's a particular niche not in competition with the National Organic Program." She's convinced that CNG members "believe in farming in harmony with nature as an expression of their values. It's not something they do to get a premium in the marketplace."[34]

That may well be true, but there's no question that organic produce—especially the gorgeous and delicious fruits and vegetables available at the Eugene Saturday Market down the street from my house—fetch top dollar, with nothing lost to the middleman grocer.

⁓

Language evolves; definitions change. The dictionary I took to boarding school so many years ago still sits on a shelf in my library: *Webster's Seventh New Collegiate*, with a 1965 copyright date. Organic is defined there as "relating to a bodily organ and derived from living organisms, containing carbon compounds and developing in the manner of a living plant or animal." There was no mention back in 1965 of anything to do with gardening or eating, fertilizers or 'cides. Another dictionary on my shelf is the *American Heritage College*, published over thirty years later in 1997. What a difference a generation (or two) makes. Organic by the 1990s included using no synthetic fertilizers or pesticides, free from antibiotics or hormones, and this sweet thought: "Simple, healthful, and close to nature, as in 'an organic lifestyle.'"

⁓

In a residential San José neighborhood, the Regiones cafe lures me with its promise of a vegetarian lunch. I order an avocado and onion sandwich with sweet red peppers on a sesame-seeded wheat roll, a tasty break from the more common rice-and-bean-based Costa Rican fare that's been keeping me nourished. The restaurant and adjacent store are a project of some three dozen groups representing fishers, farmers, and conservationists from across Costa Rica. The Regiones menu draws attention to its organic coffee, and when the relaxed manager, Isaac Rappaport, joins me for a chat while my order is being prepared, he suggests that much of what's in the kitchen meets organic standards.

"Sometimes they have a certificate," he says about his suppliers, "but not in every case." He quickly adds, "They have certificates in very few cases." Doing business with the rest—the ones selling food called organic but without certification—is based on the confidence he feels; again it's based on trust. "I know the people. I see how they act and how they live."

Organic ingredients on the menu fluctuate with availability, says the affable Rappaport, and because Costa Rican cuisine requires some ingredients that do not exist in an organic form. "It's very difficult to produce organic rice, potatoes, and organic beans," but what isn't difficult is to obtain a fraudulent organic certificate. "In Latin America it is very common, you know? You give money under the table and they give you what you want"—a phony certificate or a passing grade on a test never taken. "Inspectors go to your place, they find something wrong, and sometimes they certify you if you pay." That's not the case in Costa Rica, Rappaport says patriotically, but in the rest of Latin America, "Could be, could be." The *mordida* permeates business dealings. "That's the way it works here. It's really, really common. He offers a scenario of how the south-of-the-border bribe works. "The authorities tell you, 'Well, we have a little problem here, but . . .' They don't talk about money, but you understand and you say, 'I can help you.' You're talking the same language."

"When you go to the market and you see food marked organic," I ask Rappaport, "do you believe it?"

"Yes, I believe it," he says, laughing. "But you cannot trust everybody! It's best to know the people and make a spiritual connection with them. Then you can trust them. You have to trust somebody. You cannot live alone as if you are the perfect one and nobody else is."

Chapter Seven

The NSA ≠ Organics

With the information door slammed, double-bolted, and guarded by intellectual property security police at Trader Joe's, Natural Directions, and QAI, I sit in my office thinking about my rancid Kazakh walnuts and my elusive Bolivian black beans. Why are my suppliers intent on making it so difficult for me to ascertain their sources? What's more important than the food we eat?

Yet beyond advertising copy platitudes, the companies who produce and distribute the food refuse to disclose how they grow it, where they get it, how they manipulate it en route to the marketplace. And the government that is supposed to protect us from abuses? It is outsourcing inspections to private third-party certifiers like QAI, certifiers that hide behind the company "secrets" of the food producers they inspect (and again: those certifiers *are paid by the very outfits they certify*). What little government oversight that does exist is spread mighty thin. Once more I contemplate that sobering figure Miles McEvoy reported to me: A single overworked USDA National Organic Program employee for every billion dollars of annual retail trade in the organic sector.

I find myself thinking about secrets in our twenty-first century, information-hungry, post-9/11 world. You, dear reader, and I enjoy almost no privacy. Your address is probably two Google clicks away from anybody who cares to know where you live. Your credit rating, your Visa card number (and its three-digit "security code"), even your Social Security number—so many matters you may wish to keep private—are available to all sorts of anonymous clerks and call center operators in the contemporary globalized economy. And many of us choose—too often mindlessly—to expose ourselves and our personal data via so-called social media. (I must report I closed my Facebook account years ago, shortly after I opened it. At first I was tempted by its promise to connect me with old school chums and the potential for the service to help me attract new readers for my books. But fast I found its presence in my private life intrusive, even before I considered Facebook's predatory corporate goals.)

Yet while we live in glass houses regarding our personal privacy, our government and its corporate partners continue to clam up (to use another food metaphor cliché), keeping the most prosaic details of their antics from us—all the while insisting these tactics are for our own good. "Don't worry," they say, whether it's regarding attacks by hijackers and hackers or what's in our food. "We'll take care of you. We just can't tell you how. And that secrecy is for your own good, too. It protects your national security. Here, have another organic spirulina-spiked quinoa chip from the Bolivian Andes and wash it down with this organic, fair-trade, caffeine-infused lemon-flavored vitamin water from a pristine Kazakh spring." But don't ask too many questions about the source of that quinoa or water. That's another secret.

I'm working on this book while Bradley Manning is on trial for dumping US government secrets into WikiLeaks' databases and while Edward Snowden seeks asylum after spilling the proverbial beans about the secret National Security Administration spying on the American public's telephone calls and e-mails. The Obama administration has been vehement in its unprecedented pursuit of those who leak its secrets, and it threatens journalists who receive those secrets and report them. Thousands of Americans reportedly languish on no-fly lists, even while their government refuses to confirm or deny what names populate those lists and offers no guidance to appeal the blacklisting. Secret drone attacks kill American citizens overseas, Americans targeted in secret, far from the due process of law.

"Do you have a Safeway Club card?" the clerk asks with friendly-sounding courtesy. She waves your card's bar code under the reader and the contents of your shopping cart are recorded for . . . ? For what exactly? For Safeway, of course. To refine its merchandising: for the store to focus advertising and special offers tailored to your buying habits. And who else has access to that database? Do you care who knows what you're buying? Nordstrom and other stores may follow you as you wander through their aisles—using video cameras and tracking devices that tune in to locator signals emitted by your mobile telephone. They, too, want to better focus their marketing efforts, but in what you may tend to think of as a public space, you're being watched—just as you're being watched by closed-circuit TV in so much of the public square. The Postal Service keeps records of your mail (if you still pen letters on paper and stick stamps on envelopes).[35] Automobile manufacturers equip most new cars sold in the United States with black boxes. Tell the cops after an accident that you were wearing your seat belt while obeying the speed limit, and you may find yourself contradicted by the so-called event data recorder that you didn't even know was secreted in your car's interior (and available without your consent in many states to police, lawyers, and even insurance companies should disputes arise).[36] Of course your lies to the cops can lead to further charges against you.

While government and business embrace recording devices that keep a watch on John Q. Public, average citizens can be charged with a crime if they switch on a video recorder at the wrong time and in the wrong place. Even if it is to serve the public good. Laws have been passed or are proposed in several states making it illegal to surreptitiously record video of animal abuse on farms (or to take a job as a livestock worker without revealing one's ties to animal rights organizations).[37] In my book *No Animals Were Harmed*, I recount the story of one of those videos. Posted on YouTube by Mercy for Animals, the 2010 footage shows a worker beating a tethered dairy cow with a pipe and saying, "You're mine, motherfucker." Later his voice is heard saying, "I get going it's just like, oh, this feels good. I want to keep fucking hitting them." The abuse resulted in a fine and jail sentence for the perpetrator; the new laws would target the photographer who documented the abuser's secret life.[38]

If we are what we eat, why is it that we succumb to corporate and government control over the origin of our food? How can business secrets take priority over consumer knowledge of what goes in our bodies? Why should we trust corporate food producers and retailers, government regulators, and the organic inspectors they license when they all refuse to divulge what's on the blue plate special this week?

There was a restaurant (now out of business!) near where I lived in Sonoma County that offered a bargain surprise lunch. I frequently passed by the eatery but never was tempted to stop in and order it. Why would I want to order a mystery meal? Yet mystery meals, I'm starting to worry, are what we all make with the groceries we buy at our local supermarkets.

There is no acceptable rationale for the government to oversee a clandestine operation that regulates our food. Transparency is mandatory when what goes into our stomachs is at stake, especially when Washington repeatedly proves itself opaque. Consider the testimony to Congress by national intelligence director James Clapper, the guy who was in charge of the NSA when Edward Snowden blew the whistle. Oregon senator Ron Wyden asked

Clapper if the NSA was scooping up "any type of data at all on millions or hundreds of millions of Americans."

"No sir," lied Clapper. He added a vague and unsuccessful attempt at plausible deniability: "Not wittingly."

When Clapper was caught lying to Congress, because of the secrets Snowden revealed, he told NBC News, "I responded in what I thought was the most truthful or least untruthful manner by saying, 'No.'" That's an amazing phrase from one of the most powerful officials in the US government: "least untruthful." *Trust us, we know what's good for you* is simply not an adequate explanation for secrecy, whether it's to defend the spying on our telephone and Internet traffic or the contents of our grocery bags.

Time for an Official Complaint

I figure it's time to put my tax dollars to work. I get back in touch with Miles McEvoy, the National Organic Program chief, and follow Joe Smillie's suggestion to file a formal complaint.

From my redoubt in Vienna's Josefstadt, I send him this e-mail message:

Hello, Miles.

Again, I very much enjoyed our meeting in your office—the USDA background you provided is serving me well as I continue to research my book about the validity and credibility of organic labeling and the certification process. I write to you from Vienna where I am studying the Austrian bio labeling model.

As I hope you remember, I am attempting to trace a can of organic beans and a bag of organic walnuts back to their reputed places of origin in Bolivia and Kazakhstan, respectively.

I am running into obstacles. The retailers and the distributors are not giving the certifiers license to reveal their sources. They are citing proprietary business interests as a rationale.

However I am led to believe by credible third party sources that it is highly unlikely there are organic producers of walnuts in Kazakhstan and beans in Bolivia that could provide these goods in the quantities required by Trader Joe's (the walnuts) and Natural Directions (the black beans).

As I understand the law and USDA practices, I can file a formal complaint with your office and request that the USDA audit the products' supply chain. I would like to file such a complaint and inspect the certifiers' paperwork regarding the provenance of these products.

Please let me know, Miles, if this letter is enough to get the process initiated or if there is another protocol for me to follow. Thank you very much in advance for your help with this. (I still hope you'll join me on one or both of the treks to the source!)

I hear back from him immediately.

Hi Peter,

I'm glad your book project is moving along. Tracing organic products from final product back to the ingredient source or farm is a standard part of the certification process. Certifiers do this every day as part of the inspection audit process.

The information you have provided does not appear to be a complaint. It is certainly interesting work to trace organic ingredients back to the source but we would not consider this a complaint unless you had information about alleged violations. You mention credible third party sources. If you can provide specifics on why they allege that these ingredients are not valid then we may have sufficient information to pursue a complaint.

We receive over 200 complaints per year from a wide variety of sources. Each complaint involves considerable resources to investigate. We have a goal to close complaints within 180 days but with the volume of complaints received and limited resources we often have complaints that take much longer to resolve.

I would also encourage you to keep working with the retailers and distributors to see if they can provide you with more information. Thank you for your understanding.

Nice guy. But, of course, not what I wanted to hear. I gather my data and send him a follow-up note the next day.

Hello again, Miles. I have that third party information in hand now. Allow me here, please, to frame this note as an official complaint (and if I need a more formal style, please let me know).

I bought walnuts from Trader Joe's that were labeled organic and product of Kazakhstan. I was suspicious of the Kazakh provenance, questioning if certified organic walnuts could originate in that corruption-ridden country. I contacted Trader Joe's. They refused to provide information about the source of the walnuts. I contacted the certifier, QAI. They refused to provide such information without the approval of Trader Joe's which, predictably, refused approval, according to QAI. I requested further help from QAI tracing the nuts, offering to protect any proprietary business information as a condition of access to information verifying that the walnuts are certified organic. QAI refused.

I am unable to find any evidence of organic walnut cultivation in Kazakhstan. My research led me to a EuropeAid project in Kazakhstan that was designed to develop an organic sector in that country. It was led by the Louis Bolk Institute and it was not successful. One of the principals of that project, Peter Brul, in response to my query regarding organic walnuts in Kazakhstan, told me, "I don't know of any organic walnut project in Kazakhstan."

I believe these are grounds for a complaint:

There is no evidence of organic walnuts being grown in Kazakhstan. No grower claims to be producing organic walnuts. The retailer refuses to state its source, yet it proclaims the product it sells is organic. The certifier refuses to cooperate with a traceback of the walnuts. A prominent international NGO announces that its efforts to promote organic agriculture in the country are a failure. A principal with the NGO states that there is no sign of organic walnuts grown in Kazakhstan.

The circumstances are similar in Bolivia with the beans. In this case the distributor is Natural Directions. It is non-responsive to inquiries. Again, QAI is the certifier. The scenario is the same: QAI refuses to offer a response.

And, as is the case with the walnuts, I am unable to find any evidence of organic black bean cultivation in Bolivia. There is plenty of coffee and quinoa, but no sign of beans. I contacted Peter McFarren, longtime Associated Press news correspondent in Bolivia (with whom I worked on a project about cocaine for NBC News). He has been deeply involved in the commodities export business from Bolivia. He was emphatic that there is no organic black bean sector in Bolivian agriculture and hence no organic black beans being exported from Bolivia to the United States.

Based on these two food products, the lack of transparency expressed by the producers, retailers and certifiers, please accept this note, Miles, as a formal complaint.

Thanks very much.

Again his response is immediate. He forwards my complaint letter on to one Michael Matthew in his office with a one-line order: "Please investigate and register as a complaint." Matthew is the director of the compliance and enforcement division of the USDA Agricultural Marketing Service. In the hierarchy of the USDA, the National Organic Program is located in the space where the USDA "administers programs that facilitate the efficient, fair marketing of U.S. agriculture products."[39] Or, as President Calvin Coolidge famously noted in a 1925 speech to the American Society of Newspaper Editors, "The chief business of the American people is business."[40]

It is the end of May 2013. If the 180-day complaint investigation timeline holds true, the results of the USDA inquiry will be available a few days before my deadline for this book.

The Luxury of Eating Organic

I'm in San Francisco walking down ultrahip Valencia Street in the Mission District, where the stores feature organic this and organic that: frozen yogurt, "fair-trade" organic coffee and tea, grocery stores offering organic products, and restaurants promising organic meals. There's Herbivore, where I've eaten many a baked falafel (spending an extra seventy-five cents to add potatoes and avocados). "Since 1997," reads the menu, "100% vegan restaurant dedicated to serving healthy quality food." It doesn't advertise its food as organic, but on the other side of Valencia I stop in at the Blue Fig and load up on its Organic Irish Oats (with brown sugar, Saigon cinnamon–spiced pecans, strawberries, banana, and a splash of soy milk). On the next block is Valencia Whole Foods—not a branch of the megachain, but a local corner grocery filled with piles of organic fresh produce and shelves lined with organic canned goods. It goes on. Valencia is a Rodeo Drive for organic elitists, a Xanadu for the new-money tech troops bidding up rents to prices that drive families out of the old working-class neighborhood. Just a few doors down is a clothing store: Synergy Organic Clothing. Alongside the skirts and tops is the brochure promising that "each garment is made for women who want to look great while treading gently on our Earth." Thirsty? Time to stop in at the π bar for a glass of Two Rivers Organic Pomegranate Cider.

My Valencia Street stroll brings to mind Dr. Steven Bratman and the condition he named orthorexia nervosa, what he calls "an unhealthy obsession with eating healthy food." Bratman makes his arguments in his 2001 book *Health Food Junkies*. "One can have an unhealthy obsession with something that is otherwise healthy," says Bratman. "Think of exercise addiction, or workaholism. I never intended the expression to apply to anything other than extreme cases of over-focus, particularly where the person themselves would rather lighten up and stop thinking about it so much."[41]

Nonetheless, the good doctor generates entertaining hate mail (which he prominently posts on his website). "You are a moron. Please go to Mickey Dee's and chow down on a few Big Mac's and don't call me in the morning. I guess Monsanto's GMO products, high fructose corn syrup, aspartame, processed sugar and flour are great for us. Amazing that they give a PhD in medicine to a fucking imbecile. Have a great day and don't forget to supersize, you idiot."

Chapter Eight

GRANDFATHERS OF THE OLD-WORLD ORGANIC MOVEMENT

Austria's first laws regarding organic food date to 1983. But the roots of the global modern organic movement stretch back much further, primarily to the Austrian philosopher Rudolf Steiner (well known as the educator who created the Waldorf School) and the theories he expressed in the 1920s about the value of farming without chemical fertilizers, pesticides, and herbicides—what became known in that early era as biological-dynamic agriculture. It is a practice that continues today under various names and includes using manure and crop rotation to improve soil. "The farm is a living organism," Steiner mused,[42] and early scientific tests of his ideas began in the late 1920s on a farm called Wurzerhof in Carinthia. Steiner's theories of biological-dynamic agriculture went beyond ecologically sound farming that is free of poisons. He looked to what he saw as interplanetary influences on soil, spirituality of processes such as photosynthesis, and intimate personal relationships with cultivated land for the inspirations that led to his work as a rebel against early factory farming.

In his interpretation of Steiner's biodynamics (as the practice has become known), the organic gardening champion Wolf Storl writes that the practice "is a service to the earth and its creatures, not just a method for increasing production or for providing healthy food." Biodynamics, concludes Storl, "can be summed up as putting one's energy into supporting the good instead of fighting the bad."[43]

American practitioners who follow Steiner's biodynamic farming philosophies may apply to Demeter-USA to be certified biodynamic. That means they adhere to USDA organic standards and also engage Steiner principles such as leaving a percent of their land fallow to increase biodiversity (of course crop rotation is not a Steiner original—it's been practiced throughout history and across cultures). Once certified, their products can exhibit the Biodynamic seal.[44]

Food packaging is decorated with a growing array of such trust marks. The Food Justice Certified seal pictures a hand holding balanced scales of justice with the stem of a healthy-looking green-leafed plant wrapped around the balance. The Agriculture Justice Project sponsors the Food Justice Certified seal in an effort to, their literature explains, "ensure fair treatment of workers, fair pricing for farmers, and fair business practices."[45] Fair Trade Certified is a seal designed to assure consumers "that they are buying a quality product that improves lives and protects the environment," according to Fair Trade USA.[46] The logo is a black human figure superimposed over a green globe and carrying a large bowl or basket. The Non-GMO Project seal shows a bright red butterfly lighting on a green stalk and is an effort to provide consumers with "clearly-labeled non-GMO food and products."[47] The Animal Welfare Approved seal is a sun setting or rising over a rolling hillside, "a food label for meat and dairy products that come from farm animals raised to the highest animal welfare and environmental standards," according to the organization that offers approval.[48] Certified Humane is another animal welfare seal, this one sponsored by Humane Farm Animal Care, a group that calls itself "dedicated to improving the lives of farm animals in food production from birth to slaughter."[49] American Grassfed is a green seal illustrated with blades of grass that "defines grassfed animals as those that have eaten nothing but grass and forage from weaning to harvest, have not been raised in confinement, and have never been fed antibiotics or growth hormones," according to the American

Grassfed Association.[50] The result of this potpourri may be a better-informed consumer—depending on the credibility of the various approvals, verifications, and certifications. One thing's for sure: The seals are a challenge for package designers who need to deal with a growing number of claims announced with often conflicting typefaces and color schemes.[51]

Not long after the Austrian government established regulations regarding organic food production in the 1980s, Alois Posch was asked by the Health Ministry to create an organic certification policy for Austria. Just retired, he's happy to meet with me on a sunny spring afternoon at Café Milano, an Italian coffeehouse near the University of Vienna. The windows are wide open and our talk competes with sirens, clanging tram bells, and perpetual high-pressure hisses from the espresso machine.

In the late 1980s consumer interest in organic food was not yet common in Austria, he tells me, and farmer's organizations opposed official recognition of the slowly growing organic movement—they considered it encroaching competition. A generation later Austria, along with Switzerland and Denmark, leads the European Union in per capita consumption of organic food.[52] Now farmers organizations, such as BioAustria, set standards for organic farmers who wish to exceed the European Union rules. The Austrian marketplace demands the higher standards, as both farmers and retailers realize extreme-organic is a moneymaker.

"The most important rule," Posch says about BioAustria standards, "is that the whole farm must be organic. It is not allowed for one part of a farm to be organic and one part conventional." He, along with many other organic purists, sees philosophy as a prime ingredient of organic foodstuffs. "The man who produces organically," he states with studied precision, "cannot use poison." Full stop. No exceptions. "It doesn't fit together," he declares adamantly. European Union rules allow a farmer to split the crop—some acreage organic and other land conventional. Such a bifurcated policy, Posch tells me in his poetic English, is a non sequitur. "It doesn't fit into the same head."

Clattering dishes add to the cafe cacophony. "Why is it important that it fit in the same head?" I ask.

"For consumer trust," he says. "Trust" is a word I'm hearing more and more often as I seek the origin of my nuts and beans. "It's a question of trust." Posch believes that when farmers mix organic and conventional on their fields, consumers worry that they may mix them—intentionally or by mistake—in their silos or en route to processing plants, to warehouses, and ultimately to the marketplace. He estimates that as many as two-thirds of Austrian organic farmers restrict themselves to an organics-only policy. Farmers dedicated solely to organic crops both embrace an antipoison philosophy and offer their customers an extra guarantee: Organic produce from their fields can't get mixed up with conventional stuff since no conventional agriculture is practiced on their land.

When supermarket chains also exceed the European Union standards for their organic products, says Posch, it's because they are fighting for a share of the lucrative organic retail market. Billa and Spar and Hofer (three of the big Austrian chain store players) want to lure customers with their more-organic-than-thou promises. He takes a sip of his latte—made with conventional coffee and conventional milk. Around the corner, at the Welt Café, customers are lured inside by signs guaranteeing not just organic, but so-called fair trade organic coffee. I can't fault Posch since I'm the guy who picked this Italian joint for our meeting.

"I am a farmer's boy," Posch says. He tells about his childhood, an upbringing that's ideal for the line of work he chose as an adult, especially since the farm where he grew up was de facto organic. He recounts a pragmatic approach to biological-dynamic agriculture: "We didn't have much money, so we didn't buy poisons." At the University of Vienna he studied agriculture, and after graduation he went to work at the Agriculture Ministry, where he spent his entire career.

Contemporary Supermarket Organics

Posch dates the arrival of organics in Austrian supermarkets to 1994, the year Billa launched its *Ja! Natürlich* line. It's clever branding. *Ja natürlich* is a common German idiomatic expression meaning an enthusiastic "Yes, of course!" But literally it means "Yes. Naturally." And *Ja! Natürlich* appealed to a sizable percentage of Austrian consumers ready to pay more for what they perceived to be not just superior food but also a type of farming that benefits the nation's environment. This mentality, says Posch, led directly to government subsidies designed to encourage organic farming, a program he initiated and oversaw. "To protect the environment is not only the task of consumers who are willing to buy organic products. It's the task of the whole society," he explains from his European communitarian perspective. "So it's correct to give tax money to the farmer to compensate for the strict controls and other extra costs of organic farming. A conventional farmer is a free farmer—fewer controls and checks."

An intriguing aspect of this taxpayer subsidy system is that it creates a rigorous incentive for farmers to follow the rules—a fiscal incentive. Here's why: If a subsidized farm fails to abide by Austria's strict organic farming rules and regulations, it isn't just decertified; the farmer must pay the subsidy back to the government. Compare that to what the US government demands: Organic food producers must bear the financial burden of inspection and certification while enjoying no special organic subsidies. And don't call it a subsidy, cautions Posch. "We call it a compensation payment." The money helps keep Austrian organic farmers honest. The Health

Ministry—through third-party certification companies—checks all the farms receiving compensation payments once a year, and the Agriculture Ministry conducts its own inspections, spot-checking what it considers a representative sample of farms. As a result of these controls, Posch tells me, when Austrian consumers see their government-authorized seal guaranteeing *bio* on a label, they're confident that what they're buying is both homegrown and organic.

Discerning Austrian consumers like Posch are skeptical of organic-stamped food that comes from outside their national territory. "One hundred percent of the pedigree doesn't cross the border. A certification paper comes with the product, but it's not possible to check on the farm and the handler. We have to trust the paper." Posch and I are meeting as yet another organic-food scandal is surfacing in Italy. Huge shipments of corn and soybeans were seized by customs agents in the Adriatic port of Pesaro in the spring of 2013. Inspectors charge that the beans and corn are conventional and that fraudsters in Moldova relabeled it organic before exporting it to the European Union. "The problem is that we have no authority to check in Italy," says Posch about his Austrian colleagues at the ministries. "We have to trust the information they give us. I'm not saying Italian products are bad products," he quickly adds, "but Austrian products have a higher level of security. For Austrian consumers it's more important to have Austrian products than organic products."

"Because Austrians are chauvinistic and nationalist?"

"No," he says. "It's a question of trust."

"So when you shop you seek Austrian products?" I ask.

"Of course." But there's a limit. "You can't buy Austrian bananas. But if it's a product we produce, I buy Austrian."

"And if global warming continues," I offer, "you'll be able to buy organic Austrian bananas."

I'm rewarded with a polite laugh.

Before we say *auf Wiedersehen,* Posch says that he sees organic agriculture as being important for coming generations, and he laments the advent of pesticide- and herbicide-resistant GMOs. Genetically modified organisms are forbidden in Austrian agriculture by a policy that trumps the European Union approval of such crops. "More poison and more poison," he worries. "This poison is not just in the soil, it is in the plant. And if I eat the plant, I eat poison. It cannot be very healthy. We have to try and do it without poison."

Kazakh and Bolivian Organics as a Laugh Line

"Austria's organic pioneer" is how Werner Lampert bills himself, and he acts the part with flair. His salt-and-pepper beard and bushy, graying full head of hair, along with his wire-rimmed spectacles and trademark black three-piece Edwardian-looking suits, make him an easily recognizable figure, especially since he stars in lighthearted TV commercials for the Hofer supermarket's *Zurück zum Ursprung* (meaning "back to the original") line of organic products. In one he appears in a bakery, kneading dough, but making a mess of it as it sticks to his hands. The narrator formally announces that "perfect handwork" is needed for Hofer organic breads, along with a lot of time. In the next scene he is reading while he and a baker watch the dough rise. The spot closes with a satisfied-looking Lampert telling the camera, "*So weit muss Bio gehen*"—loosely translated: "Ya gotta go far for organic," reminding me of "I'd walk a mile for a Camel." Lampert developed the *Ja! Natürlich* brand for Billa. Austrian supermarkets recognized the value of organic food to both their images and bottom line early because of Lampert's marketing savvy and prowess.

Austria's organic pioneer and I meet at his offices in swank downtown Vienna, around the corner from St. Stephan's Cathedral. The inside of the elevator I take up to his floor matches his suit. It's a dark-wood-paneled paternoster, that jump-on-and-jump-off

European invention without doors that moves slowly between floors. For me the paternoster adds to the romance of the organic food movement—*Zurück zum Ursprung*: back to those compelling days before Big Agra, DDT, and tomatoes as hard as baseballs.

I tell Lampert the story now familiar to you, dear reader, regarding my quest.

He laughs. "I would never buy a product of Kazakhstan or Bolivia," he says with a smugness that fits well with his formal attire. Lampert makes it clear that he finds it impossible to trust claims of organic from countries famous for corruption—even if the farmers themselves meet the highest international standards for producing organic crops.

"It is rather easy to convert the farming itself to organic farming," he says. "But the products are processed, packaged, and cleaned. The people who clean the products, process and package them also have to work properly. That's the even bigger risk. And then we have to think about what happens during transport. There are many risks in the process." He leans back in his chair and thinks about the likelihood of my black beans and walnuts passing muster as organic. "I don't want to deny the farmers in Kazakhstan and Bolivia their honor, but there are many risks en route." He brings his concerns much closer to home. "We have the same problems with products from Italy, Romania, and Bulgaria." As an example he cites a case from a couple of years before our meeting, five thousand tons of conventional foodstuffs from Romania that were certified organic in Italy and shipped on to England, Germany, Switzerland, and Austria to be sold as organic.

"Laundered," I say.

"Yes. I totally agree: It is very difficult to get proper products from corrupt countries—especially organic products. It is very, very difficult. I don't trust these products. But the problem," he lectures, "lies elsewhere." Lampert faults consumers who seek whatever they want whenever they want it. If broccoli is out of season in Oregon, I can buy it shipped up from Mexico.

"That is a basic error," he says. "Reliable organic work is only possible regionally. There is no other way than regional farming—that's where you can build up confidence, and confidence occurs only when relationships exist. You're a farmer and I'm the consumer. I look you in the eye. I come visit you. I see your five children. You see my needs—and we can work with each other."

Of course this idyllic one-to-one relationship is not possible for everyone. Most of us simply do not have the time and resources to get to know the producers of all the foodstuffs jammed into our cupboards and the fridge. If we can't shake hands with the farmers, we must rely on a trusted third party to do the crucial job food tasters once performed for medieval monarchs.

Marketing Organics to the Masses

"We have an urban area with four million people," Lampert says about Vienna, "and they have to eat every day. They cannot drive to the countryside and build relationships with the farmers." And now he touts *Zurück zum Ursprung*. "For them we developed a system of transparency."

I ask him what transparency means to him in the complex business world of supplying groceries to the masses.

"The first thing that has to be destroyed is the anonymity of the origin of products. Nothing good hides behind anonymity—ever. Transparency means the consumer has to be able to trace back a product through all the methods of transport, all the methods of processing, until he gets to the original producer."

He's describing my odyssey. "So each consumer should be able to do what I'm trying to do with the beans and the nuts," I say. "But they can't and they won't—so should they trust the certification process?"

Lampert explains that *Zurück zum Ursprung* is designed to allow Hofer customers to find out exactly where anything with that catchy slogan originates. Each product marketed with his label is marked with a code number. Customers are encouraged to use the code to track the product back to its original producer via the Internet. That fork-back-to-farm option defines transparency, Lampert boasts.

I tell him about how Trader Joe's and Natural Directions are opaque, not transparent.

"Of course," and he lets out another belly laugh.

"They claim business secrets prevent them from disclosing their sources."

"Naturally." He keeps laughing. "Trust is only possible when things are open and accessible for everyone. If a business needs secrets, you have to give it a wide berth and buy nothing from them."

Hmm. Trader Joe's is owned by Aldi, and Hofer is an Aldi brand. There are the two Aldi companies founded the Albrecht brothers, Aldi Nord and Aldi Sud. Aldi Nord owns Trader Joe's, and Hofer is a subsidiary of Aldi Sud. How can the *Zurück zum Ursprung* brand operate with transparency in the opaque Aldi environment?

"Aldi did not develop this," Lampert says about his consumer trackback system, "and we didn't develop it for Aldi. We cooperate with Aldi. That means all the work we do—the transparency, the quality management, the backtracking—we do all this in this very building. We are an independent company." He is intense as he tries to make clear the difference between himself and the retailer he promotes on the TV ads. "We are not owned by Aldi. Aldi has no shares. This is my company. I own 100 percent. We developed the trademark. We created the concept. We find the farmers. We ensure the quality of the farming on-site. We develop the products. We have the product know-how. All the transparency measures happen here." This declaration of independence gets him revved up. "My God! There wouldn't be any other way."

Traditional traders, he says, aren't optimized for quality. Rather they seek anonymity and interchangeability. That's certainly what I've been encountering on my search. "So if I go to Hofer and I buy a bag of walnuts or a can of beans with your trademark on it, I can trace them back to the source?"

"Of course, yes. Responsibility. That's the capital of the future," Lampert says with missionary zeal. "The brand brings a lot of consumers to Hofer."

But Lampert's company is not vetting beans from Bolivia or nuts from Kazakhstan. Places where corruption is common, he says, defy transparency. "In countries like Sicily, Bolivia, or Kazakhstan, organic farming can only exist if there are buyers in the West." But as soon as such sales begin, he says, corrupted officials and protection rackets demand bribes. When extortion saps profits, quality suffers. "That means," says Lampert, "mixing organic with conventional in order to earn more money. Nothing good can come from corrupt systems."

I ask him why he thinks such a high percentage of Austrians choose organics. He gives credit to the work of Alois Posch and his colleagues at the Agriculture Ministry. But just as important, he theorizes, is that Austrians (along with the Swiss and French) "still have a good sense for natural food and every Austrian has some kind of relationship to the mountains, or to the Waldviertel or Mühlviertel—to the countryside. The Austrian loves nature and spends a lot of time there. He goes into the mountains. He takes a walk. He spends his vacation there. He has an intense emotional relationship to nature." He adds, "Agriculture in Austria evolved very slowly and modernized very late. So a lot of the old knowledge is still here." As is the acquired taste for fresh heirloom tomatoes instead of those factory-farmed lipstick-red ones.

It sounds much like my Oregon home: a lust for the natural world and the food it can provide.

"I don't know about Oregon," he says, announcing to me, "In Oregon there are many hippies."

Now it's my turn to laugh. "Many hippies?"

"I read a wonderful novel by Pynchon about Oregon. Must be paradise."

"It is," I agree, inviting him to visit without disturbing his fantasy about Thomas Pynchon's *Vineland;* it's set in Northern California.

"I always thought I might go to Oregon."

"We share your sense of belonging to the land, to our Cascade Mountains and Pacific Ocean and to our breadbasket, the fertile Willamette Valley—fat with organic agriculture."

"Wonderful!" he exudes. I feel as if I'm making a friend.

I ask Lampert if I should make the trips to Kazakhstan and Bolivia, seeking wisdom from his experiences. He responds with a story.

"When I started doing business with Billa in 1994, I started with organic milk products, with yogurt. In the yogurt there were strawberries. The organic certification was from Poland. I assigned a Swiss certification group to track back where those strawberries were grown. They wrote letters to Poland, and they were referred from one company to the next. In the end it became apparent that the strawberries were bought somewhere in Canada and nobody was able to tell us the origin of the strawberries. I think that's global business; it disguises everything. I think you will never find where in Kazakhstan or Bolivia those nuts and beans originated. Never, ever."

Before we part and I head out of his office to try my luck again on the paternoster, I ask Lampert about what continues to baffle me regarding the credibility and the legitimacy of the organic certification system as it operates in much of the world: the certifiers are paid by those they certify.

"That is a tremendous problem," he says without hesitation.

"A direct conflict of interest?"

He answers with another story, this one about telling a certification company the standards he wanted checked at a supplier. "The man looked at me and said, 'That's impossible.' Why is it impossible? 'They pay me. They will never let this happen.' The certification is always to the benefit of the one who pays—and not to the benefit of the consumer," Lampert says with certitude. "It's a tremendous problem."

"So do you think my wife is wasting all that extra grocery money buying food that's certified organic if it's not from Oregon?"

"Yes." I mentally note that it's easy for him to make that harsh judgment surrounded as he is by the cornucopia of Austrian organics.

"What do you buy? What does your grocery cart look like? What's in it? Where do you shop?" I ask this organic pioneer. He describes the organic market where he shops near his Salzburg home, buying directly from farmers. It sounds like the Saturday Market in Eugene. The two of us live privileged lifestyles. We live in places where the highest-quality food is easily available and we can afford to pay premium prices for it while the rest of the world eats poison. Our obligation in the face of such luxury, insists Lampert, is to work for change.

When I returned to America, I encountered a variation on Lampert's *Zurück zum Ursprung* concept. I bought a cantaloupe with a hefty sticker slapped on it advising me that it was "organically grown in Hermiston, Oregon," by John Walchli, and that if I wanted further information I could "connect to the farm" via HarvestMark.com. I punched my melon's sixteen-character code into the form on the website. Harvest Mark suggested I made a typo. I tried it again. Twice. No luck.

Zurück to the Hofer Supermarket

After hearing from an impassioned Werner Lampert that shoppers at Hofer—the Austrian Aldi—can use smartphones and websites to trace the food they buy at Hofer back to its source, I leave his office impatient to test his system. I glance up at the gaudy tiled roof of St.

Stephan's Cathedral and fight the cold, wind, and a late spring drizzle up to the Kärntner Ring. There I jump on the Number 2 tram to the Volkstheater, transfer to the 46, and three stops later am at my flat. I am starving—not a good time to visit a supermarket, even an Aldi type. I make a sandwich: smoked wild Alaskan sockeye, wondering if wild counts as organic, on sweet Austrian pumpernickel. Next stop is the Hofer a few blocks down Lerchenfelderstraße.

The organic pickings at the Hofer are slim. A banner in the produce department promotes Lampert's *Zurück zum Ursprung* program. Zap the *Chargencode* with your phone, it advises, or enter the sell-by date codes on the website. The Hofer slogan is *So weit muss Bio gehen,* and it's posted with the fruits and vegetables. "Organic must be inclusive of all factors" is a better loose translation than "Ya gotta go far for organic." ONE HUNDRED PERCENT TRANSPARENT, a sign trumpets. *Prüf nach!* (Prove it now!) *Exclusiv bei Hofer* (Exclusively at Hofer). This sounds promising. But the organic stuff on offer makes the old Bethesda Co-op's ugly fruits and vegetables look like Blue Ribbon winners for best looking at the county fair. A few bunches of radishes with wilted greens and one package of white asparagus—nine stalks, one missing its tip—for over five bucks American.

I move on to the dry goods aisle, where the number of organic items offered also is inconsequential. Two types of flour and a bag of pumpkin seeds. In the bakery section I find a loaf of organic walnut bread! So I am close to a couple of samples that compare—more or less—with my Kazakh nuts and Bolivian beans. The pumpkin seeds will be my stand-in for black beans, and the bread is *Walnussbrot.* I grab them both, along with two bottles of Italian Chardonnay (not organic) and head for the checkout stand.

Just like in Germany, Austrian grocery stores make you work for your dinner. The clerks not only do not bag what you buy, they shove it across the counter at you (often with sneers). As soon as your money is in the cash register, no matter how much stuff of yours is stacked up, they immediately begin checking out the next guy in line, shoving his stuff unceremoniously into yours. Buying groceries in Austria is an exercise that makes me appreciate the saccharine practiced lines of American clerks like, "Did you find everything you wanted?" and "How's your day going?" and what seems especially incongruous as the Austrian cans, bottles, bags, and bananas come flying at you faster than you can bag them, "Would you like help out to your car with that?" Ha! Instead, I head out into the nasty weather, lugging my bag, and climb aboard the 46 for the trip back to my flat, anxious to log onto the Hofer website and learn the origin and farm-to-fork path of my pumpkin seeds and walnut bread.

Amazing. As I'm eating handfuls of delicious black pumpkin seeds and after a couple of easy clicks, I'm reading a list of the farms where pumpkin seeds are harvested for Hofer. It's a short list. Franz Hoesch's place in Pillischdorf. And Hans and Ursula Lembacher's spread in Sitzendorf. Perhaps the ones I'm eating are from Paasdorf and the fields of Gerhard Thüringer, or his neighbor Christian Seltenhammer. A few more. Along with the names are the street addresses of the farms. And a map, showing their proximity to Vienna, where I bought two hundred grams of the snack for two euros and ninety-nine cents—just shy of four American dollars. Not only can I find the farms, but with another couple of clicks I can check on the middleman. Agervita Handels is the company in St. Ruprecht an der Raab, just east of Graz, hired to truck the seeds to market.

Here in Austria, while I wait for the bureaucracy of the USDA to process my formal complaint on the nuts and beans, I can sit in the comfort of my Tigergasse flat, drinking Italian wine, and find the likely source of the food I'm eating. I could call up Franz Hoesch tomorrow and ask to come out to tour his Pillischdorf farm. Or request that Agervita Handels show its facilities to me. I punch up my walnut bread, and another list of suppliers appears on the screen of my laptop (not a one of them is in Kazakhstan!). Hofer is showing off its supply chain while Trader Joe's and Natural Directions hide behind the excuse of proprietary business secrets.

Not that the Hofer *Zurück zum Ursprung* system is perfect. The Hofer products on offer at my local branch of the chain are limited in both quantity and variety. Were I to eat only organic products that passed the Hofer source machine, I'd starve! But I'm mighty impressed. And depressed that not only are my suspicions about Kazakhstan and Bolivia reinforced, I'm also experiencing a tracing system that's been operating for several years here in Austria while monster American retailers like Trader Joe's dismiss basic inquiries into their practices. Funny that the Aldi family of stores owns both Trader Joe's and Hofer. But then again, General Mills makes Chocolate Lucky Charms and it packages Muir Glen organic tomatoes. Coca-Cola bought Odwalla, and the wholly owned subsidiary still makes organic carrot juice. Or so it claims. Of course corporate cross-ownership is commonplace, and just because General Mills owns Muir Glen doesn't mean the cereal division of the company is convincing the organic division to add high-fructose corn syrup to its stewed tomatoes. But I am surprised that so few of the shoppers I talk with who fill their carts with organic bother to learn who owns the farms, factories, and stores. Instead they seem to be comforted by brown packaging and green copywriting while they convince themselves that some starry-eyed idealists fresh squeeze their Odwalla.

The Austrian Skeptic

If Joe Smillie considers organic purists to be the Taliban of the food industry, he probably would consider Austrian author Clemens Arvay—who identifies himself as an agricultural biologist—its Mullah Mohammed Omar. Arvay's titles include *Der Grosse Bio Schmäh:* in English, *The Great Organic Con.* He suggests we meet at the Welt Café ("100% fair trade and organic," says the menu, which promises that all the food and drink served tastes good and is ethical). Arvay is not impressed by Werner Lampert's *Zurück zum Ursprung* campaign. No surprise since Arvay seems to assess supermarkets much like the Taliban felt about the Bamiyan Buddhas.

"Usually the things labeled organic are legally organic," Arvay says above the clatter of coffee cups and conversation, "but they are not organic if you compare mass production to the original ideas and ideals of the organic movement." The Welt Café is a student hangout, and with his youthful good looks, scraggly beard, and trademark ponytail coiffed around his neck and dangling down the front of his shoulder, Arvay fits in seamlessly. I'm sipping a cup of allegedly organic green tea as he calls some certifiers corrupt but identifies most as honest and proud of their work. "I know there are cheaters. I'm totally aware of the fact that not everything labeled organic is really organic." But even food showing off legitimate organic seals is suspect for him; certifiers check farms infrequently and focus on auditing files in offices instead of the agricultural practices in fields.

He's convinced that some organic purveyors rationalize fudging the rules. He offers an example he found at a farm in Germany. "They used more conventional feed for the chickens than European organic standards allow. They said they were forced to do it because they had a cannibalism problem." The conventional feed provided the chickens with more protein than they received from the organic feed; hence they weren't tempted to eat their cousins for a dietary supplement. "In their view it was absolutely okay to use a little bit of conventional feed just for a few weeks because they needed it for the welfare of the chickens. They don't see it as a violation. I don't think they're criminals."

Nonetheless, Arvay is convinced that most factory farms work hard to ensure that their products are what they claim to be. "They all know it would be a real scandal if it turned out that they cheated on the consumer." The credibility of the organic seal on a label is not his worry. His villains are mass production on organic farms—especially farms that produce both organic and conventional crops—along with mass marketing in supermarket organic sections. "It is not true that there is an organic food industry," worries Arvay, because the conventional food industry dominates organic production, distribution, and retail sales. "They're buying the image." Buying the image *and* buying the trusted trademarks in many cases, like the corporate takeovers of famous organic brands: Santa Cruz Organic and Cascadian Farms, Erewhon and Garden of Eatin'—the list of corporate ownership of trusted brands is long and suspect, at least for me. I can't help but question the allegiances of Big Business. If there is a conflict between next quarter profits and what goes into my stomach, my gut fears for my gut.

Keeping the Chickens Chickenly

The potential exists for cross-contamination from the conventional facilities to the organic. But Arvay figures that's a rare occurrence. His outcry is more philosophical, and he offers chicken as an example. "Big companies with their centralized slaughterhouses, usually they process about 95 percent conventional, plus 5 percent organic. I asked many of them," he says, "why they bother with the organic, and the answer is almost always the same. So that they can show that they're green." Image again. "You can feel the philosophy of those conventional food industry managers . . ."

"You mean their soul isn't in it?" I'm hearing a religious-like binding of soul and food across organic Austria.

"Their soul isn't in it," Arvay agrees, "but it has real practical consequences. Let's stay with the example of chickens." He describes how a chicken producer can obey the letter of the European Union organic law while violating its spirit: The population in chicken stalls is limited to six chickens for each square meter of floor space, but Arvay says hustling producers build stalls with more than one floor, allowing them to stack the chickens. Standardization is not limited to housing. The supermarket chains, he says, demand a particular breed of chicken (and specific breeds of other animals and farm products). The result is bland bad news at the dinner table. "People don't know what tomatoes taste like!" he laments, and they are deceived by the organic claim. He says he traced back *Ja! Natürlich* organic tomatoes, the Billa supermarket organic brand, to the farmer and found tomatoes grown out of conventional Monsanto seeds.

"The seeds were mislabeled," I suggest.

"No, they *weren't* mislabeled! That's the point. The European Union doesn't say that you must use organic seeds; it says you must you use them *when you can*." And the Monsanto seeds are hybrids. Farmers must go back to Monsanto, the world's largest seed purveyor, for each planting.

Monsanto's GMO corn and soybeans carpet vast acreage of American farmland. The global Big Agra monster (which calls itself, Newspeak-like, a "sustainable agriculture company") designed its genetically modified seeds to grow crops that tolerate the herbicide glyphosate. Glyphosate is another product of Monsanto's laboratories and is better known by its trade name, Roundup. Farmers keep weeds away from their Monsanto GMO corn and soybeans with glyphosate sprayed on their land. The GMO crops thrive, but most anything else that gets hit with targeted spray or spray spread around the landscape by wind or accidental overspraying quickly withers and dies.

The organic compromises plague Arvay. He's an idealist and longs for the mom-and-pop organic farming featured in the *Whole Earth Catalog*'s heyday. "No hybrids—that was one of the main ideas. And keeping animals so that it's *artgerecht*," he says in German, searching for the English word. "Species appropriate" is the literal translation.

"Humane," I offer, but he rejects the word.

"Not humane," he insists. "Chickenly!" We laugh, but he's happy with his word choice and elaborates: "Keeping the chickens chickenly. Not humane. You know what I mean? Keeping the cows like a cow. So they can live out their natural desires of how to behave as a chicken or a cow. That becomes nearly impossible if you have a farm with eighteen thousand laying hens."

In his books Arvay calls for a reorganization of global food production and distribution. "The problem is that the big players control and centralize food systems." Replace centralization with regionalism, he says. Farms can flourish in urban centers like Vienna and Detroit. "I have a very radical position: I think we have to get over the food industry. We have to leave it behind. I don't care what the companies want and I don't care what's good for their profit. Agriculture is the domain of farmers. What I care about is the agriculture itself and the food that we eat. If we have a system that is not able to produce real organic sustainable food, let's leave it behind." He also wants to get rid of the factory farms, and once that's accomplished, "There's no space for supermarkets."

It's a heartfelt idealistic speech, but who's going to get those sweet heirloom tomatoes and chickenly chickens from the farmer to the stomachs of the millions of people who live in our cities?

"I don't need a supermarket to get the food from the field into my stomach. I don't go to supermarkets. I don't buy anything in supermarkets except in emergencies."

"Easy for you to say," I respond. "You and I have the luxury of time to find farmers' markets, even in big cities. But what about the harried and exhausted worker, rushing home from the office, who only has a few minutes before dinner to rush into a supermarket and buy groceries?" Our debate fits well in the cafe atmosphere, although the students at the tables surrounding us look as if they're enjoying much more lighthearted chats.

"This could become a really intense philosophical discussion," he interrupts me, "because I don't think that is the way humans should live."

He's correct, and I need to stay focused on my quest. Survival of the supermarket culture is not a question for this trek. Besides, I must admit that I'm happy that Market of Choice (where Sheila bought the Bolivian beans) opens at seven in the morning and stays open until midnight. I'm glad I can buy everything from toilet paper to vitamins (from bean soup to nuts!) minutes from my home. I like it that Market of Choice lines up yellow bottles of French's mustard right next to esoteric bottles of organic Dijon. I am more than okay with convenience and variety. I am spoiled.

A Marketing Duel

I am intrigued to learn that Arvay once worked for Werner Lampert and his *Zurück zum Ursprung* label.

"I would never want to work for that guy ever again," he tells me. I'm surprised. I enjoyed my encounter with Lampert. I considered his responses to my queries thoughtful and candid. Arvay feels otherwise. "He's one of the most inhumane people to his employees that I've ever met in my whole life." His tone of voice is thick with disdain, and he quickly adds, "That's just a personal thing that has nothing to do with the food itself."

Whatever happened between them as employee and employer is, of course, their business. But Arvay doesn't only reject Lampert as a boss, he rejects the *Zurück zum Ursprung* campaign as just another supermarket marketing hustle and one that depends on factory farming. "What's the benefit?" he asks with renewed disdain. "Who does it?" he asks about the opportunity *Zurück zum Ursprung* offers consumers to trace organic products back to their source. "What the concept mainly effects is that people have a good feeling. Wow! It's so transparent!" He mocks how a naïve consumer might react. "I *could* check this number. I *could* go to the Internet and I *could* type it in and I would find the name of a farmer there. And then I *could* call the farmer and I *could* visit the farmer. But nobody does that." I don't consider myself naïve. I *was* impressed when I punched in the number of my pumpkin seeds and found the farmers' names and addresses. I *could* introduce myself to them and ask to visit their farms. That's a much better option than being told to buzz off by Trader Joe's and QAI.

I acknowledge that few Hofer shoppers will bother contacting farmers, "but isn't that better than what I've been facing with the walnuts and the black beans—zero cooperation? At least Hofer customers have the opportunity to check on sources even if they don't bother to take advantage of it."

"But what do you really find in the end?" is Arvay's caustic reply. "I traced back eggs, for example. I ended up at a farm where they keep eighteen thousand laying hens. What happens to the eggs? They are sold to supermarkets. They are sold to all supermarkets— to all organic brands. But what do you hear in the marketing? That they are unique. There is such a big difference between reality and advertising. They're all the same. They're faking pictures in advertising and hiding the reality. That's how those supermarkets work."

As we depart the cafe, I hear from Arvay appreciation for small farmers who follow organic principles but do not bother with certification. "They do a better sustainable job than some industrialized organic farmers." Don't think in black and white, he cautions: Organic isn't always better than conventional.

Chapter Nine

Us and Them

If Clemens Arvay represents the Taliban wing of the organic food industry according to Joe Smillie's criteria, Joachim Massani—the chief of the quality assurance department for the Spar supermarket chain—could be a candidate for secretary-general of the United Nations of Organics. He is the epitome of reasoned compromise. Despite their disparate camps, Arvay and Massani agree that the *Zurück zum Ursprung* marketing scheme is of questionable value to consumers concerned about the purity of food labeled organic. "When you have bread and you think about the wheat, does it make sense to know there are two hundred growers?" Massani asks me. "What are you doing with the information? What are you doing as a consumer when you see there are two hundred, three hundred wheat growers listed? They always are mixing the wheat together. What are you doing with this information?" It's a valid point. Maybe the list of growers provides some psychological boost to the credibility of the *bio* label. "I think nobody's looking at it. You have to trust."

We're talking in the Spar corporate offices in Salzburg. I made the glorious trip into the Austrian Alps, past pristine mountain lakes and storybook villages, to meet the man who signs my food. I feel as if I should already know Massani since his signature decorates the packages of Spar *bio* products that fill my pantry and refrigerator. The Spar *bio* guarantee to its customers is written in the first person ("I guarantee this product is organic in the name of Spar") and signed in his flowing cursive. Massani's shock of white hair belies his youthful appearance and animated responses to my questions. He leans back with a casual comfort in his conference room chair, answering my queries with refreshing candor.

"I've been in Moldavia," Massani tells me when I express skepticism about the "organic" walnuts Trader Joe's sells marked "Product of Kazakhstan." Spar was, I'm intrigued to learn, buying walnuts in the former Soviet republic now known as Moldova—not organic walnuts, but at least my search is moving toward Kazakhstan and finding walnuts en route in a place with a recent political and social history similar to Kazakhstan's. Massani journeyed east to inspect the Moldovan walnut-processing plant after reports reached Salzburg that the place failed to meet Austrian hygiene standards. "When you see how they are living," he says, "it's understandable." He was appalled by his hotel, calling it "the worst hotel I ever stayed in" and was shocked to see how the walnut workers lived. "They have no water in their houses, no toilets in their houses." The walnut operation was in the countryside near the Ukraine border. "The streets were not paved. It was simple living. The walnut-processing plant was the only building in the village with a flush toilet. They needed to teach the workers how to use the toilet." Massani showed the Moldovans how to satisfy Austrian food safety standards and raced back home to Salzburg.

Not just because of his harrowing experiences in Moldova, Massani tells me I'm right to be suspicious of the walnuts, and he suggests I'll never learn where they originated. The global food trade is so complex, even Spar can't determine with certainty the provenance of all the food it sells.

"We don't always go back to the origin," he says about the company's research into the products on its shelves. "What's sourced from Austria is no problem. All that comes from Europe is also possible to locate. But all the other things, we don't have the possibility to trace to the end." When Spar's own tests identify a problem with an item it sells, like traces of pesticides, then the company attempts to determine where it was tainted. "Very often the suppliers mix it. They buy a little bit from here; they buy a little bit from there. Even they themselves don't know where the problem comes from." As long as any traces of pesticides are below the limits set by European Union regulations, there's no need to ask questions. That means that an organic shipment could be infected with some conventional material but that the ratio of organic to conventional is high enough to satisfy legal requirements.

"You have to compromise," Massani believes, and decide when it makes sense to trace products back to their origin and when such checks are not worth the time and expense. *Bio* products for sale at Spar "will never be 100 percent organic, in my opinion," he says, because suppliers knowingly mix conventional with organic—cutting the more expensive organic with the cheaper conventional and banking on the fact that the rules allow for enough pesticide residue in food labeled organic for the supplier to make a few extra bucks.

"They do this intentionally?" I check to make sure that I understand that what he's talking about is a conscious scam.

"Yes, yes, yes. They're doing it to increase their profits," he affirms, as if it should be obvious. "They have maybe one thousand kilos of conventional wheat. They put it together with ten thousand kilos of organic."

"Because they know it will pass an inspection?"

"You'll never find them," he says about the hustlers. "There will always be holes in the inspection systems. Therefore you have to make compromises."

Okay. I'm ready to make compromises. But I want to make well-informed compromises. What Trader Joe's, Natural Directions, and QAI are trying to force down my throat are compromises on their terms: They claim their stuff is organic while refusing to pull back their curtains.

Italy: A Nice Place to Visit

Massani offers a tale of Italian broccoli contaminated with pesticides, contamination that showed up during one of the routine spot checks that Spar makes as standard procedure. "Italy is a country where we always, again and again, have problems." He complained to the certification outfit that had verified the vegetable to Spar as organic, which then queried its Italian counterpart. The result? No response from the certifier on the other side of the Alps. "When you do it the official way, it leads to nothing."

It's an astounding statement to hear from a supermarket executive. Or anyone for that matter. "When you do it the official way, it leads to *nothing?*" I repeat his conclusion back to him just to make sure I heard him right.

"Yes, yes," he says, perhaps with some resignation—or maybe impatience. "It leads to nothing. You have to trace it for yourself. You have to go there and learn where it comes from. The problem is, when you are in Italy, they speak Italian. They don't like to speak English, as we do. They say, 'We don't understand.' The suppliers say they don't know where the broccoli comes from. They can't explain the pesticide. When you have the language barrier, it's really not easy." I try to image a Hawaiian shirt–clad Trader Joe's representative traveling the Silk Road, vetting the Kazakh walnuts with a Russian or Kazakh phrasebook in hand, and what keeps replaying in my mind is the mistranslated Hungarian phrasebook sketch from *Monty Python.* ("My hovercraft is full of eels.")

Massani agrees that I'm correct to suspect the Kazakh walnuts because the country may lack First World standards and mimic what he found in rural Moldova. "Italy also is suspect. Italy is always a problem, and it's the First World. It's a nice country, but organic is always a problem in Italy," Massani reiterates with a laugh, "maybe because they are trying to make more of a profit. They see it the Italian way."

I ask him what makes it the Italian way.

"The Italian way is that they take it a little bit easier." He dismisses his neighbors with the wink of an eye. "It's a different mentality." But he quickly makes it clear that Austria also suffers scandals in the organic sector—recent ones involving wheat and potatoes. "They aren't so strict in Italy. Everybody loves it when you go to Italy and make holiday there. It's easy living. But doing business with them is a little bit complicated, especially when you have problems. Nevertheless, you always have to smile," he says with a smile, "because they take it with a smile. It's easy."

It's not just overt scammers that Massani marks as problematic. He, too, cites the rules that allow farmers to raise both organic and conventional crops and animals on the same properties. Such a mix sets the stage for crossover, by intent or by mistake. When the same storage and processing facilities are used for both crops and the same varieties are grown, it stretches his credulity to imagine that the conventional strawberries—the example he chooses—don't get mixed up with those certified organic.

"You have to trust your supplier. I can't assign one of my employees to stand there all day and look at what they're doing. That's impossible." Of course. "We do our checks. We do our audits. But it's also important which supplier our buying department chooses. You have to trust." Developing personal relationships, he says, is more important than bureaucratic checks and audits. Responsibility also rests on the buyers. If supermarkets negotiate brutal financial terms with producers, producers may feel more inclined to break the rules—to cut organic loads with conventional content, especially since the likelihood of being caught in the act is negligible. "You have to give them the money they need. If you always try to make the cheapest price, you force them to do tricks."

Massani is not an evangelist for organic food; he can take it or leave it. "This is marketing!" he says with enthusiasm when I ask him why his signature is on the packages of *bio* products I buy at Spar. He laughs when I call him a *bio* celebrity and says again, "This is only marketing." The integrity of the organics line is critical, but just as important for him is the origin of the conventional foods on the shelves. "When we write on pumpkin seeds, 'This comes from Austria,' then we also have to check that they come from Austria. I love my job and I do not distinguish between the different articles. Organic is only one of them."

"But for your own stomach," I ask him, "when you're pushing a cart through the market, are you buying *bio?*"

"I try to buy *bio* where I think it's important. Although it's more expensive, I try to buy *bio* meat because I think it makes the biggest difference. You really see the difference in animal welfare. The organic chickens really can go outside; a conventional chicken will never see outside. For me this is the most important thing—animal welfare."

"What about fruits and vegetables? Don't you care if they're sprayed with poisons?"

"I do not care that much," he says. "I know that the pesticide levels are not really a problem for me. It also depends on the season. In the summer if I buy tomatoes from Austria, I know that the pesticides are not a problem." But when he is buying imported tomatoes in the winter, he tends to pick the organic, worried that the imports may be dosed with too much pesticide.

I ask Massani, from his standpoint as a supermarket chain quality control officer, how he would define organic.

He hesitates, thinking about his answer. This meeting is an invigorating encounter for me. Massani is not spewing rehearsed corporate talking points, a rarity in today's controlled environment of media-trained executives. "*Bio*, for me, very often is not what it should be. It should be, I think, a kind of living. I think the best *bio* would a farm where everything is *bio* and you have your menu that comes from the animals and the fields, where you have a closed system. This would be the best *bio*." Many farmers raise *bio* products for the money, he says, expecting higher profits. "I think most people buy *bio* because they think they are doing something good for their health." They may buy *bio* for their health, but they want that *bio* to look pretty. They don't subscribe to the Bethesda Co-op "Buy ugly, it's organic" philosophy. "When consumers buy organic food in our shops, they want organic food that looks like conventional food," Massani says. Ugly produce cannot command the premium prices Spar charges for its organics, and organic sales account for as much as 10 percent of the gross at the chain's upscale Spar Gourmet outlets.

I ask Massani if he thinks I'll find the origin of my Bolivian beans and Kazakh nuts.

"You don't have a chance" is his simple reply. And he does not understand why Trader Joe's and Natural Directions refuse to direct me to their suppliers. Something's wrong when companies do not disclose their sources, and that suggests problems, he says.

"If I took a bag of walnuts and a can of black beans off a Spar shelf and asked you where they came from, would you tell me?"

"Yes, I would give you the information." And his name is on the packages, promising that his personal integrity backs the products. "Although my signature is on the articles, we never get asked, 'Who is the supplier? Where did it come from?' Consumers never ask."

Is that silence a measure of trust? Or of complacency? Maybe it's a lack of interest.

I head off from Spar headquarters to a relaxing evening in Mondsee. A sign is posted on the local Mexican joint announcing that the beef served is *bio* and so local you can visit its still-grazing relatives at a nearby ranch.

Double-Checking
Back in Vienna I meet Natalie Kirchbaumer early one morning at Café Raimund, another typically charming Viennese coffeehouse, just a

block off the city's famous Ring. Kirchbaumer works with Global 2000, a group of Austrian environmentalists linked with Friends of the Earth. I'm fascinated to learn more about her assignment: She's a detective for the supermarket chain Billa and other food-importing companies, checking out the sources of products that the company fears may not meet organic (or other) standards. Hers sounds like a dream job. She travels to exotic foreign lands. But once arrived at her faraway destinations, she's not relaxing poolside at a swank resort sipping an umbrella drink. Instead Kirchbaumer is busy in farm fields, offices, and processing plants, double-checking not just the validity of organic certificates but also the working conditions of the laborers responsible for the food products Billa imports.

"They want to have more guarantees about what they're actually buying," she tells me about Billa. More guarantees than can be provided by a third-party certifier. "They want a guarantee so that they don't advertise something, and then a journalist"—she looks at me with a knowing smile—"a journalist travels and finds out it's completely the contrary!"

It's been a cold and wet, gray and windy spring in Austria—for the most part terrible weather. I ask her about her last inspection trip.

"I just came from Spain," she tells me. Kirchbaumer, her blonde hair cascading over her shoulders, combines a bubbly, free-spirited personality with serious analyses of her professional responsibilities. She was out in the field—literally—inspecting melons and clementines. She studied certification paperwork, got her hands dirty visiting orchards and vineyards, washed up, and analyzed the logs that document the path fruit takes from Spain to Austria. She tracked the fruit in order to learn how Billa's supplier can guarantee that the clementines from that specific farm end up in Austria at the Billa supermarkets. It's work important to her personal life. "I'm almost buying 100 percent organic," she says about her diet.

"If you're buying almost all organic food, you must believe in the integrity of the process. You must believe that the stuff on the shelves in the stores labeled organic is really organic."

Not so fast, she cautions. "It's like in every business. There are dark sides. There are people who think they're really clever and they want to make money," she says. "But this really happens everywhere." She accepts the fact that some food marked organic won't pass her tests. "This is human." Otherwise there would be no need for jobs like hers. "But in general, yes, I believe in the system."

The clementines and oranges checked out clean. That's good news, but I'm seeking the anomalies. As the saying goes, dog bites man isn't the news; the news is man bites dog. I ask her for an example of a horror story from her fieldwork. She denies ever being witness to what could be called a catastrophe, though everywhere she visits can use improvement. But from Kirchbaumer I hear a complaint I've heard from others in Austria and elsewhere. Because each country and every certifier interprets mandated organic standards independently, the de facto result is an inevitable one: Standards differ from country to country, from certifier to certifier. "Different cultural backgrounds influence how people read the regulations." If there is wiggle room or if the letter of the law should be followed, "this is a very cultural thing. If you don't really have an organic farming heart, maybe you interpret it as 'I should do it, but I don't have to do it.'"

I tell her about the continuing reports I'm hearing that Italy is an organic disaster. And certainly there are news stories breaking to add to that reputation. "Italian Police Uncover Organic Food Fraud" is a typical headline, this one from the English-language service of Xinhua, the Chinese news agency perhaps relieved to be reporting about tainted food not connected to China. The summer 2013 bust was for one hundred thousand tons of conventional grain sold as organic.[53] Kirchbaumer offers an intriguing commentary. Italy produces a great deal of organic food for export and—especially compared with Austria—not much organic food is purchased for domestic consumption. "People are not so conscious about organics if they are just producing it for export." She tells me about visiting a strawberry farm and tasting organic strawberries in the field, berries bound for export. "They were not really nice. Then we walked to a smaller area and I said, 'Ah, I want to try these,' and they were fantastic." But her guide quashed her enthusiasm, informing her that the tastier berries were not heading for Austria; they were grown for Italians. The farm, she figured, was more interested in making money from the berries that were "not really nice" than they were concerned about the taste. The berries marked for export met organic standards, but the overall quality was poor. Of course there are exceptions to that negative stereotype, she says, citing examples of Italian farms producing fine products for export while taking good care of the land.

"I can tell you what I would like organic to be," she says. "But reality is different."

And what would she like?

"I like the vision of Rudolf Steiner," she says, referring to the Austrian founder of biological-dynamic agriculture, "for a self-sufficient farm. This would be the perfect organic farm. They exist, but not many," she says of this utopia. Her *realpolitik* compromise is that food producers simply follow the European Union regulations.

"If you go to a market and you see a tomato from Kazakhstan and a tomato from Salzburg, which tomato are you going to buy?"

"That's a good question," she parries, laughing again and favoring the local product. "When I see peppers from Israel, then I just decide I won't have peppers today. When it comes to tomatoes, I just eat tomatoes during the season. The rest of the year I don't eat tomatoes because they don't have any taste. I just quit them from my diet. I really love tomatoes, but most of them are really horrible. They taste like water."

"And they're as tough as a baseball," I add.

"The problem is that the supermarkets are interested in shelf life. When you have a long shelf life, there is a direct correlation that the tomato is losing taste. This is a very simple equation. The consumer has to tell the supermarkets, 'We're not content anymore with these kinds of products.' Kids are growing up with these tomatoes, so they really don't know how tomatoes taste. There has to be this perfect tomato," she says about the supermarket produce, "and they have to be the same size. This is just ridiculous. Organic is not perfect."

The Organic Parliamentarian

Just down the street from Café Raimund is the massive neoclassical Austrian Parliament building, where Green Party MP Wolfgang Pirklhuber advocates for organic agriculture. The organic food business is not just an abstract political agenda item for him. Pirklhuber is a farmer and he owns and operates one of Austria's organic certification companies. He and I sit down in the ornate *Parlamentscafeteria*—Parliament is in session and Pirklhuber is keeping track of the time so that he doesn't miss a vote.

Certification is risk management, he says, embracing the skepticism I express about my search. "It could work," he speculates optimistically about my beans and nuts passing muster as organic. "When the collaboration of companies in the so-called developed countries is based on quite good cooperation with transparent partners in Third World countries and both are winning, it can work. But anonymous markets are dangerous." Hard to imagine anything more anonymous than my Kazakh nuts. Pirklhuber offers his own example. "Let's say I'm a Romanian worker and I sell some cereal to a wholesaler and that wholesaler sells organic cereal and the two get mixed up. That's a problem."

"Laundering," I offer. "Fraud."

"The big risks," he agrees, "are between First and Third World countries, when the trade involves First World retailers." The distances—cultural and geographical—invite fraud. He's quick to offer examples of clean trade between developing and developed countries, and to spread the blame, noting that some profit-hungry First World retailers instigate fraud across the borders. "They're looking for cheaper imports. Can they get it from Kazakhstan or some other country where nobody knows what's going on?" There is some First World oversight of operations in developing countries, but for Pirklhuber it's inadequate and not likely to improve. "It costs a lot, and it's getting more and more expensive."

Pirklhuber talks fast. He's packed with energy, and drinking not a Viennese coffee but apple juice.

"It's not organic," I point out.

"No," he acknowledges, "but there always is some *bio* on the menu." We take a look and, indeed, this day a steak touted as organic is offered at the Parliament restaurant. "I wrote a letter to our Speaker calling for more choices." But we look at the menu more closely and realize that, although the steak is called organic, there is no mention that it is *certified* organic.

"Please don't write that in your book," Pirklhuber pleads, laughing about the Parliament's reputation because Austrian restaurants should note that food offered as organic is certified (if it in fact is).

"I must write it," I counter.

The vote call sounds and Pirklhuber excuses himself after making it clear he trusts most of the food labeled organic in Austria because he studies test results.

Near the Vienna city limits is the city's organic farm and organic agriculture institute, Bio Forschung Austria. Bernard Kromp is the chief scientist at the institute, and one of his proudest accomplishments is a partnership with the Vienna garbage service to process household refuse and deconstruct it into compost that meets European Union organic standards. The compost is given away to Viennese backyard gardeners and sold to commercial farms. Looking out over the city's farmland, Kromp tells me that too many of those eating organic food are not thinking globally while they act locally. "To buy organic products is a very selfish attitude." He characterizes what motivates the average shopper: "I want better products for myself and my children, because they are healthy." Consumers, he says, must understand that even if organic food is not statistically better for those who eat it than conventional food, organic farming is better for the earth.

Better Living through Organic Chemistry

Back in Oregon we just finished eating dinner and I'm cleaning up the kitchen. A few random cans and bottles left over from the last couple of trips to grocery stores need to be shoved into the cupboards. I pick up a bottle of olive oil I bought at Whole Foods up in Portland. The back label is packed with reference points. The ubiquitous Quality Assurance International Q is there, along with— what we call in the radio business—its liner: "Certified Organic" in tiny uppercase letters. It reminds me of "More Music, Less Talk," or "Traffic and Weather Together."

Below it is another seal, and this one reads, "Non GMO Project Verified" and adds the website nongmoproject.org under what looks like their image of a butterfly lighting on a plant sprout. Next to it is a sign I've not noticed before, a V inside a circle with a plus sign after it and the simple word "Vegan." At the top of the back label is an illustration of an olive branch sporting two plump olives—also inside a circle, a circle lined with the copy "North American Olive Oil Association Certified Quality"—and alongside the trademark are these comforting words (whatever they may mean): "Tested for Quality to Meet International Olive Council Standards." I turn the big (33.8 fluid ounces), dark glass bottle around and am greeted by the USDA Organic seal, along with a *U* inside an *O*—alerting me that the Union of Orthodox Congregations supervised its preparation. All these organizations are expecting me to trust their stamp of approval, and why should I?

The North American Olive Oil Association reminds me of an article I once wrote about diploma mills, those post office box universities that sell degrees and promote themselves as accredited (by organizations that are as much of a shell as the "universities" are). Its rules for affixing its seal to olive products add another layer to its mystique: "In order to use the seal, a company must be a member in good standing of the NAOOA and the type of oil bearing the seal must be tested and must meet the International Olive Council standard for olive oil. The IOC, a quasi-United Nations organization, is recognized worldwide as the quality-standard-setting body for the olive oil industry."[54]

That announcement sends me, of course, to the International Olive Council, wondering what exactly constitutes a "quasi-United Nations organization." Aren't you either a United Nations organization or not? The council identifies itself with a fleeting UN reference: "The International Olive Council is the world's only international intergovernmental organisation in the field of olive oil and table olives. It was set up in Madrid, Spain, in 1959, under the auspices of the United Nations. It used to be known as the International Olive Oil Council or IOOC until 2006, when its name was changed. The Council is a decisive player in contributing to the sustainable and responsible development of olive growing and it serves as a world forum for discussing policymaking issues and tackling present and future challenges."[55] IOC members, it claims, account for 98 percent of world olive production. Not a very exclusive club. It's a trade organization. Nothing wrong with trade organizations. But its seal on the Whole Foods brand bottle of "organic extra virgin 100% Italian cold pressed" on my kitchen counter is designed to impress me that the oil is blessed and sanctified as something special (along with 98 percent of the rest of the olive oil in the world).

Douglas Powell is a former professor of food safety at Kansas State University and the lead author of a study that analyzes third-party food safety audits. An inordinate number of the inspectors checking to make sure the food Americans eat isn't going to make us sick are hired by the very food producers they vet. He says those audits are "meaningless."[56] Powell's work probes food safety inspections, but the seals promising "organic" suffer similar credibility questions.

"Who Is Certifying the Certifiers?"

A sparkling late fall day greets me when I arrive in Oakland to meet with Charlie Margulis at the Center for Environmental Health, a not-for-profit organization that, according to its literature, "protects people from toxic chemicals and promotes business products and practices that are safe for public health and the environment." Margulis's title is food program director, appropriate for a University of California at Berkeley–educated (peace and conflict studies) activist who also graduated from the California Culinary Academy and takes pride in his work as a chef. A mutual friend introduced us—a friend I met during an out-of-the-ordinary experience. We were sitting next to each other on a flight about to land in Moscow when the captain came on the intercom to tell us that the plane ahead of us had crashed as its pilot was attempting to touch down. We would be circling Sheremetyevo International Airport while crews cleaned the debris off the runway. Much later we heard from our captain again. We were running out of fuel and the runway was still blocked. Our flight was now destined for Helsinki, where we would spend the night.

As tends to be the case during such anomalies, my seatmate and I started talking. We hung out together during the dinner British Air provided us, and we exchanged contact information. Over the years our shared interests in the former Soviet Union and post-Soviet Eastern Europe brought us together for lunches and conferences. We traded ideas and contacts. When I mentioned years later that I was researching the credibility of food sold as organic, my old friend figured the Center for Environmental Health would be a worthwhile source to check.

"Who is certifying the certifiers?" Margulis asks rhetorically when we sit down to chat. It's a relaxed office environment. I'm wearing a suit but no tie. Margulis shows up in silver running shoes, cargo pants, and a shirt that looks like it never met an iron; he flashes a wide grin. He expresses concern about giant Quality Assurance International and what he calls their lack of transparency, and he isn't happy about the lack of transparency at Oregon Tilth—even as he understands that both are businesses worried about what they perceive as needed confidentiality between them and their clients. Those clients are now the giants in the food industry, giants that bought successful start-ups. "Big players do what business does," he laments. "They cut corners."

I ask Margulis if I'm right to suspect the credibility of organic labels.

"Absolutely," he says without hesitation. "I think 90 percent of what is on the shelf is completely legitimate. But when you see labels from Bolivia and Kazakhstan, it's suspect." Suspect, he says, because those countries don't have years of experience regulating organic food production. "It's really complicated to do organics right. People who do it right have been doing it for a long time."

Margulis adds to the list of concerns consumers should consider when buying food labeled organic. He worries about social justice for organic industry laborers. He wants sustainability issues addressed regarding the resources required to produce organic food. Water use is one example he offers. He opposes megafarms devoted to a single "organic" crop and asks how monoculture can be embraced as organic.

"I think they will tell you"—Margulis smiles as he covers up his eyes and pretends he is a food producer seeking organic status for his products—"'We rely on our certifiers.'" I leave Margulis's office in an anonymous art deco downtown building with a sheaf of new contacts and a deepened sense of skepticism.

It's skepticism fueled by some isolated stories in the popular press. From the *Independent* in London comes the question, Do you know the real origin of your food? "Every time there's an exchange of goods and services along the food supply chain there's an opportunity for fraud," the newspaper quotes University of Michigan professor John Spink, who researches food safety and fraud, as saying. "When food passes from producer to processor, or from manufacturer to distributor, globalization and our growing willingness in the West to pay a premium for certain products has made food fraud a pressing concern," worries Dr. Spink—who dates early corruption at least to Roman Empire hustlers watering down wine. The newspaper cites a 2010 case in the English Midlands: One hundred million conventional eggs were sold to supermarket chains as free range and organic. Authorities managed to note the three-million-pound hustle and catch (and lock up) the crook.[57]

Chapter Ten

More Than Nuts and Beans

Back home, I am in the market buying apples and come home with standard-issue Red Delicious (labeled organic) because the other varieties were from other continents. It makes zero sense for me to buy apples from Chile, especially in the middle of summer when they're ripening on trees across my state. And especially when the foreign-born apples are $3.99 a pound and the local Delicious are $1.99. Yet half the fruit and 20 percent of the vegetables eaten by Americans—organic and conventional—are grown elsewhere.

Those imports are unnecessary. We Americans are spoiled. We don't want to wait for asparagus season in North America, so we fly the tender stalks up from Peru in the dead of our winter. We don't want to pay decent wages to farmworkers or deal with our broken immigration policies, so US-based avocado and tomato growers buy acreage south of the border and outsource our food. The result? We buy groceries in markets filled with rock-hard avocados and those infamous grown-to-withstand-the-rigors-of-shipping tomatoes instead of waiting for succulent in-season local produce.

Although the USDA is responsible for verifying that food labeled organic is, in fact, organic, it is the federal Food and Drug Administration that oversees most of our food for health and safety issues (the USDA is in charge of meat purity). Our record isn't great. Each year well over a hundred thousand of us check into hospitals, sick from contaminated food, and bad food kills about three thousand Americans annually. Despite these numbers, the FDA inspects only 1 to 2 percent of those apples from Chile, those mandarins from Israel, those tomatoes from Mexico—not to mention any Bolivian beans that may be en route to your dinner table.[58] With those numbers, what's amazing is that more of us don't get sick from what we eat.

The FDA wants more inspectors in the field. "We must work toward global solutions to food safety so that whether you serve your family food grown locally or imported you can be confident that it is safe," FDA commissioner Dr. Margaret Hamburg told Americans in the summer of 2013 as her agency grappled with ideas for more thorough inspection in an era of reduced government spending on consumer affairs.[59] One FDA option is for importers to inspect their own products, a scenario that can be likened to organic certification procedures. If the government adopts that policy, it would again be the proverbial fox guarding the henhouse.

"I don't trust the FDA or the USDA. I'm sorry," says schoolteacher Amy McKendrick, who is party to a suit against General Mills that charges the conglomerate with a bogus package design because it promotes its Nature Valley granola bars as "naturally flavored." Nature Valley, she says, fooled her into believing that their slogan "100% Natural," plastered on the snack's label, was a claim that nothing "processed" was in the box. "I have to trust what's on the labels. I can't test it," she laments. "I'm not a chemist. I can't go to the factory, obviously, and see what's going on there. I have to trust the labels. What else can you do?"

It's almost one hundred degrees in the California San Joaquin Valley summer shade as McKendrick explains her complaints with gusto in downtown Bakersfield. Sitting at a sidewalk table, she sips her iced latte, convinced locally owned Dagny's dosed her with nothing unexpected. She shuns Starbucks, concerned that

Big Coffee works with Big Agra and hence may well sell coffee and cakes containing unlabeled GMOs. McKendrick's deep tan, long blonde hair, and cotton lace blouse would make her look at home on the California coast back when the first *Whole Earth Catalog* was published. She made the forty-mile drive down from her mountain home in Tehachapi—an oasis at four thousand feet between the valley and the Mojave Desert—anxious to explain the links she sees between her daughter's behavior and diet.

"When my daughter Kalie was five, she was diagnosed with bipolar disorder, anxiety, and OCD. They put her on some highly antipsychotic drugs."

"And a powder," adds Kalie. The eight-year-old is sitting with her ma, actively listening to the familiar story.

"After a month there were so many serious side effects," says the single mother. She sought alternative treatments, intent on finding options that would wean her daughter from the psychotropic medications. The drugs were replaced with vitamins, augmented with a diet that precluded food preservatives and food additives. After two years of the changed regimen, McKendrick is pleased to report, the negative diagnoses were reversed. And throughout the hour of adult talk about the lawsuit, diet, labeling, and trust, Kalie proves to be a well-behaved child, punctuating her mother's story periodically and showing her off her new stuffed sheep plush toy.

"It's all because we raise our own chickens in our backyard," McKendrick says, summing up her back-to-the-land lifestyle.

"We get lots of eggs," Kalie chimes in.

"And you learn to butcher your own, right?" prompts McKendrick.

"Yeah," acknowledges Kalie, with markedly less enthusiasm.

Small-town Tehachapi (the population is about fifteen thousand) doesn't support a grocery store packed with the organic products McKendrick wants for her dinner table. She belongs to a food co-op and shares a truckload of goods that arrives monthly in the isolated community, supplies she augments with periodic trips down to

Bakersfield. So what the heck was she doing buying granola bars without reading the ingredients?

"It was my ignorance and lack of due diligence—just seeing that it said 'natural' in front, I assumed that it was. I never really looked at the actual ingredients." But the Center for Science in the Public Interest did. They filed the suit against General Mills, with McKendrick and another frustrated California mother as plaintiffs. As a member of the public health advocacy organization, McKendrick responded to a query from the group asking consumers if they felt duped by the Nature Valley liner notes. Indeed, McKendrick points to the granola bars as what slowed Kalie's recovery because they are not "natural," a word she considers synonymous with organic—even if the law imposes no restrictions on the use of the word "natural." Even when it is describing food that may be highly processed and filled with chemical additives and preservatives. Organic, she says, means "no chemicals, no additives, no preservatives." Period.

Back in Eugene I find Nature Valley granola bars in the cereal aisle of my regular market. The front label of the "oats 'n honey"[60] flavor announces that they're "made with 100% NATURAL whole grain OATS," with two words in a larger typeface than the rest of the legend. On a side panel General Mills lists the ingredients: whole grain oats, sugar, canola oil, yellow corn flour, honey, soy flour, brown sugar syrup, salt, soy lecithin, baking soda, and natural flavor.

McKendrick studied agriculture, and now she teaches it. Her experience with the Nature Valley granola bars resulted in further studies. "I have to educate myself on who owns what. Kashi, for instance, when it first came out: excellent product. Got bought out by the big people. It's not the same. It's not the same product." Kashi is now owned by Kellogg. "We all know that it boils down to money. Who is getting paid for what? I know that. I refuse to purchase anything that I know is connected with Monsanto. Won't do it. I know that in today's world, government is not the way to go about changing rules."

She's disgusted by the amount of money the food industry spent to defeat the 2012 California ballot proposition that would have mandated that GMO ingredients be identified as such on labels. "Money drives it. My buying power is what's going to change it. If people stop buying, they won't make any money," she says of companies like Kellogg and General Mills. "I would have never guessed that the things I was feeding my child were actually sending her down a path of life that would have been horrible."

The lawsuit charges General Mills with false advertising, a violation of California law. "By marketing its products as 'Natural,' General Mills takes wrongful advantage of consumers' strong preference for foods made entirely of natural ingredients," reads the suit. "General Mills profits in this lucrative market for natural foods by dressing up its Nature Valley products as 'Natural' and selling them to consumers who seek to purchase products made from ingredients that are found in nature and who are willing to pay more for such foods."[61]

McKendrick's is just one of scores of lawsuits filed against food companies that slap "natural" and "all natural" on their labels, lawsuits that are starting to scare the processed food industry. In 2013 PepsiCo paid out nine million dollars to settle complaints against its Naked Juice brand. The bottles promised "all-natural fruits and vegetables" as the ingredients, but juice drinkers complained they were being dosed with artificial vitamins along with GMO fruits and vegetables. As a result, "all natural" is no longer claimed by Naked, and other food conglomerates are deleting the meaningless sales pitch from their labels.[62]

As for plaintiff Amy McKendrick, she says she seeks none of the General Mills profits. "I'm not looking for any kind of compensation. I told them I do not want any money. If there is any settlement, I want it all to go toward an organization that is working for GMO labeling." McKendrick was born and raised in Germany. She applauds the European countries that ban GMO crops and enforce strict food-labeling laws. "Why are we so far behind?" she asks of the United States. "That almost makes me not want to be an American anymore, and go somewhere where they're actually doing something about the things that are destroying our planet and our people." She doesn't even trust her favorite Bakersfield natural food store. "I've gone there and tried to ask questions," she says, "and there are people that work there that have no idea what I'm talking about. So, no. I've learned the hard way. I need to be my own advocate." She points to healthy-looking and charming Kalie. "I need to be her advocate. I'm not going to rely on the store as a source."

Although California's proposed GMO labeling law was defeated in 2012, a radical marketing change not mandated by government regulation occurred in early 2013 when Whole Foods announced it would label all the GMO foods it sells by 2018. Foul, cried the anti–GMO labeling Grocery Manufacturing Association. The trade organization's executive director, Louis Finkel, offered a convoluted argument that claimed it's dangerous for us to know if our food contains GMOs. "These labels could mislead consumers into believing that these food products are somehow different or present a special risk or a potential risk," he said in an official statement from the GMA.[63] Finkel is experienced dealing with delicate PR matters. Before lobbying for grocers and groceries, he worked in the government relations office at Exxon Mobil.[64] The alphabet soup can be confusing. The GMOs—the genetically modified foods—should not be labeled according to the GMA—the Grocery Manufacturing Association. It's a confusion that Jeremy Seifert uses to great advantage in *GMO OMG*, his anti-GMO film polemic. The movie chronicles his family's horror as they travel across America learning about Monsanto's Roundup-resistant soybeans and pesticide-producing corn—a terrifying journey he manages to temper with humor. "The corn we see growing around here is actually registered as a pesticide," he reports before he and his two young sons don hazmat suits to protect themselves as they run off and play amid the towering cornstalks.

I'm thinking of Amy and little Kalie as I study a box of organic microwave popcorn. Maybe the corn is organic as claimed, and perhaps the other ingredient is organic, too: palm oil (a fat that constitutes social and health controversies outside the purview of this study). But what's not mentioned on the label is the perfluorooctanoic acid (known in the food industry as PFOA) that undoubtedly lines the magic little bag that spins in the microwave as it fills with the popped corn. Getting dosed by perfluorooctanoic acid from popcorn bags certainly violates one of Michael Pollan's basic food rules. Rule number three, insists the food writer and University of California professor, is that one "avoid food products containing ingredients that no ordinary human would keep in the pantry."[65] The chemical is used to keep popcorn from sticking to the microwave bag and manifests in another wonder: Teflon. It's also caused liver, testicular, and pancreatic cancer in laboratory tests with nonhuman animals,[66] and research conducted at the West Virginia University School of Public Health suggests the more PFOA in your blood, the greater your risk for heart disease.[67]

There's nothing much easier to cook than popcorn using the old-fashioned stovetop method, and a hot air electric popper is one of the least expensive kitchen appliances you can buy. If you're hooked on using the microwave, another food writer, *New York Times* reporter Mark Bittman, suggests just using a plain old brown paper bag. But a parent who apparently does not share Amy McKendrick's worries for the next generation is Dan Turner, a PR manager for the PFOA manufacturer DuPont. When the PFOA-popcorn scare first surfaced, he announced loyally in 2008, "I serve microwave popcorn to my three-year-old."[68]

I drop Turner a note. "I am curious to know if that is still the case," I write of his offspring's popcorn diet, "or if, because of continuing concerns expressed by some about PFOA, your child (who must be about eight now), no longer eats microwave popcorn." A couple of days later Turner responds. "Hi Peter," is his cheerful greeting. "Thanks so much for your email, but I am not going to comment on such a personal inquiry." Fascinating how a "no comment" can speak volumes.

We exchange a few more notes. I ask Turner if he would advise me to avoid or enjoy microwaved popcorn. "I think you can make your own decision," he responds, and to help me he refers me to an Environmental Protection Agency report that concludes, "The information that EPA has available does not indicate that the routine use of consumer products [containing PFOA] poses a concern. At present, there are no steps that EPA recommends that consumers take to reduce exposures to PFOA."[69] Of course I can make up my own mind, I write back to Turner, but because of your unique professional position and your reference to your three-year-old's popcorn-eating habits, I seek your advice. Thus ends our pen pal relationship; I seem to bring out the bad cop side of the food industry's PR corps.

The microwave popcorn bag tussle makes me consider what else leaches into food labeled organic. What about those ubiquitous stickers plastered on fruits and vegetables? What's in the glue that sticks them to the delicate skin of an heirloom tomato? No worries, says Scott Howarth, the director of research and development at Sinclair Systems, a global provider of labels headquartered a couple of freeway hours north of Bakersfield, in Fresno. "Our labels are scrutinized pretty heavily," he says, "and adhere to FDA regulations." The chemicals in the labels come from the GRAS list. GRAS is FDA shorthand for "generally regarded as safe." Sinclair labels get stuck on billions and billions of pieces of produce every year, including that which is certified organic.

"Our adhesive is never intended to be part of the fruit," says Howarth. "They're fine to use on organic products." Maybe so, but I've pulled plenty of labels off of fruit only to see glue residue or pieces of the label still blemishing the apple or whatever. Perhaps those sticky labels aren't one of Sinclair's, but since the label makers are not identified on the sticker, tracing the glue residue probably would make my search for nuts and beans look like a cakewalk.

Back to the 1960s

One of my favorite food stores is an example of the explosive growth of the organic marketplace. Good Earth is where I stopped when I was in high school in the late 1960s and needed trail mix before a hike. That was when the Marin County, California, retailer occupied its hole-in-the-wall storefront in Fairfax, at the base of Mount Tamalpais. Flower boxes on the sidewalk in front of its Bolinas Avenue shop windows doubled as benches where customers ate from cartons filled at the take-out counter. The salad bar featured exquisite marinated and fried squares of tofu. The limited produce section offered basic local fruits and vegetables touted as organic long before the USDA considered controlling organic labels, along with what were then exotic choices (by supermarket standards) like bok choy and Jerusalem artichokes. On the dry goods shelves were spaghetti made from corn for those experimenting with wheat-free diets, organic peanut butter, and whole-grain breads with no preservatives. The bulk bins offered organic flour and grains and nuts. A corner near the checkout stands was stacked with cookbooks and magazines such as the *Utne Reader, Shambala,* and the *Sun* ("Personal. Political. Provocative. Ad-free."). It was a completely alternative shopping experience for the times, offering now-commonplace products decades before mainstream America embraced them. The place was—pick your stereotype: Bohemian? A health food store? A hippie hangout? What it definitely wasn't was a Safeway.

Around the year 2000 Good Earth worked out a deal with the old-fashioned Food Villa, a couple of blocks down Bolinas on Sir Francis Drake Boulevard. The Food Villa *was* your father's neighborhood grocery store. Or your grandfather's. When we lived up the street, we shopped there, and if we forgot our cash at home in those pre–ATM card days, we signed a tab (it was just a piece of paper on a pad with the amount owed noted) and paid later. The offerings were basic Americana, from French's mustard to the all-beef hot dogs to spread it on. The clerks carried your bags of groceries to your car, placed them gently in the back of your station wagon, and petted your dog (whose name they knew). Without asking. I learned an important lesson in customer service from Larry, the congenial owner. "Make eye contact with the customer you're serving," he told me once when he was explaining his business philosophy. "Let them know that they're the only thing that matters to you while the two of you are talking." But the ancient (early 1950s?) linoleum floor tiles were chipped and cracked. The whole place needed a paint job. And fancier stores a couple of miles distant were enticing the Food Villa's clientele with a wider variety of intriguing mustards and frankfurters—some of those dogs meatless and organic.

One of the Food Villa box boys was Al Baylacq. He was paying attention to the lines at the Good Earth cash registers and the bags full of organic groceries carried out of the competing store. When Larry was ready to retire, Baylacq helped midwife a deal that brought Good Earth to the larger Food Villa quarters. A dozen years later, as one of the Good Earth owners, Baylacq was instrumental in moving Good Earth once again, this time to a vast and vacant supersize property at the Fairfax city limits, an eyesore of a building long abandoned by the Lucky supermarket chain. The old Lucky was gutted and revitalized into a luxury food emporium that offers a massive selection of organic food at often-ludicrous prices. "We always endeavor to remember that food contains spirit" is how Baylacq summarizes his store's philosophy.

The two of us meet on the porch of the latest Good Earth incarnation for an organic talk. The store he presides over is teeming with customers; the cash registers are eating dollars as ravenously as I used to eat those delicious marinated hunks of tofu at the old storefront on Bolinas Avenue. Streaks of gray are sneaking into his hair and neatly trimmed beard, but he exhibits no overt signs of business stress as we talk groceries.

I'm intrigued by the metamorphosis of both him and his store, especially since its full name is Good Earth Natural Foods. "Natural": that ambiguous word that really can mean most anything.

"The easy and most common thing you hear and I say all the time is that organic is mostly free of chemicals and insecticides. I'm most comfortable being a part of that, both personally eating foods free of chemicals and from a business standpoint," Baylacq says. "As you know I kind of fell into this; it wasn't what I thought I was going to do with my life, but if I've got to make money doing something, I'd like to feel good about it."

And he clearly does. Baylacq preaches organic food to me on this sunny afternoon like an evangelist at a revival meeting.

"Both my boys, twenty-one and nineteen, see a difference in quality and they feel a difference when they are eating the crap versus when they are eating healthily. My oldest now hits the salad bar at least the days he works here, so I see Dakota eating a big old salad and appreciating its value. High-quality food that makes him feel good. I really feel the quality matters physiologically to me." He pauses for a few seconds and considers his sermon. "I'm sure there is a level of placebo effect to it. But I value it so much, I want to share it with others."

His organic lifestyle is not limited to food. He points to his T-shirt (festooned with the legend "Hang Loose Maui") and indicates that his definition of an organic lifestyle extends to clothing and whatever else is possible. "I support the more idealistic model. Whether we can scale it up to the rest of the world in time to save the planet, I'm not sure." He watches affluent Marin County customers leaving his store with their organic bundles, heading for their hybrid SUVs, and he's pleased to see them joining him in what he calls "Living better. Eating better. Eating fresher. Eating with taste in mind. I don't know if you get that shopping at the Costcos and Safeways of the world."

"Easy for you to say," I banter. "You're making piles of money because everything costs a whole heck of a lot more in your store than at those Costcos and Safeways."

No argument from grocer Baylacq. "Yeah, I do think it's 15 to 20 percent more. Why do you pay more?" he muses, and then answers his own question. "We pay a little more attention to the subject of your book." He's anxious to talk about how sure his crew is about the provenance of the food Good Earth sells that's marked organic. "We look for bullshit because bullshit comes out of greed. Somebody out there is trying to make a buck, and they put something out there with a level of bullshit that needs to be packaged with it in order to make it successful. At the same time some cloak what the bullshit is about, and some do it really well. Some don't even try and you can see it right off."

The Good Earth staff visits some local producers and inspects their operations, but when it comes to national brands and imports from places like Bolivia and Kazakhstan, the store trusts the USDA Organic seal and stocks the shelves. "If there's a news story about something to worry about, then we may be prompted to dig a little further." But Baylacq is sanguine that those QAI-certified, General Mills–made Muir Glen brand organic tomatoes for sale in his store are organic. "I firmly believe in the USDA National Organic Program. We have to have some trust in what we have built," he says about the organic industry. "There is enough scrutiny in the annual audits to make sure enough is tracked by the ingredient suppliers. We have to trust that to some degree." Maybe. But as my investigation continues, I'm less and less confident that the USDA Organic sticker deserves our trust. Our farm-to-fork food chain is too complex for much comfort.

Baylacq and I leave the porch and head into the store. I want to take a random sample of a few items and hear from him why he's convinced they're organic. We stop in front of a bin overflowing with lovely-looking just-ripe avocados. The price card announces that they come from Rancho Vasquez in Azuza, California. The card indicates the mileage from Azuza to Fairfax (395 air miles) and the price (a sobering $2.89 a pound). The sign indicates that the avocados are certified organic in accordance with the Organic Food Act of 1990.

"What do you know about Rancho Vasquez?" I ask.

"I don't personally know anything about Rancho Vasquez," he says. "My produce buyer may. Distance is key. I've visited every farm in western Marin County." He's checked out farms in nearby Petaluma and the Capay Valley, where the store's cherry tomatoes are grown. "I walked that farm and talked with the pickers picking. It was 103 degrees and these guys are dripping and sweating in the middle of the day. But I got a nice, firsthand look at that farm. We will keenly look for the signs of not playing by the rules, like guys with masks on out in the field." But his visits are not de facto certification trips. They are meet-and-greet opportunities to develop the relationship between the store and the producer. "I want to talk to the grower about what the customer would be interested in knowing."

We head over to the meat counter. There's a tray marked Marin Sun Farms "100% grass fed" and "local," but it doesn't say organic.

"That's because it's not organic," says Baylacq. He knows the owner and operator of Marin Sun Farms, a cattle operation on lands west of Fairfax out toward the Pacific Ocean, and he's watched the animals graze. His butchers have been assigned to rewrite the card and change "100% grass fed" to "100% pasture fed" because "we know they're not just eating grass. They're eating all kinds of little things. Weeds and thistles. We're technically wrong. This came up yesterday in a meeting. That's how seriously we take the labels."

Next stop is the canned and bottled tomatoes and pasta sauces. We look at the Washington State Department of Agriculture–certified Muir Glen products lining the shelves.

"General Mills makes Trix," I mention to Baylacq. "Does it bother you to sell General Mills–made Muir Glen tomatoes and indirectly support a product you would never stock, like Trix?"

"There's something to be said for supporting companies like General Mills and Smuckers." Smuckers owns the Santa Cruz Organic juices line and R.W. Knudsen Family juices. "A half a dozen big companies have bought into our industry because that's where the growth is. You look at conventional brands, they're flat in sales. Organic has been double digit every year I've been in it." If the goal is to increase production and consumption of organics, says Baylacq, it makes sense to welcome all players. "The number one seller of organic food in this county is Costco. There's a place for them because they're doing it. The direct result, I am positive, is more organic acreage."

Check out Costco for yourself. From boneless rib eye to Turkish towels, from baby formula to Hiball brand energy drinks, from Yummi Bears multivitamins to Muy Macho(!) blend coffee, Costco is an emporium of big box bargain organics. But Costco mixes the organic stuff with whatever else America buys. Good Earth's mission is to sell 100 percent organic food. The store claims its produce already meets this standard, and all the rest of the food stock for sale is over 95 percent organic. But its customers want the stuff to be tasty, not just healthy. "Quality," Baylacq says, "or how it eats, does count." I love encountering the jargon of a subculture: "How it eats." What a great phrase for defining taste from the point of view of the food instead of our mouths. "Shelf talker" is another phrase I picked up from Good Earth. A shelf talker is the sign below a product that promotes and/or explains it. An example might read like the advertising copy for Sea Snax brand seaweed snacks: "Nutrient packed roasted seaweed snack made using 100% olive oil and just a pinch of salt. Vegan, gluten free & strangely addictive."

Back in the Willamette Valley I visit the Europeanesque chateau of the vintner King Estate for a leisurely lunch overlooking the rolling hills south of Eugene. When developing an advertising campaign for its organic wine, marketing manager Sasha Kadey says she and owner Ed King "lamented the fact that organic agriculture is treated as a hippy-fueled pseudoscience while chemical farming is referred to as 'conventional.'" From that irritated point of view came their advertisement that reminds us, "From 10,000 B.C. to 1945 A.D. all agriculture was organic. We owe the future."

Fishy Fish

I am sitting at the desk in my room on the fifth floor of the Hotel Fifty—my regular stopover when I teach at the University of Oregon campus in Portland. I love this hotel just a few blocks from the university's refurbished quarters in the White Stag Block, the now-gleaming example of nineteenth-century industrial architecture—a marriage of gothic and Italianate, and famous for the huge neon PORTLAND OREGON sign on its roof, decorated with a prancing stag. The Fifty is vintage "Portlandia"—a remodeled mid-twentieth-century motel with a bar featuring fine Oregon Pinot Noir and Pinot Gris. Gas-fueled flames dance on rock-floored fireplaces, and the late-night menu offers eats far from what the coffee shop was serving when this place opened back in the days when seat belts were a novelty and cigarettes were ubiquitous with watered-down morning coffee. The contemporary fare, though, is far from my usual midnight snack. French fries, for example, are served with truffle oil, parmesan, and a "hint of spice." The tacos are filled with "pork belly, arugula, and pickled carrots." There's saffron in the hummus and "crispy chicken skin" with the deviled eggs.

Last night I chose the soy-cured salmon with wasabi tobiko caviar and pickled ginger. Delicious. And this morning, as I write, looking out over the typical cloud-laden Oregon winter skies and the fast-flowing Willamette, I feel confident that the salmon I ate with relish really was salmon—despite the distressing headline in this morning's *Oregonian,* "Labels Often Tell a Fish Story: Much of the Seafood Sold in Restaurants and Stores in the U.S. is Mislabeled, Study Finds."

More than 20 percent of seafood bought in Portland markets and restaurants was mislabeled, according to the story. The not-for-profit group Oceana is credited with the statistics, based on a two-year study conducted by the conservation organization. "Everywhere we looked for seafood fraud, we found it," Beth Lowell, an Oceana campaign director, told the newspaper. "Consumers are being ripped off."[70] Exposing fish-labeling fraud is a major goal for Oceana out of concern for both the sustainability of fisheries and human health. "Swapping one fish species for another that may be riddled with contaminants, toxins or allergens can make people sick," Oceana's report warns as it lobbies for strict legislation requiring that the traceability of commercial fish be available for consumers.[71]

The story only exacerbates my suspicions about organic food labels. If 20 percent of Portland fish is mislabeled, why should I believe my beans and nuts are correctly labeled? And Portland is one of the most food-conscious cities in America. "Trust, but verify," cautioned President Reagan, quoting a Russian proverb to the Soviet leader Mikhail Gorbachev as the two signed a treaty.[72] Just trust us, say Trader Joe's and Natural Directions. And we'll do everything we can to keep you from verifying.

Chapter Eleven

ON THE GREAT SILK ROAD . . .
TO WALNUTS

Not long after Chernobyl blew in the mid-1980s, I arrived in Belarus to work with journalism colleagues at the Minsk Mass Media Center on a project designed to develop free and independent news reporting in the nation still considered to be Europe's last dictatorship. The de facto dictator since 1994 has been Alexandr Lukashenko, who wins elections with ludicrous margins after locking away his opponents. Years after my brief experiences in Belarus, censors continue to shackle the news media; Internet use is tapped along with telephones. As long as Lukashenko uses Soviet-era techniques (he still calls his secret police the KGB) to stay in power, a free Belarus press remains a fantasy.

The journalists I worked with in the early 1990s in Minsk told me back then that it was dangerous for them to speak about politics, and that they expected life in Belarus to deteriorate. It did. The country remains a relic of its Soviet past. Participating in an unauthorized demonstration against government policies is a crime; police break up those few that occur, arresting participants and hauling them off to what can be long prison terms. Belarusians respond to the police state creatively. One technique they used is like a flash mob: They gathered not to hear forbidden speeches or to carry illegal placards, but just stood in public squares and simply clapped their hands. The message was clear: a call for democracy. The illegitimacy of the Lukashenko regime was reinforced when it responded by threatening to arrest Belarusians who were clapping in public without authorization.

Something I saw on that trip still haunts me. It was one of those illuminated signs common in front of banks, flashing the time and the temperature. But the one in downtown Minsk, so close to Chernobyl, offered a third factoid. It showed the time and the temperature and recorded the *current level of background radiation*.

I'm all for detailed weather reports, even if the news is dreadful. But what exactly do we do with such killer information when it informs us of danger to ourselves? (The Monty Python rule for war comes to mind: "Run away, run away, run away!") Of course most of us cannot escape our immediate environments and we're forced to cope with what sometimes are horrifying realities. A television news cameraman I spent time with in Minsk was one of the first on the scene of the Chernobyl disaster. He told me he worked days at the poisoned site wearing just street clothes because he felt obligated to document the story and no protective gear was available to him. Soon after the extent of the radioactive fallout plume was known, his family and others were issued devices to measure the poisons in their food.

"I never used it," he told me. "It just sat in our flat."

I was shocked. "Why not?"

"For the first few days we tested everything," he said, "and all the food registered as unsafe. But there was nothing else to buy. We either ate the contaminated food or we ate nothing."

A generation after the collapse of the Soviet Union, what I witnessed in Belarus typifies ongoing crises in former Soviet republics. Questionable elections empower easily corrupted leaders who hold on to power by limiting free expression with brute force. Just ask Lukpan Akmedyarov, a reporter who was shot twice and stabbed eight times in the spring of 2012 after he published stories in the newspaper *Uralskaya Nedelya* that criticized the Kazakhstan government. His wife and his editor were warned that Akmedyarov should stop his reporting about government and business corruption. Other reporters doing similar work had been arrested in the months leading up to the attack on the newspaperman. "I think they wanted to kill me," Akmedyarov said after the attack. "They would have said something if they wanted to warn me."[73]

Committee to Protect Journalists deputy director Robert Mahoney said the attack "shows just how dangerous it is to be an independent investigative journalist in Kazakhstan."[74] Four men were charged and convicted in 2013 of attempted murder for the Akmedyarov attack; not long after, another Kazakh journalist critical of government officials, Igor Larra, was seriously injured—he suffered a concussion and sustained severe cuts and abrasions after being hit in the head with a crowbar and kicked in the face.[75]

A couple of months prior to the attack on Akmedyarov, the former foreign minister and customs chief for the country—an official directly engaged in the business of exporting Kazakh goods to the rest of the world—was arrested on corruption charges. Serik Baimaganbetov was charged with taking bribes. Riches from the region's oil boom combined with weak business laws "breed corruption" in Kazakhstan according to the Global Advice Network, a nongovernmental organization that works with business, the United Nations, and the World Bank on issues of worldwide corruption. About the same time, the mayor of Zhanaozen was arrested on suspicion of embezzling money from the government. And in addition to Mayor Orak Sarbopeyev being hauled into the station house, former Zhanaozen mayor Zhalgas Babahanov was picked up and charged with embezzling money from the government.[76] Were the two mayors the corrupt ones, or were the ones who arrested them the criminals? It was in Zhanaozen that police shot and killed striking oil workers in 2011 when a police sweep through a city square filled with peaceful strikers turned into a riot that killed and injured unarmed civilians. Strikers charged with aiding and abetting mass unrest told horrific stories of their pretrial detention. "I was repeatedly suffocated with a plastic bag," oil worker Roza Tuletayeva testified at his trial. "They hung me by my hair . . . There were other things done to me, but I am too ashamed to talk about it here."[77]

"Corruption on a grand scale" is how the Global Advice Network sums up Kazakh government and business affairs. The watchdog group blames that status of affairs on a nasty stew of vast oil and mineral wealth combined with the behind-the-scenes wheeler-dealer scams perpetrated when state-owned businesses were privatized in the immediate post-Soviet era. "Corruption in Kazakhstan is systemic, even within the country's anti-corruption agency, and no public office is free from executive interference" is the sorry assessment of Global Advice Network investigators. Sure, Kazakhstan's laws cry out for criminal penalties whenever corrupt practices are perpetrated, but when the bad guys are in charge of catching the bad guys, the result is impunity.[78]

Huge and rich Kazakhstan, the size of Western Europe and flooded with oil and gas, has been ruled by its autocratic president Nursultan Nazarbayev since the collapse of the Soviet Union in 1991. It's difficult to imagine such world-class corruption could exist there without him knowing about it and at least tacitly approving of it— even as he rails against it. "The uncompromising war on corruption is an important aspect of enforcing law and order," Nazarbayev said in a speech to his parliament when its September 2011 session opened. "We should improve our anti-corruption legislation removing loopholes for the evil."[79]

It was an understandable assessment since in 2012 Transparency International, an NGO that tracks corruption and works to reverse it, ranked Kazakhstan near the bottom of its list—133 out of 176 countries checked—in terms of government corruption. In its 2010 study of how well Kazakhstan controlled corruption, Transparency International marked it at 15 percent. Compare those numbers with Austria, for example, since I've been studying the organic sector there. Austria ranks number 25 out of 176 on the Corrupt-O-Meter and enjoys a striking 92 percent regarding corruption control.[80]

Hence trade along the Great Silk Road in Kazakhstan must be viewed with more than a tad of skepticism—despite what may be Trader Joe's best intentions—and in the Wild West–like environment of contemporary Central Asia, there's much to doubt about the growing conditions for any walnuts stuffed into bags labeled "organic," destined to travel over six thousand miles to my grocer's shelves from the orchard where they were grown.

Nevertheless, my initial research seemed promising. Kazakhstan is home to forests of wild walnuts. I found evidence of a EuropeAid project dating back to 2007 with lofty goals set by the European Union. "The project," promised EuropeAid, "will strengthen the organic sector in southern Kazakhstan, encompassing the development of organic products, organic certification, training in organics etc. It will not only consider the production side but also the marketing and, whenever possible, the export."[81] To get the work started, a half a million euros and two years were budgeted. The kickoff contract was secured by the Louis Bolk Institute in the Netherlands, an outfit named after a University of Amsterdam human anatomy professor who mused, "How much broader would be our view of life, if we could study it through reducing glasses?" The institute specializes in food and health improvements for the developing world. "Our clients choose us," the institute is proud to proclaim, "because of our expertise in sustainable agriculture, nutrition, and health." Growing organic food in developing countries is its specialty.

I tracked down Peter Brul, who was a coordinator of the Kazakh project for the Louis Bolk Institute. His message back to me—which I quoted to the USDA when I filed my complaint—was not encouraging.

"I worked in different parts of Kazakhstan," he told me, "in the mountains near the Chinese and Kyrgyz borders, and near Astana." Astana is the relatively new capital city. Brul reported to me that he didn't know of any organic walnut projects in the country. Further, he said his studies found the struggling organic sector in Kazakhstan tainted. "In Kazakhstan there is a small group of large-scale arable farms, certified by an Italian certifier and exporting via an Italian company. Unfortunately, it is not transparent at all. We did not get any contacts: no names, no addresses. This is not how organic should function," he lamented, "but sometimes it is due to competition between importers and competition between certifiers."

The Kazakhstan embassy in Washington is no more encouraging. It touts Kazakh agriculture and shows off its high-protein wheat along with cotton, leather, and wool all as valuable exports. The government lists other crops with pride: barley, maize, rice, potatoes, soybeans, sugar beets, cotton, tobacco, sunflowers, flax, and mustard. It suggests corn and bean yields are developing in importance. But other than the vague mention in its literature that "orchards and vineyards are widespread," there is no hint from the government of walnuts for export, organic or otherwise.[82]

Studying back issues of the *Astana Times* only adds to the sense of the exotic I feel for the country, despite the seeming lack of organic walnuts. For whatever reason I've always been a trolley car aficionado, and I learn that Almaty is home to a restored streetcar that serves as a rolling restaurant. "Passengers sip coffee and drink champagne, savor quality desserts and even listen to soft music," reports the newspaper, "as they ride around town enjoying the sites outside and the soft, ambient lighting within."[83] But the English-language newspaper offers no news about local walnut orchards, organic or otherwise.

I find a bed-and-breakfast—Zhenja and Lyuda's Boarding House— in Zhabagly, a village in the Tulkubas region of South Kazakhstan (about a hundred miles from Tashkent), and I write to Zhenja and Lyuda, even though they seem to specialize in tours for bird-watchers. Theirs is one of the few Kazakh businesses that mentions walnuts ("Relax under the walnut trees in the garden," their advertising suggests). I write:

> Hello, Zhenja and Lyuda,
> I am interested in the walnut industry in Kazakhstan, and am considering a trip to Kazakhstan. I saw from one of the reviews of your boarding house that there are walnut trees in your garden. Are you located in a walnut growing region? I am specifically interested in organically grown walnuts harvested for export. Any information you can provide very much is appreciated and I look forward to the possibility of staying at your boarding house.

I never hear back from Zhenja and Lyuda.

I check in with WWOOF—the Worldwide Opportunities on Organic Farms group. "In return for volunteer help," the organization arranges with farmers to offer travelers "food, accommodation and opportunities to learn about organic lifestyles." WWOOF's mission is to connect "people who want to volunteer on organic farms with people who are looking for volunteer help."[84] The only WWOOFers I can find who managed to connect with farmers remotely entertaining organic standards in Kazakhstan are Pierre and Danielle from Normandy. The two posted a note on the WWOOF website back in August 2009 relating their frustration in Almaty trying to find an organic Kazakh farm where they could live as volunteers. "There is almost no organic farm in Kazakhstan," wrote Pierre. "Almost nobody cares about organic products in Kazakhstan."[85]

From the other side of the globe, I am coming to the same conclusion.

My cynicism is fueled by a line from a film a colleague shot about tea growing in China. He witnessed the use in production facilities of "organic" labels on tea, tea adjacent to bags of chemical fertilizers. When he asked the owner of the facility about the discrepancy, he received the flip and honest response, "Oh, Americans like the word 'organic.'" Chinese authorities announced that they uncovered a fake meat scheme at the same time horsemeat was sold as beef across Europe. According to police, the conspirators mixed rat, fox, and mink meat and added gelatin, coloring, and a variety of chemicals—and then sold the concoction as mutton. "China has many laws," said Beijing's Renmin University agriculture professor Zhen Fengtian about food safety. "If nobody is checking, then there are no consequences for people who break the law."[86]

It's easy to criticize China, especially after considering the rat-as-mutton story. China's vast economy exports a lot of junk. We can see that with a quick trip down a few Wal-Mart aisles. But Professor Fengtian's analysis is germane from Shanghai to San Francisco and back. And there is a First World corollary to his statement: When checking is superficial, it's an invitation to break the law.

Unnatural Directions

My branch of Market of Choice is just down the street from my house in Eugene and from my office at the University of Oregon. Since its buyers mix organic products with all-American standards, the shelves are lined with fancy and pricey Oregon-made organic specialties alongside bottles of that familiar French's bright-yellow mustard and bags full of Oreos.

Not long before the Ducks beat the Wisconsin Badgers in the 2012 Rose Bowl, I noticed a new label on some of the staples that I often grab on my short commute home from the campus. I was impressed by the bargain prices for Natural Directions organic ketchup and Natural Directions organic oatmeal, Natural Directions organic salsa and Natural Directions organic black beans. It seemed like every time I went to the market something else I needed to buy was suddenly available for a better price if I chose the Natural Directions brand.

Natural Directions is a private label established by Unified Grocers, a wholesale grocery cooperative owned by retail grocers operating in the western states. Founded in Portland in 1915, it provides its member stores with brands long familiar to us on the Left Coast and in Hawaii, brands like Western Family.

Some Western Family products sport the claim "100% natural" on the label, and Unified promises its customers that means they're made with "only natural ingredients" and "without the use of synthetic substances and flavors." Of course that still leaves consumers in a vague haze regarding the meaning of "natural" and "synthetic."

"Natural and organic products are no longer the exclusive domain of specialty retailers," Unified Grocers tells its members in promotional literature drawing attention to its Natural Directions product line. The company cites meteoric growth in "organic, natural and earth-friendly products" and insists, "We carefully screen our producers and suppliers and each is required to meet or exceed rigorous quality control standards." Unified contracts with Quality Assurance International to certify that its products meet USDA organic standards. Keep "profitable customers in your store," advises Unified, by stocking Natural Directions.

Natural Directions brand indeed helps (or helped?) keep me in Market of Choice, but despite the promises of Unified, when I saw "Product of Bolivia" stamped on the can of their black beans, it was difficult for me to imagine those "rigorous quality control standards" in what the US government calls "one of the poorest and least developed countries in Latin America."[87] My doubt is reinforced by my own experiences tracing cocaine from the coca farms of the Chaparé jungle to the crack-plagued streets of West Oakland. The Drug Enforcement Administration agents I was traveling with, for example, were chased out of the small

Amazonian city of Santa Ana by a crowd yelling, "Death to the Yankees!"—the agents' "secret" mission foiled by townspeople corrupted with cocaine cash.

If the illegal drug business is protected by the traffickers' neighbors, just what is the chance that the Natural Directions Bolivian black beans I pull off the Market of Choice shelf are organic? Can I trust the farmer? Can I trust the inspector who works for a Quality Assurance International partner certifier in Bolivia to assure that the growing and canning process meets QAI's organic standards? What due diligence is QAI engaged in to check on the Bolivian certifier? What due diligence is Natural Directions engaged in to check on QAI? A myriad of unanswered questions fill our supermarkets and our stomachs.

I figure those questions will be easy to answer with a quick trip down to Unified's Los Angeles basin headquarters and a meeting with the cooperative's chief marketing and procurement officer and/or the executive in charge of securing the food sold under the Natural Directions label. I will ask if the black beans from various countries are considered by Unified to be an identical product. I will wonder aloud how Unified can feel sanguine about leaving assurance regarding the provenance of the beans sold behind its label to QAI. I will seek a site visit to the Natural Directions bean-processing plant(s). And I plan to invite my Unified colleague to join me on a road trip to the bean sources in Bolivia.

Ha! Fat chance.

It's a summer Saturday morning in Oregon and I'm sitting in my kitchen, drinking allegedly organic green tea and contemplating the can of Natural Directions beans in front me, the one stamped "Product of Bolivia" on the lid. I'm reading the fine print on the label, and I see a line of type I've missed on previous readings: "See end of can for country of origin." That message must be a government regulation. Why else would Natural Directions direct me to the note on the lid with the curious message that informs me I've bought beans here in the fertile Willamette Valley that were shipped over five thousand miles to my local grocer?

"From Mt. Rainer to the Apennines, Natural Directions searches the world over to find the finest organic crops and products," reads generic copy on the side of the can. "Our products meet the high standards of the USDA, and are certified by Quality Assurance International. Your satisfaction is guaranteed." What would have prompted the copywriter—with the world to choose from—to pick the Apennines as an example locale for Natural Directions products? Perhaps it was the lure of Italian cuisine or the romance of the Slow Food movement, which was founded in Italy. But Natural Directions, the Unified Grocers division based in Tigard, Oregon, might consider a change to "From Mt. Rainer to Mt. Ashland, Natural Directions searches Oregon to find the finest organic crops and products," especially on its cans of beans. If Natural Directions looked in its backyard, it would find organic beans growing close to its home, but perhaps not at the bargain prices the company negotiates in Bolivia.

"Your satisfaction is guaranteed," it says on the label. Well, I ain't satisfied. Researcher Charles Deitz has been working to arrange a meeting at Unified's headquarters. Yesterday the outfit's spokesman, Bob Hutchins, asked for some details about the upcoming meeting. Deitz responded with a gracious e-mail message listing some of the questions I intend to pose: How do you guarantee the safety of your organic products? How do you know your certifying agencies are trustworthy? What do you believe the consumer thinks "organic" means? Do you use independent organic certifiers in addition to the government-approved certifying agencies? Unified's Hutchins called Deitz back with a terse response. "We have regretfully chosen to decline the interview request," he said. Regretfully? Wouldn't "deliberately" be a better choice, or even "prudently," if the corporate goal is—in the best case—to keep company policies secret, or—in the worst case—to hide questionable (or worse) business practices? Deitz, of course, asked why the closed corporate mouth. Hutchins hemmed and hawed for a moment and then referred to Unified's playbook. "Participating in this project," he said before hanging up the phone, "doesn't meet our needs right now." I think about that arrogant line whenever I'm tempted to save a few pennies buying Natural Directions.

That's two huge distributors of "organic" products refusing to discuss the pedigree of the products they want me to buy and eat: Trader Joe's and Natural Directions. Where does Unified Grocers get its "organic" beans for its Natural Directions brand? Their only answer: "From Mt. Rainer to the Apennines."

We Don't Know Beans about Our Beans

Harry MacCormack's Sunbow Farm in Corvallis is an easy hour's drive up old Highway 99 from my home in Eugene. MacCormack is a hard-core organic farmer who's been tilling the fertile Willamette Valley soil for over forty years, experimenting with crops and promoting organic fruits and vegetables. He is one of the founders of both Oregon Tilth and the Willamette Valley Bean and Grain Project, a long-term effort to bring food production back close to home. A graduate of Oregon's Lewis and Clark College, MacCormack went on to Harvard and the University of Iowa Writer's Workshop before returning to Oregon and farming. Along the route he was an early member of Students for a Democratic Society, and a civil rights and anti–Vietnam War activist.

It's a hot and humid summer day when I arrive in Corvallis, early for my appointment with MacCormack and hungry. The sun is playing hide-and-seek with a soft Oregon drizzle. I don't feel like getting wet looking for lunch and allow myself to be seduced into the convenient parking lot of a just-opened Panera outlet at the edge of downtown. "We are bakers of bread," announces the St. Louis–based chain in its glib promotional literature. "We are fresh from the oven. We are a symbol of warmth and welcome. We are a simple pleasure, honest and genuine. We are the kindest gesture of neighbors. We are home. We are family. We are friends." Yeah, sure. As long as you don't ask too many questions.

I look up at the Panera menu board and know immediately what I'm going to order: the vegetarian black bean soup. I'm in Corvallis as part of my black bean search, and here they are on offer. "Plump black beans," promises the menu, "simmered in a spicy vegetarian broth with onion, red bell pepper, garlic and cumin." The warm and friendly Jess serves me; she's the outlet's general manager, according to her name tag. I ask her the origin of the beans, telling her I must order them because I'm studying black beans. "I don't know where they come from," she answers honestly. But with the genuine, kind gesture of a neighbor, she pulls a loose-leaf binder out from under the cash register and looks up the soup ingredients. We linger over the list together.

Water is the number one ingredient, followed by black beans. In brackets after "black beans," the list notes "may contain soy." There's no hint about the percentages of black beans to soy I should expect in my bowl. Nothing odd about the rest of the list unless "modified food starch" creeps you out. But there's no clue about the source of the beans. Jess tells me she's curious herself. The soups she serves come to Corvallis from Panera's soup kitchen—wherever that is—and they come ready for lunch. She suggests I check with Panera customer relations and asks me to let her know what I learn. That the soup doesn't come from Italy, I'm sure, despite Panera's Italianesque name. The chain formerly was known as the St. Louis Bread Company. Don't tell our friends in the Show Me state, but apparently the consultants at Panera don't think St. Louis sounds romantic enough to sell soup.

A call to Panera headquarters in St. Louis is like ringing up the NSA. Panera, Quality Assurance International, Trader Joe's, Natural Directions—they all could use an Edward Snowden in their midst.

"I just ate the black bean soup at your Corvallis restaurant," I tell Mr. Customer Relations. "I'm wondering where you get the beans."

"Where do the beans come from?" He repeats my question, sounding flummoxed by the request.

I repeat the query, adding that the soup was delicious, which it was. I don't want him to be suspicious of my intent.

After a long pause he says, "May I put you on hold for a minute?"

When he comes back on the line, his answer is succinct. "That information," he says about the soup I just put in my stomach, "is proprietary."

Skinny as a beanpole himself, Harry MacCormack looks as if he could have been a model for the fellow with the pitchfork in Grant Wood's *American Gothic,* except for his long gray hair tied back in a vintage ponytail. Wearing a blue work shirt, dirty jeans, and an Oregon State University baseball cap calling out "Beavers" (OSU is just a few miles from the farm, and he taught there for several years), he welcomes me with what seems to be an unenthusiastic acceptance of duty. Sunbow Farm is toured often as an example of a successful family organic farm; MacCormack is interviewed often as a back-to-the-organic-land spokesman. We sit on the back porch of his farmhouse. He munches on chips directly out of the bag (offering me none). His message is a sober one. "We need to localize as much of our food as we can," he preaches. "We are in the situation right now of cheap oil not being available and it getting more and more expensive. The availability of oil is what's allowed our food system to run at the cheap level it's run at and have all the international shipping going back and forth." Witness the long ride my black beans took from Bolivia to my future burritos.

It's late August and MacCormack has just finished harvesting the beans he's experimenting with—favas, pintos, garbanzos, and blacks. As the drizzle turns to rain and he crunches chips, he tells me that the beans are early this year. His answers to my questions ramble with intriguing streams of consciousness. I ask if his bean crop is a success this year, and within a few sentences I've heard his opinions on global warming, devastated European grain harvests in the years 1645 and 1200, and O. J. Simpson's yardage for USC in the mud of Oregon State's stadium. When MacCormack stuffs more chips in his mouth, I take advantage of the lull to move our conversation back to prosaic beans. "We can grow so much here," he says about the Willamette Valley, with what I soon learn is characteristic enthusiasm. "We've got so much land in the valley." And much of it grows grass seed for export, not food for the locals. Linn County, just north of Eugene, boasts of being "the Grass Seed Capital of the World."

MacCormack and some curious farmer neighbors founded the Bean and Grain Project in 2008, convinced that the potential exists in the hundred miles of dirt between Eugene and Portland to feed the valley, even though over 95 percent of what we who live here eat, he tells me, comes from elsewhere. Not all the farmers at the project's early meetings were convinced that beans—especially organically grown beans—could thrive along the Willamette River. MacCormack enjoys talking about what he calls the Nozzleheads— organic skeptics who sprayed their lands for years—and how one Nozzlehead joined the project and became an organic bean convert after planting a test crop in a fallow field. "What we're doing is we're starting to build a microclimate agriculture that has beans and grains as a possibility for a base, and it's organic."

Just a few years after the experiments began, small growers were harvesting commercial Willamette Valley beans and selling their yield at local farmers' markets. "The flavors in all this stuff are amazing," MacCormack says about the beans and grains, "and it could change the valley. The one that is the survival food for here," says MacCormack, "is fava bean. They're 30 percent protein and they grow here in cold weather."

"And they're delicious," I offer, remembering a fava-filled dish I ate when I was working in Egypt.

"And they're delicious," he echoes. But it's black beans I came looking for. "I've got beans that taste way better than black beans," he says, pushing his Indian Woman variety. "We eat them here on the farm, and we sell some of them." This year's black beans are on a tarp in a greenhouse. "We do the bean dance," he says about what happens next. Workers stomp on the pods as if they are doing the Mashed Potato. "That breaks open the pod and rolls the beans out on the tarp. Then we sit around and talk." The stems and chaff are saved for the compost pile. Some chaff remains mixed with the beans along with some soil that gets picked up when the pods are pulled by hand out in the field. The beans are dumped in a tabletop seed cleaner that blows off the chaff, leaving piles of mostly clean beans. A quick rinse before cooking brings the remainder of the chaff to the surface of a pot filled with beans and water.

Sunbow Farm sells its beans for four dollars a pound. Here's a sobering look at the local versus global debate. Amazon sells those Natural Directions "organic" black beans I'm trying to trace back to Bolivia. Fifteen ounces of beans are in each can. Amazon sells them twelve cans at a time for $22.74, which means almost a pound of the canned Bolivian beans can be had for $1.90. Amazon wants another $15.89 for shipping, but if I add a few more cans of this and that to my virtual cart, the shipping charge disappears. Nonetheless, I want to buy a couple of pounds of Sunbow beans from MacCormack. I want to cook them at home and taste-test them against a can of Natural Directions beans. And I want to take them to Bolivia and trade them to a Bolivian farmer for a bag of his beans. The globalized economy works against my family budget and my desire to support local farmers; beans from a few miles up the road cost more than twice the price of legumes from half a world away.

Founding Oregon Tilth

"It started upstairs here in the barn." MacCormack, a cofounder of Oregon Tilth, points from his back porch across a driveway to his barn. "Five bucks out of my pocket and five bucks out of another person's pocket," he says about the initial capitalization of what is now a multimillion-dollar organic certification concern. Though Oregon Tilth was founded in 1984, a local precursor began operating in 1973, just a year after MacCormack started farming in Corvallis. A hand-lettered, rainbow-colored sign from those early days adorns the side of the barn: SUNBOW CERTIFIED SINCE 1972. "The thing that Oregon Tilth is known for," he says, thinking back to its origins, "is that it had a close tie to the land." That reputation, he says, appealed to corporate players like General Mills when they began using organic ingredients for their processed foods. "They looked at Oregon Tilth—and this still goes on—saw that it's tied back to this kind of hippie culture out here on the West Coast. These are straight guys in suits, you know?" He's laughing at the memory. "They tended to trust the fact that these old-line organic people were putting these organic standards together.

"That still goes on," the veteran farmer says, "and it's total bullshit, this image that Oregon Tilth is tied to the old hippie culture. It isn't." His voice rises in protest. "That's where it started, and it has the word 'Oregon' in it." He appreciates the brands—both Oregon Tilth and the romance of Oregon as a place with an organic heritage.

"You lived in California," he says to me. "Oregon is this place you go for a vacation. It's like Wonderland." I'm reminded of Oregon governor (and journalist) Tom McCall's ode about Californians in a

1971 speech: "I urge them to come and come many, many times to enjoy the beauty of Oregon. But I also ask them, for heaven's sake, don't move here to live."[88]

Certifying the food processors is where Oregon Tilth, QAI, and the others make their money, according to MacCormack. Certifying the farmers, however, is small potatoes. "It's all this stuff out of the country, and people bringing stuff in. It's huge money in certification. Huge money." MacCormack embraces the USDA organic standards as better than the patchwork of different standards that existed prior to the National Organic Program. He accepts the outsourcing of certification work to inspectors in developing countries because those freelancers must pass examinations that prove they understand international and USDA organic regulations and requirements.

"Sure they do," the cynical journalist in me responds, "and then they go back to places like Kazakhstan and Bolivia where there is blatant corruption."

"Blatant," he agrees. "I know inspectors who have inspected in China and they said they wouldn't eat anything from China." But MacCormack isn't disheartened. Progress made by the organic movement—a cause that he's been an integral part of since he first planted vegetables at Sunbow—pleases him. The questions remaining deal with personal ethics. "Do these people have enough integrity to do the job that they're being paid to do? That's part of what Oregon Tilth is known for, its integrity. I would say that's still pretty true. Even though they're hiring all these contract inspectors, Oregon Tilth trains them, too. It's a little looser than it was ten years ago," he figures as we talk in 2013, a worry he attributes to the sheer volume of work faced by certifiers as the organic sector continues to boom. "When the forms come in from the inspectors, they're gone over with a fine-tooth comb by high-paid reviewers."

MacCormack says that his fellow farmers making a transition to organic crops are heroes. "He took one helluva risk planting those beans," he says about his neighbor the Nozzlehead. "It sounds stupid, but it isn't. He's in the coffee shop with all the guys he's grown up with and he takes more ribbing—they think he's fucking nuts doing this organic stuff. Now he's got five hundred acres of organic stuff, and a positive cash flow from it." Being appreciated by consumers "changes a farmer's whole attitude about going out and doing the stuff we do hour after hour, taking on the risks we take on, because we know we have people backing us. That's huge. That's a huge, huge change in everybody's consciousness." He gestures toward his own flourishing organic acres. "It makes all this possible."

The rain lets up, and summer songbirds are serenading. Before I head back to Eugene, I buy a couple of pounds of Sunbow Farm black beans. MacCormack weighs them in a plastic baggie, and I ask him if he wants me to deliver a message to his Bolivian bean-growing compatriot. "My message for him is, 'Feed your community. Don't worry about people in the U.S. Feed your community!'"

"But what if he says to me, 'This is how I make my living, by selling beans to you gringos.'"

"Yeah, but part of what we have to do is focus on learning how to live locally again. This whole thing about shipping stuff all over the world just isn't going to be affordable." Later I look at my airline ticket. From Santa Cruz in Bolivia to Eugene is 5,775 miles. The trip for beans from Sunbow Farm in Corvallis down the freeway to my house in Eugene is a leisurely fifty miles.

Chapter Twelve

THE OREGON TILTH CERTIFICATION ROUTINE

Andrew Black's place in Eugene reminds me of Harry MacCormack's house. Both are typical Western-style simple frame bungalows painted in festive colors, and both feel immediately welcoming. Black escorts me to his office in an outbuilding behind his farmhouse and immediately tries to assuage my concerns about the integrity of the organic certification system. He kicks off his shoes ("You can leave yours on," he tells me). Along with his Columbia brand jacket, blue jeans, and wire-rimmed glasses, he fits that stereotype MacCormack referred to about Oregon Tilth being "tied to the old hippie culture."

Immersed in the organic food business and lifestyle, Black wants to tell success stories, not draw attention to what's wrong. He tells me he's convinced that the good guys vastly outnumber the Harold Chases.

"I've done hundreds of organic inspections," he says, "and I inspected Harold Chase's farm. Most people are obviously complying with the regulations. They have good record-keeping. They're earnest. They're honest. They're trying hard to make an income from their farm. We go back year after year and things get better and better. While at some, like at Harold Chase's farm, things weren't getting better and better. They were . . ." he trails off.

"Getting worse and worse?" I prompt him.

"Yeah," he says, "and less transparent. But my personal experience is that most of the time things are getting better and better as years go on. You can go out to a farm and see it getting better. You can see it with your own eyes. If you go out to one of these vegetable farmers here in the Willamette Valley, like Groundworks Organics, you will see biodiversity. You will see cover cropping. You will see practices that maintain or improve the quality of the soil. You will see beautiful vegetables and not a lot of dependence on pesticides. There's a lot of what we call 'cultural practices' to control pests, like floating row covers." Floating row covers consist of movable sheeting that protects crops (floating row covers protected the young radishes at the Adamah farm outside Vienna).

I want to embrace Black's bubbly optimism, but from what I've learned about organic food production thus far in my quest, it's clear to me that the certification routine is much too easy to game. Greed is a mighty seductive mistress.

"Obviously we can't detect fraud," Black says about Oregon Tilth inspections. "We couldn't with Harold Chase know for certain what was going on, but there were questions about record-keeping." Chase was not responsive enough to Tilth's queries, concerns, and demands for change. He was not submitting a required annual "organic system plan" for the farm, and he delayed inspection dates, citing heart problems. "It's not normal behavior for an organic farmer to try and put us off. So we dropped him."

"Just as you can go out to a place like Groundworks and see that it's going to be good, can you go out to a place and see that it's bad?"

Black assures me that he can.

But I want to know how. How can he tell things are not as they should be with just a visual inspection of the place? A farmer can just pretty up the landscape, I imagine, and hide the boxes, bags, and cans of illegal toxic junk that increase the yield.

"You could go out to a farm and notice if it's really weedy; that tells you something about the work that's being put into it. If their records don't match the scale of production—for example if they say they're producing five hundred pounds of potatoes but they don't have the land area or they don't look organized enough for five hundred pounds—that tells you something. These are all very vague, subjective observations that we're making. But the first thing that I do as an experienced organic farm inspector when I set foot on the property is look at it and pick up on just the vibe of the farm itself." These first impressions fuel the detailed inspection that follows. "If it's dirty and unorganized, that might translate to their farming practices and the organic integrity of the place." But not necessarily, so he goes out into the fields for a closer look. He interviews the farmer and asks questions not just about specific procedures but also about the farmer's organic agriculture philosophy. He wants to know how committed the farmer is to organic farming practices.

An Oregon Tilth inspection, according to Black's criteria, relies on more than those vibes he picks up, and on more than the quick glance at the landscape and documents that sources tell me constitutes typical field trips by inspectors. "I'm also asking, 'What inputs are you using?'" "Inputs" is the industry term of art for additives to soil, from fertilizers to pesticides, which include insecticides, fungicides, and herbicides. "We have a list of allowed materials. I'm asking them what they're using, and if they say something that's not on their organic system plan list, then," he snaps his fingers, "I note it down. They're using this, they haven't asked us for approval to use this, but they're using this. Basically we're having a conversation about organic farming. You can't detect fraud by just chatting to someone about subjective opinions about what organic farming is or should be. But interspersed with their philosophy, when you ask them pointed questions like 'Are you using liquid fertilizers?' or 'How do you get such a big plant here?' you begin to understand their system.

"Then we go and look at records. We look at receipts for the inputs they purchased. I'll say, 'Show me your receipts for all the fertility materials you purchased in the last year.' They pull out a folder, we flip through it, and we know exactly what materials are allowed. We can just flip through it and say, 'Oh, you purchased herbicide.' And then we'll have a conversation about what they bought and why. That's how inspection works." A typical Tilth inspection, Black says, lasts two to four hours from initial vibe to formal records.

But the once-a-year visit is not necessarily adversarial. "If they're really committed to organic farming, it's also a time to show off what they've done and to take some pride and ownership of it, and to talk with somebody else involved in agriculture about how to grow food without using chemical fertilizers or how to combat a certain pest. A lot of these organic farmers don't have a lot of like-minded individuals around to talk with in farming communities. Some of them do, but a lot are really, really ready to share."

That sounds pretty chummy to me: the inspector as visiting confidante. What's the psychology of that dynamic? Is it easy for a conniving farmer to bamboozle a visitor while showering the inspector with tales about how tough it is to be growing organics surrounded by Monsanto junkie neighbors? Not a chance, says Black. He insists that while personal relationships between inspectors and growers tend toward the collaborative and even communal, Tilth's rigorous standards transcend friendships.

An Oregon Tilth inspection is a farm-to-fork inspection. Or almost to the fork. You're boss of your own dinner from the grocery store checkout counter to your stomach. But Tilth inspects trucks and trains that carry organic foodstuffs, to make sure their cargo holds are clean of contaminants. Tilth inspections extend to what's called "tracebacks" in the industry—like trying to find the origin of Kazakh nuts.

Black offers an example from breakfast cereal. "I would say to the producer, 'Okay, you have a multi-ingredient product here.' This is a cereal that has corn, it has wheat, and, let's say, amaranth. We say, 'Okay, who did you purchase the corn, wheat, and amaranth from?'

Then they show us the receipts, and I want to see bills of lading. 'When did this arrive?' I ask. 'Show me the organic certificate that proves that this ingredient that's in this product is really organic. How much of it did you buy? How much was in inventory?' I want to know the only thing that went into this breakfast cereal was the organic amaranth, that you didn't purchase any other nonorganic amaranth to spike it, so to speak. If something came up fishy or didn't seem right, we would report those observations and issue a noncompliance. Or maybe it's so severe that we would move to suspend or revoke the operation's certificate."

Compromised at the Paycheck?

But just as is the case with Quality Assurance International, Oregon Tilth is paid by the food-to-market operators it certifies as organic. In most cases, Black says, the charge is based on a percentage of gross sales. That seems to double the potential for conflict of interest. First, the certifier relies on the company it's inspecting for its fee, and second, the more product that passes inspection, the fatter the check. "We try to keep certification fees as low as possible," says Black, "and the percentage is lower for farmers than it is for food processors." Nonetheless, inspecting those who keep you in business by paying for your inspections makes me think of police departments investigating corruption in their own ranks. These are codependent relationships, much too cozy—even if there is no corruption—to inspire confidence and credibility.

Consider the difference between the potential for compromise when the inspected pays the inspectors and how organic operators are inspected in someplace like Denmark. A department of the Danish government handles inspections and assumes the costs for the work, unless fraud is suspected.[89] Although the USDA licenses Oregon Tilth (and all other certifiers doing business in America), details of what Tilth and the others find on the farm (and on the rest of the journey to the fork) are none of your business—even though the food Tilth certified ends up in your stomach.

"We sign confidentiality agreements to be able to do this work," Black explains patiently, "and the information we deal with, some of it's trade secrets, so it needs to be confidential."

He offers the breakfast cereal as evidence.

"We would have that recipe in our records."

"Right."

"We sign confidentiality agreements that say we won't share your company's information. It's the same for that breakfast cereal manufacturer or Groundworks Organics. I can't tell you where he's getting his seed or what his seed is. I can't talk to you about the outcome of the inspection. I can't say, 'Oh that farmer? His compost isn't compliant to the National Organic Program standards because he didn't record the temperatures and the compost pile didn't get hot enough.' I can't disclose that text."

Trust us, says the industry and its overseers. Where my black beans were grown is none of my business.

Virtual Bolivia

"It's protected information," explains Black. "If you go to Natural Directions and say you want to know where those beans were grown, how do they know you're not a competitor?"

But Black's natural inspector instincts are piqued. He swings his chair over to his computer and punches the keyboard. Up pops the USDA website. He tells me he thinks he can click through the spreadsheets of data the government posts and determine from his office if there are any farms producing black beans in Bolivia. He taps more at the keyboard and locates the National Organic Program pages. With a click on "Bolivia" we see 132 companies listed as operating in Bolivia and certified organic.

"Right." I'm not surprised as I read over his shoulder what crops they produce and process. "Coffee, coffee, coffee, coffee, coffee."

"I don't see beans," he reports.

"Nope," I agree.

He looks further and finally finds one Bolivian farm listed as a black bean grower. Later, when I am back in my office, I check the list and find two: Bolivian Shoji and Alimentos Naturales Latco International, both headquartered in Santa Cruz de la Sierra, and both certified to import organic black beans into the United States. Despite the silence from Natural Directions, despite the dismissal from QAI, might I have found the source of my can of beans? And might the Kazakh walnuts, despite the closed-door policies at Trader Joe's, in fact be certified organic? Of course just because there might be legitimate organic beans in Bolivia doesn't mean those are the ones I ate.

I dig further into the bean fields of Bolivia. According to the USDA records, and despite the skepticism of the colleague of mine who worked as the Associated Press Bolivia correspondent, there are those two companies in Bolivia authorized to send beans to us gringos. Bolivian Shoji ignores my repeated efforts at contact. Alimentos Naturales Latco responds immediately to my inquiry. It seems an intriguing operation. Founded in 1997, its primary crop is organic black sesame seeds, and its mission statement is flawless: "We at Latco endeavor to provide products of the highest quality at competitive prices with service designed to ensure customer satisfaction. We focus our effort on organic and natural products to protect the environment and we will work with small farmers to fight poverty with fair prices."[90] The founder, Ray Ramiro Clavel, earned two master's degrees in the United States, an MBA from Florida International University and one in information resource management from George Washington University.

Latco responds to my inquiry posthaste. "We do not have organic beans this year," company spokesman Yoshiko Clavel informs me. While I consider possible options for contacting the elusive Bolivian Shoji company, I turn my attention to walnuts.

I hit the drop-down menu on the National Organic Program site and click "Kazakhstan." Chickpeas are on the list, along with soybeans, peas, lentils, and wheat. But no walnuts. In fact, no nuts of any kind. I check one more USDA website page, as Andrew Black suggested. It's a listing of operators out of compliance with USDA organic standards. But no company in Kazakhstan suffers from suspended or canceled organic nut certification.

If I'm reading these statistics correctly, the walnuts Trader Joe's peddled to me that were labeled organic, and certified by Quality Assurance International as organic, fail to pass this simple credibility test. There are no exporters approved by the USDA to sell organic walnuts into the American market. No wonder Trader Joe's won't talk about where it sources the "organic" walnuts it sells marked "Product of Kazakhstan."

Hispanic Organic Bolivian Beans

When I was in Bolivia the last time chasing drugs, the crack cocaine epidemic was surging, and the US government was sending Black Hawk helicopters and Drug Enforcement Administration agents to Bolivia in what turned out to be a failed effort to stop the northward cocaine traffic. My impressions of the corrupt and impoverished country remain vivid these many years later.

I drank coca tea (legal, of course) in the American embassy. I met with the Bolivian president, Victor Paz Estenssoro, at his fancy La Paz palace to talk about his decision to invite the US military into the country to fight the so-called War on Drugs. I wandered around La Paz, visiting Americans in prison on drug charges and checking out the Witches' Market, where dried llama fetuses were on offer. I arranged for a tank of oxygen for my Marlboro-smoking colleague who was gasping for breath at eleven thousand feet above sea level. We took a train over the top of the Andes and down to Cochabamba, a city awash in cocaine money, and visited a care facility for teenagers addicted to brain-rotting *pasta*—a precursor to the white powder cocaine that's exported. *Pasta* is junk that's filled with toxic processing chemicals.

At a mom-and-pop coca farm we interviewed the farmer while helping him spread out his crop to dry in the jungle sun, and we sent his wife—pregnant with their thirteenth child—off to Cochabamba for prenatal care, paid for with a hundred dollars out of our NBC News expense account. Drugs and poverty were everywhere, punctuated by examples of extreme wealth like the rows of private airplanes in the cocaine-manufacturing crossroads where the locals chased us out, chanting, "Kill the Yankees."

When I was searching for cocaine in Bolivia, the Associated Press stringer was Peter McFarren, a Bolivian-born American who spent much of his career in South America as a journalist and businessman. He is a natural source to contact when I start tracing the Natural Directions beans back toward Bolivia. I find him in Alexandria, Virginia, where he is finishing a book about Klaus Barbie—the Gestapo torturer who lived in Bolivia until he was extradited to France in 1983, to be tried and convicted of crimes against humanity.

"Bolivia does not export beans," McFarren tells me without hesitation. And he is in a place to know. McFarren was on the board of the Bolivian Export Foundation, a World Bank–financed project designed to help Bolivian farmers produce and export high-quality food crops. Beans, he says, were never on the agenda. Even if beans are being exported from Bolivia, he says, he knows of no government department or private organization engaged in oversight of any Bolivian organic bean farming. Bolivia is well known for its export of coffee and quinoa. He suggests there may be a trickle of garlic, soy, and bananas heading north from Bolivia. But he is emphatic: No beans.

However, I do in my digging find evidence of a trickle of Bolivian beans coming north. They show up on an esoteric Michigan State University Department of Agricultural Economics report titled "Common Beans in Bolivia," and the Instituto Boliviano de Comercio

Exterior reports that a modest amount of beans is, in fact, exported from the country—primarily to China, Spain, and Canada—but not to the United States.

There is a market worldwide for a type of organic beans from Bolivia—coffee beans. Organic quinoa is a growing market sector. But other than the label on the can of black beans in my kitchen, there is scant evidence supporting the likelihood that Bolivia is the place to search for organic black beans.

Do I pack my bags and head back to one of the poorest nations in South America, to the land where Butch Cassidy and the Sundance Kid escaped until they supposedly were killed in a gunfight with the army, where Che Guevara tried to foment another revolution but ended up captured and shot dead by a Green Beret–trained Bolivian soldier, and where Klaus Barbie was arrested?

Do I head south and just search Bolivia for what may be my bean field with no hint about it save for the street address in Santa Cruz listed by the USDA for Bolivian Shoji? Do I inspect the farm if it's at that address, interview whatever farmer I can find, try to talk with the processor who buys from the farmer, and attempt to follow the trail of the beans off the farm and out of Bolivia? If I find the beans and the farmer and the processing plant, how will I determine—as an uninvited outsider—if the beans meet Oregon standards for organic and if they're being sold to Natural Directions?

The Bolivian farmer, like the phantom Kazakh walnut grower, is either hero or villain—a determination that cannot be made unless we're face-to-face and until the crop is analyzed. Or the farmer could be neither hero nor villain, but merely an unwitting coconspirator, unaware that the conventional beans he or she is growing are sold in *El Norte* as organic.

Chapter Thirteen

THE CORN HUSTLER

"You made a big mistake to commit this crime in Lane County."

US District Court judge Ann Aiken reprimanded the defendant in front of her bench. His crime: selling conventionally grown corn and claiming it organic. "The food supply and the water supply of this country and other countries are sacred," she continued. "It is to be respected, period. It's going into the bodies of our children." Her succinct speech completed, the judge sentenced Springfield, Oregon, businessman Harold Chase to over two years in federal prison.

Springfield is just across the river from my Eugene home, both in Oregon's Lane County, the original home for one of the icons of the organic food world: Nancy's Yogurt made at the Springfield Creamery. The business is a local legend. Author Ken Kesey's brother Chuck and Chuck's wife, Sue, founded it in the 1960s. The Grateful Dead came to Springfield in the 1970s to play a benefit concert for the struggling creamery, and in the 1990s organic yogurt was added to the product line. The creamery is just one of a long list of Lane County businesses catering to a population ready to pay extra for organic food. Judge Aiken knows her constituency. Lane County was in fact one of the worst places to be caught committing organic food fraud, and from the bench she drew attention to local farmers'

markets and the long-running and fast-growing subculture in Lane County that is hungry for pesticide- and herbicide-free food.

Harold Chase didn't just sell a few ears of mismarked corn from a roadside stand. He was convicted of misrepresenting over four million pounds of conventional corn as organic, corn that he inserted into the food chain in order to reap an extra profit of almost two hundred thousand dollars, a near doubling of his usual take. He hid the conventional source of the corn with false documents and by dumping it from one truck into another, which made it difficult to trace its origin by the time it was delivered from Idaho and Washington growers to an Oregon feed supplier. The duped supplier sold it to dairies that used it as feed for their herds of cows, cows producing supposedly organic milk. The crime jeopardized the organic rating of the dairies and resulted in deceived milk-drinking consumers. The case was a prime example of how a single bad apple in the organic food chain literally can ruin the barrel. Given lax government oversight and the cozy relationships binding organic food producers and the companies they pay to certify them, should we be surprised?

The USDA Agent and the Federal Prosecutor

The US Courthouse in Eugene is a gleaming glass-and-steel fortress that sits between downtown and the University of Oregon—imposing on a strip of otherwise trite urban sprawl. Its neighbors are motels catering to campus visitors, the Goodwill retail store, and a steak house that occupies an old Victorian-style house. I like the suggestion of urbanity the courthouse brings to sleepy Eugene, but it's viewed with disdain by some of my neighbors who are offended by its airportlike security and see it as out of scale for the locale.

I empty my pockets at the front entrance and successfully pass through the metal detector en route to a meeting with Scott Bradford, the assistant US attorney who prosecuted Harold Chase. The guards want to store my cigarette pack–size audio recorder but tell me I can keep my mobile phone. "Those are the rules," one of them explains. I patiently explain in return that it would be a challenge to find a telephone in 2013 that doesn't double as a recording device. "Those are the rules," I'm told again.

The windowless courthouse conference room is decorated by images of Lincoln and JFK, accented with an American flag. I tell my tale of nuts-and-beans woe; the tough prosecutor lets out a cynical laugh. Also laughing is Kevin Porter, the USDA special agent who led the criminal investigation that resulted in the fraud charges against Chase. Both of them sport shaved heads, and their partnership reminds me of Mutt and Jeff. I'd wager Porter played tackle on his high school football team while Bradford covered sports for the school newspaper.

A tip from a wronged citizen—a conventional corn grower in Washington State—sent Agent Porter after Chase. Chase used several aliases when he was making his conventional corn purchases from growers, and then he sold it as organic under his own name to Grain Millers, a company that supplies feed corn to farmers and ranchers. His modus operandi was to transfer the conventional corn from trucks that hauled it from the cornfields into trucks he hired that hauled it to Grain Millers—where it was delivered along with fraudulent certificates identifying it as organic. In the end it wasn't the fraud that caused Harold Chase's downfall; it was his greed. One of the conventional corn growers followed a shipment because Chase was in arrears on his payments to the corn farmer. "The grower discovered that the trucks were going to a transload site, which is pretty unusual. You don't transload corn unless there is a reason to," Porter says. The suspicious grower kept following his corn and checked in with the company handling the transloaded shipment. "They told him they were hauling organic corn, which he knew it wasn't because it was *his* corn." The grower contacted the authorities, and Agent Porter was on the case.

The bust sounds like a lucky break. "If Chase had paid his bills to the grower, there would have been no reason for him to follow the corn?" I ask.

"Yep," says Porter. It was the kind of break that cops seek, depend on, even, and Chase left a paper trail that included a fax between Oregon and Washington—wire fraud across state lines—making it a federal case. Once Chase was arrested and news reports about the case circulated, the USDA received more tips from the public. Some of these charged Chase with laundering conventional onions as organic. By that time he had already pleaded guilty to the corn fraud and prosecutor Bradford was content with the hefty sentence that sent Chase to federal prison. He didn't go after him for onions.

"Do you think Chase is a rogue one-off," I ask the agent and the prosecutor, "or do you guys think he's an example of an endemic problem within the organic farming sector? Are we plagued with false certificates? Is my wife wasting our grocery money on high-priced stuff just masquerading as organic?"

"I'm not aware of any other complaints about this kind of fraud," Agent Porter says. "In this case he was pretty crafty, using the different aliases." Before he was caught Chase shipped close to a hundred truckloads carrying nearly four million pounds of conventional corn—moved in an unconventional manner. Porter assures me this is rare.

But both Porter and Bradford might run into Sheila at the market. "We buy organic," Porter says in answer to my question about his eating habits at home. "It really hit home." Bradford says his family also chooses organic products at the market.

There was no trial. The prosecutor's office contacted Chase and informed him that he was under investigation. When Chase saw the evidence gathered against him, he came to the courthouse and acknowledged his guilt. "It was a fairly easy fraud to perpetrate," says Bradford. Chase knew the ins and outs of the organic business since he had been a certified organic farmer himself—until Oregon Tilth yanked its approval of his operation. For the corn scam he contacted a legitimate organic corn farm, said he was considering making a purchase, and asked for a copy of their certificate as proof that the corn passed muster as organic. "He gets their certificate," says Bradford, "and then he uses that certificate to disguise his conventional corn, telling everybody, 'This is where I bought it from. Here's their certificate. It's organic corn.'" The prosecutor amends his assessment. "It was a fraud very easy to perpetrate. If you're an organic farmer and you want to sell your stuff, you proudly display that certificate. You give it out to people and say, 'Look. I'm USDA certified. Here you go.' If another broker like Chase takes it and runs with it, it's going to be easy to perpetrate fraud."

Here I am, just a few miles from Andrew Black's Oregon Tilth office, and two tough lawmen are reinforcing my concern that Black and his organic inspector colleagues are too trusting—and maybe a tad naïve. If a crook studies the certification system and employs some moxie, the organic marketplace is vulnerable on a grand scale. The USDA National Organic Program is based on trust and operates with little oversight in a capitalist economy—a capitalistic economy that's too often predatory, as the 2007 Great Recession reminded us with long-lasting grief.

A Look at the Con Man

I ask Bradford if Chase looked the part of a fraudster. "He looked like a ranch hand or a farmer." Porter heard otherwise. "A lot of the folks who dealt with him described him as being kind of shifty," he says. Based on exchanges over the telephone, Porter figures "he's the type of person who could sell anything to anyone."

The prosecutor says the motive for the crime is obvious. "If you sell something that's conventional as organic, you basically double your money." Flimsy oversight along with fat profits lure crooks, and Bradford sees a chain of victims. The corn was fed to animals being raised as organic. White-collar crimes are laborious and time-consuming to investigate and prosecute. That means meat or dairy products perceived to be organic could have gone to market tainted by the conventional feed. Since certifiers routinely inspect only once a year, a year could have passed before the polluted feed might have been discovered. In the Chase case, had the farmer he stiffed not followed him, certifiers might not have discovered the conventional feed at all. They would have had no reason to suspect the organic certification document Chase attached to the corn. "It's not just that Chase was ripping off Grain Millers," Bradford says. "He was ripping off the end consumer: you and your wife in the grocery store."

Scott Bradford's wife, too.

"My wife asked me, 'Should we keep buying organics, Scott?' I said, 'We have to trust the labels.' We have to believe that people tell the truth. We have to trust that everybody marketing organics is properly certified. We have to rely on the USDA to do their enforcement job and decertify people when they're no longer organic. That's the system we have."

The integrity of organic food should be a nationwide concern from farm to fork, says Bradford. "We want to ensure that our food system is safe and that the labeling system is accurate. We want to ensure that we're paying for and getting what we want." He believes the Chase case is important not just because it brought a bad guy to justice, but also because it spotlights flaws in the National Organic Program. "This case highlights that we need a better way to police the industry to ensure that organic products are truly organic, that they meet the USDA organic standards and that the inspectors of the certifiers are doing their job correctly." He considers those points for a second and quickly adds, "It might be boiling down to a resource issue." I'm thinking again about that incredible number Miles McEvoy told me in his office at the Agriculture Department headquarters in Washington: The National Organic Program fields one staffer for every billion dollars of revenue the industry generates.

Before I leave the courthouse I chat with the prosecutor and the agent about my interest in meeting Harold Chase and hearing his side of the story. They think he'll want to talk to me, and I agree. When I was an NBC News correspondent, I traveled to twenty-one countries around the world, interviewing Americans in prisons—research for a radio documentary and for my book *Nightmare Abroad*. Most of the incarcerated expats I found wanted to talk, not just to tell their own tales but also for the diversion meeting with me provided from their tedious daily routines.

A bemused Porter wonders about Chase's relationships with his fellow inmates. "I don't know how he's explaining to people that he's in prison for organic food fraud when he's walking around with everyone else." It might be an entertaining first question to consider if I manage to get into the Federal Correctional Institute, Sheridan, for a jailhouse interview with Chase. It's a two-step process for a journalist to get behind bars to talk with inmates. The inmate needs to okay the meeting, as does, of course, the warden. While I wait for Chase to answer my letter (the prison would not allow a telephone call), the warden denies my request. When I ask for an explanation, his assistant, Paul Thompson, writes, "It is the opinion of the warden that inmate Chase's interview could disturb the good order of the institution."

More institutional nonsense. Not that I'm much surprised by government-driven secrecy, but that explanation literally makes no sense. When I ask for some elaboration, the response from the prison is ludicrous. "Sheridan has inmate work details that operate inside and outside of the facility. Additionally, the visiting room is visible from within and outside the institution. Therefore, the inmate population is able to monitor the traffic of the visiting room. Any nonroutine activities such as legal depositions, interviews, etc. not only disrupt the regular institutional programming schedule but draw undue attention to the inmate."

Nonsense, for sure. Chase is in a minimum-security camp at the prison. The idea that it would disrupt the joint were he seen talking with a journalist in the visiting room is absurd. It's one more example of the government inappropriately exercising and abusing its power to keep us citizens underinformed. "Trust us," says the government. "Trust us, Americans. Just keep walking. Nothing to worry about is happening here. Go home and watch your television. Surf YouTube. Check your e-mail." Of course the NSA may have already checked your e-mail.

One of the farmers whose organic certification was threatened by Chase's crime noted for the prosecutor's sentencing report to the judge that organic and conventional commodities often share the same appearance—and that neither farmers nor the government have the resources to test every shipment. The organic farming business, he said, is based on integrity. Harold Chase is an example of one self-serving criminal fouling the works for the rest of us.

Chapter Fourteen

THE TUNISIAN OLIVE POET AND THE HUNGARIAN CORN BURNER

Shortly before the 2011 revolution in Tunisia, its president, Zine el-Abidine Ben Ali, showed up in research I was conducting about animal abuse for my book *No Animals Were Harmed*. Among the seemingly endless stacks of secret documents released by WikiLeaks was a cable that then–US ambassador to Tunisia Robert Godec sent back to Washington dealing with the unusual use of animals. In the message he noted that the dictator's son-in-law kept a "pet" tiger in a cage and fed it four chickens daily.

At the time, it never would have occurred to me that just over a year later I would find myself in what had been Ben Ali's Carthage palace-by-the-sea, chatting with Ambassador Godec's successor, Gordon Gray, with no tigers in sight. The occasion for my visit was UNESCO's World Press Freedom Day, staged symbolically in Tunisia specifically to support the free and independent journalism flourishing in the post–Ben Ali atmosphere.

Well, mostly free.

On the day that journalists from around the globe were celebrating Tunisian news media, the owner of Nessma TV was found guilty of "violating sacred values" and "disturbing public order" for airing a scene from the film *Persepolis* that briefly shows an imagined graphic portrayal of God. Ambassador Gray expressed concern that the verdict "raises questions about the future of freedom of expression" in Tunisia.

"It's important for friends of Tunisia to raise the red flag," he tells me, making it clear that we Americans consider ourselves among those friends of the former French colony. "It's very important that all defenders of liberty speak up on behalf of the Tunisian people," he states firmly, and we walk into the sparkling palace for an evening of official speeches praising press freedom, and an opulent banquet.

Contradictions fuel my delightful stay in Tunisia, contradictions and tears.

The vibrant streetscape along Tunis's Avenue Habib Bourguiba makes me think of how the California Parks Department describes its maintaining of the old Gold Rush ghost town of Bodie: It says it keeps the area in "an arrested state of decay." The combination of the bustling cafes, the colonial-era architecture, and the rapid chatter in French reflects Paris in an arrested state of decay. Armored military vehicles are on patrol behind rolls of concertina wire in Place de L'indépendance, all manned by relaxed soldiers. The Medina is remarkably free of tourist traffic—a disaster for its merchants, but refreshing for those of us lucky enough to visit at a time when most vacationers worried about postrevolutionary stability and went elsewhere.

Nights at the swank Hotel Karthago Le Palace, I read from two Albert Memmi books in an attempt to jump-start my assimilation into the local culture. Believe me that *Strangers* is not the best book to read when you're living six thousand miles from your wife. The conflicts Memmi details in the plagued marriage he chronicles of a European and a Tunisian add to my list of contradictions, as does his sobering *Colonizer and the Colonized*. His conclusion in that 1957 book foreshadows the Jasmine Revolution. "Having reconquered all his dimensions," Memmi writes with hope, "the former colonized will have become a man like an other. There will be the ups and downs of all men to be sure, but at least he will be a whole and free man."

Hungry, and tired of hotel cuisine, I hail a taxi to La Goulette for a leisurely fresh fish luncheon. En route the taxi driver and I share a few stories and I invite him to join me in the restaurant. As the meal progresses he tells me stories of growing up in the desert near Gafsa. He pulls out his wallet and shows me a faded photograph of his father, an image that looks like my Hollywood idea of a Berber. "He was 103 when he died," he says with a son's pride. Ziyed stares out the window of the restaurant as he tells the tale of his father saving Ziyed and his sister from a flood by holding them high in the air while he trekked through water over his head. Ziyed grabs at some napkins. He is sobbing over the memory.

But moments later, eyes again dry, he tells me how his father beat him when he learned that Ziyed was drinking beer.

I keep Ziyed's business card. Not only did we like swapping stories, his family home is near the route of the Lezard Rouge, the luxury train that winds through the lunarlike landscape near Gafsa, a must for my next trip to Tunisia.

Perhaps the most lively and poignant moment of the UNESCO events comes when the 2011 Nobel Peace Prize laureate Tawakkol Karman strides to the World Press Freedom conference podium and leads the audience in a rousing chorus from the Tunisian national anthem. Once the singing is over, she takes on the verdict against Nessma TV and dismisses it with vigor. "You feeble tyrants," she proclaims. "No laws will put us down even if it takes us ten more revolutions."

Inspiring words for me to take back to America, where our responsibility is to guard the press, speech, and religion rights we've enjoyed since our own revolution, rights that remain—these generations later—under attack.

After a week in Tunis and Carthage, I head across the North African countryside toward the fertile Medjerda Valley. There the fourth generation of the Mahjoub family grows organic olives, and their crews handpick and cold-press the fruit into what must be the best olive oil I've ever tasted. But perhaps I am influenced by the cherubic character of the Mahjoub family patriarch, Abdelmajid.

When we are inching along the highway leaving Tunis en route to his farm and orchard, I ask Mahjoub what's causing the traffic jam.

"Because business is going more and more fast," he says in his endearing English.

"So it's good news that we're stuck in the traffic?

"Yeah, yeah," he smiles. "Very good news!"

It's a typical example of Mahjoub's energetic optimism. We're making small talk. Getting to know one another. He's invited me to join him for lunch at Les Moulins Mahjoub and, to avoid an uncomfortable scene at the table, I've told him I don't eat meat.

"At midday," he says, "we will eat couscous with no meat."

"That sounds great." I love couscous.

"We will eat couscous with no meat," he repeats, adding, "with sheep."

"Sheep are meat," I'm forced to note, an edit he accepts.

Row after row of vibrant verdant olive trees stand majestically deep in what looks to me like out-of-control weeds and wildflowers.

"Look at the grass," Mahjoub instructs me. The orchard is reflected in his dark glasses. His smile matches his upbeat personality, which exudes a love for his land and its bounty. "We cannot use herbicide." It's delightful to see that the orchard grounds are not denuded to the dirt of anything but olives. The trees look robust, craggily big, and old.

"The olive tree is the only thing in the world that never dies," Mahjoub says slowly, enunciating each word clearly to make sure I understand. "It is for this reason that in Genesis the bird comes with a branch of the olive tree." I think about those lines in Genesis

(8:11): "And the dove came in to him in the evening; and, lo, in her mouth was an olive leaf pluckt off: so Noah knew that the waters were abated from off the earth."

"And the olive tree always produces," Mahjoub confirms. He waves at one of his workers and greets him in Arabic. The trees are flowering. In a month the white flowers will drop and the fruit will appear. "We want *une bonne nouaison,* the jump from the flower to the fruit." We're looking at a tree Mahjoub estimates is sixty years old.

"But this has not been an organic orchard for sixty years, right?" I'm thinking like an American, I guess, figuring that sixty years ago, before the contemporary organic food surge, these trees must have been sprayed with pesticides, this land must have been fertilized with chemicals and doused with herbicides.

Wrong.

"Almost all olive trees in Tunisia are organic," Mahjoub tells me. "The olive tree doesn't need a lot of treatment." That's not the whole story. "Since independence, Tunisia has been a clean country," he says about its agriculture since 1956. Mahjoub agrees that what he calls the "tsunami of chemicals" dates to the end of the Second World War, but he says it was not until the late 1990s that the poisons arrived en masse in Tunisia. "We've come very late to modernization, to the chemical process." His family decided to stick with the old ways. "No chemicals. We said no because we wanted to be certified organic. We were organic, but not certified."

"Why did so much of Tunisia and the world abandon its old traditions?" I ask. "What caused us to go down that wrong road?"

Mahjoub, standing in a the middle of a bucolic dirt road in his orchard, the hills around the Medjerda Valley green under the clear blue North African sky, hesitates. "Because," he starts, and then he stops with a half smile on his face before continuing. "I will say something and you won't like it. Because of the American Dream. We want to be as rich as the States. Every country wants to produce more and more. They learn how they can do it the same as in the States. That's how it started." The smile is gone; he looks contemplative. "The example of the big producer country was the States; it wasn't Russia."

"So we're the devil infidels?" I make him laugh again.

"No," he protests, American prosperity was quite attractive. "It was a dream. It wasn't wrong. It was the best choice at the time. But the dream, you have to stop it when it becomes a *cauchemar,* a nightmare. So we are stopping it today." Again America is driving the marketplace, Mahjoub believes, and this time without the *cauchemar.* "The States are the organic leader. We are following this trend, and we have to correct what happened at the end of the Second World War."

Mahjoub bends and grabs a handful of soil. "This is our earth," he says, holding it with evident respect in his palm. "It has very good filtration. It is aerated. The water goes through it very easily, to the plants' roots." He and I walk through the remains of harvested tomatoes and artichokes, piled up for compost. The smell is like fresh-turned rich earth. We're far from the stink of the Tunis traffic. Mahjoub leads me to a pile of what he calls "olive rubbish"—what remains after the oil is pressed out of the fruit. He holds up a dried slab that looks like a roof shingle. He tells me they use it as compost because it is more than 5 percent olive oil. Even after two pressings the oil lingers, and it nourishes next year's crop.

The springtime Mediterranean sun is hot. Mahjoub points out the locals he hires as farmhands, women walking through the tomato fields, pulling weeds by hand. In addition to olives, tomatoes, and artichokes, his family grows garlic and figs. The other crops are used to flavor tapenades Les Moulins Mahjoub manufactures along with the olive oil in a facility in the middle of the fields, fields alive with wildflowers and butterflies.

"Poppies mean healthy earth," Mahjoub tells me.

Birds are singing; a frog croaks from an irrigation ditch. The scene is idyllic.

Wheat grown adjacent to the olive orchard is used to make the family company's couscous. At a processing building we look through a door window at three women workers preparing the couscous for market. The grain is rolled into tiny balls by hand. Mixed with olive oil, water, and salt. I reach for the door handle so that I can open the door and capture a photograph without shooting through the glass. Mahjoub stops me. It's a clean room. Entering it without protective clothing would jeopardize the integrity of the batch. Sloppy practices or accidents can foul organic purity—another example of the power of the bad apple to despoil the rest, no matter the intentions.

The tour ends and Mahjoub sits me down in a conference room for a tasting session. He pours some "early harvest extra virgin" oil on a piece of fresh-baked bread. Heavenly. We taste delectable olives. "Never aggressive in your mouth," Mahjoub says.

"Sweet," I add.

"Sweet," he agrees, "with a finish of dark chocolate." I'm enraptured, but I'm not convinced about the dark chocolate. Mahjoub offers another description of his olive oil's role on the label that accompanies it to markets worldwide. "Bread has never been strong enough to cope with its invading yet friendly demands. Mixed up with other ingredients, it still controls the situation, without allowing others to feel its authority." Ninety-nine percent of commercial olives cure in two weeks, he tells me, the process sped up with solvents. His take nine months to finish, sitting under the Tunisian sun in a solution of nothing but water and salt.

"All may play solo," he says about food that is cooked with or served with olive oil, and he holds up the oil bottle as if it were a religious totem. "This is the conductor. But he doesn't impose. He harmonizes and makes the meal a symphony." The moment feels like a worship service where food is the venerated godhead. And I feel blessedly distant from Costco's crowded organic aisles.

But I'm not Mahjoub's only audience. He serenades his olive oil with poetry that decorates company brochures:

> *Its lemon scented perfume smothers garlic, salt and cumin.*
> *I can still hear the enchantment of women crying out of pleasure.*
> *They weep out in ecstasy when they see it,*
> *Unfolding its charms on a slice of bread.*

"My work is the same as the poet," he says about the olive oil his family has been pressing for well over a century. "Taste is in the mind. When I don't find the word, I don't find the taste." The family olive oil is sold in gourmet outlets like Dean & DeLuca; it's famous for its delicate and complex taste, and it's appreciated as organic. As we eat the sweet couscous (no sheep, but a delicious mix of fresh vegetables), Mahjoub peppers his answers to my questions about his family's operation with tossed-off philosophy lines.

"Life is not for making money," Mahjoub instructs me. "It is for making ourselves. We are never made; we are always making."

Back in Tunis I meet with Zina Aouam, and over tea we talk about her routine when she visits the Mahjoub orchard in order to certify it as organic. She travels to the Medjerda Valley twice a year in her role as a certifier for France-based Ecocert, once with an appointment and once unannounced. She takes soil samples and collects leaves and olives for analysis in a Berlin laboratory used by Ecocert for an independent check. She says she loves her field trips to Les Moulins Mahjoub, confident that each inspection trip will be like the last: a visit that immerses her in a pristine organic operation creating delicious, high-quality products.

The French Connection

On a warm Southern California winter afternoon, I meet with Ecocert's general manager, Vincent Morel. He was in charge of the company's Africa operations for years; now North America is his territory. He chose the venue for our chat: a restaurant on Venice's gentrifying Rose Avenue, just down the street from the huge Whole Foods Market—the first branch of the chain I've visited that's patrolled by armed and uniformed guards. The Whole Foods guards are eying the customers with suspicion. Me, I'm wondering about the faraway hometown of the blueberries and the cost of the journey to get the organic fruit from places like Chile to West L.A.

"They're here for your protection," the checkout clerk tells me as she rings me up. "And for our protection." She regales me with tales of customer harassment and says she feared for her till and her safety without the private police on duty. As *Los Angeles Times* reporter Matt Stevens says about the rapidly changing Rose Avenue, "Skid Rose meets Restaurant Rose."[91] Morel and I meet at one of those new Rose Avenue eateries, Café Gratitude, where the menu promises "100% organic vegan" fare.

I know the restaurant chain. I stumbled into a branch in Marin County where the waiter dripped, "What are you grateful for?" as his introduction to Sheila and me. My New York roots wanted to scream, but I knew such an outburst would not be appreciated; in deference to our lunch date, I simply ignored the invasive query. The poor waiter likely wasn't happy being ordered to open with such an insipidly pat line. Or at least I hope he wasn't. It's supposed to be an eatery, not group therapy. The company's mission statement cloyingly claims:

> We select the finest organic ingredients to honor the earth and ourselves, as we are one and the same. We support local farmers, sustainable agriculture and environmentally friendly products. Our

food is prepared with love. We invite you to step inside and enjoy being someone that chooses: loving your life, adoring yourself, accepting the world, being generous and grateful every day, and experiencing being provided for. Have fun and enjoy being nourished. Welcome to Cafe Gratitude![92]

I skip the thirteen-dollar enchiladas (titled "I Am Elated," rolled in "live[?!] spinach flax tortillas") and order a green tea (called "I Am Glorious," which it better be for four and a half bucks). Frenchman Morel picks coffee, and he looks like an extra in a French New Wave film, with his few-days-old beard. Sounds like one, too, with his Paris accent. Where is his Citroën Traction Avant?

Ecocert, he tells me, was founded in the late 1980s to certify organic products in France. Just after the turn of the century it went global and now inspects organic farms and food production facilities in countries around the world, including Tunisia. The company makes announced and unannounced visits to its clients, usually one of each once a year. He tells me the unannounced inspections are of particular importance when there's a risk that organic products may be contaminated at a farm or factory that deals with both organic and conventional products.

Again, I'm skeptical of this conflict; it's a business model that serves two masters. "But speaking of risk, if you are paid by your clients and your clients are being inspected by you, isn't there an inherent risk that you will be compromised by a conflict of interest?"

Not a chance, he insists. "We are independent, transparent, and," he is emphatic, "there is no conflict of interest."

Yet my jaundiced journalist's mentality keeps pondering: What further conflicts of interest may tempt those who certify the certifiers? Operations like Ecocert and Quality Assurance International are accredited annually in the United States by the Department of Agriculture, whose inspectors shadow Ecocert agents in the field, observing their techniques—but again, for a fee.

I sip my overpriced tea and express further questions about the checks and balances. Only a couple of inspections a year to ensure compliance? A USDA already stretched by budget cuts is policing a multibillion-dollar industry? Producers pay the certifiers for approval? Certifiers pay the government for accreditation? Opportunities to game the system seem abundant: a payoff here, a wink there.

Morel says he's heard it all before. "I'm always meeting people who say, 'Organic? Bullshit!'" But he insists the USDA oversight works, and he credits the organic industry with strict internal controls. Of course there are cheats and crooks, he tells me, just as in any business. "But if you're working hard to create a quality product," he points out, "you report your neighbors if they violate standards." He calls the formal and informal tests that determine what is and what is not organic some of the most severe and successful in the food industry. "Importers are skeptical of Third World suppliers," for example, "and do their own analysis."

Understandably, Morel wants to talk success, not scam. He tells me stories from Burkina Faso, where impoverished women formed a company and after just a few years were living well, operating a flourishing organic shea butter production and exporting business. He notes that only 2 to 3 percent of the American food supply is organic (closer to 4 percent, according to others I've interviewed). Of the twenty thousand or so companies in France producing certified organic food, he says, only about a hundred have lost their certifications. "That means the system works!" he says, gratified.

Inspector Morel stumbled into the organic business; he didn't come to it as an evangelist for pure eating. He studied political science, worked for UNICEF in Asia, and met his Ecocert boss by chance. "To be honest," he says, "I'm more into eating organic food here in the US than back home in Europe." Morel says he picks organic in L.A. because he fears that conventional US food is tainted with dangers besides herbicides and pesticides. "I'm more scared about what I can find in the food here than in Europe, like corn—because of the GMOs." He worries about what might be tainting his American vegetables and eggs and chicken.

I'm reminded of a day Sheila and I took a break from Interstate 5 for lunch near the capitol building in Salem, Oregon. We were at Venti's Cafe + Basement Bar on Court Street, a welcoming place with friendly folks behind the counter. The menu looked promising for a quick bite, with offerings like Veggie Deluxe (steamed with black beans and pineapple) and Garlic Sesame Tofu (suggested pairing: Brown Ale). But with a rare carnivore hankering, Sheila asked the clerk, "Where does your chicken come from?" She was not expecting to get a file on her chicken's name and heritage nor to visit the farm where her potential lunch was raised. But neither was she expecting the candid answer offered by the smiling help. "It comes frozen off the Sysco truck," he reported. She ordered the veggies.

"Monsanto," Morel tells me as we part. "Monsanto for us is the bad guy."

Killing Monsanto Corn in Hungary

I head east out of Vienna for the other capital of the Hapsburg Empire, Budapest—my favorite city on the Danube. On a previous reporting trip there I spent time with self-taught lion tamer Vladislav Goncharov and watched his famous trick. He sticks his head deep into the yawning mouth of a cat.

"What are you thinking about when your head is inside that guy's mouth?" I asked Goncharov.

"When this moment will end," he said.

That's how I'm feeling the more I consider genetically modified organisms, the opposite of organic agriculture. Ubiquitous Monsanto is the lion, and it's a struggle to keep our heads out of its mouthful of GMOs as we forage for our food worldwide. But I want to practice the precautionary principle with predatory Monsanto. We know old-fashioned organic corn is good for us, and we don't know what Monsanto's GMO corn may do to us. I'm in Budapest to catch up with the Hungarian agriculture minister, a bureaucrat who I've learned agrees that Monsanto is a bad guy, or at least that some of its products fit that category. Monsanto's GMOs are not welcome in my Magyar brethren's homeland.

A contemplative walk from my hotel across the Danube over the Chain Bridge and along the Pest side of the river brings me to the Hungarian Agriculture Ministry headquarters, a massive hulk in the shadow of the sprawling neo-Gothic Parliament building. While I wait for Lajos Bognár to return to his office from lunch, I'm entertained by his outgoing assistant and by the pastoral pictures on the wall. Bognár, who trained as a veterinary epidemiologist, is a deputy secretary of state in the Rural Development Ministry; he is the official who ordered flourishing fields of Monsanto GMO corn burned and ploughed under. Growing genetically modified fruits, vegetables, and grains is illegal in Hungary, as it is in neighboring Austria. The deputy secretary is a gregarious fellow, happy to talk about his role in GMO history.

As I start talking to him, an image flashes through my mind of Hungary's corn, as high as an elephant's eye, destroyed by a fleet of old Soviet-era tractors plowing across the Magyar plains, torched like books in *Fahrenheit 451*. "That was a radical thing to do," I say.

"Yes, it was radical," Bognár agrees, his voice soft but authoritative. It was radical, but because Hungary outlawed GMO crops in 2011, he considered it necessary. "There is zero tolerance in Hungary regarding GMO." Inspectors found GMO seeds in a shipment of corn seed that was imported into Hungary. "Because of Hungarian laws we had to confiscate these corn seeds." But some of the batch had already been planted and was growing. "Of course we had to take measures regarding the plants. We destroyed the plants—burned it or made silage."

Crews from Bognár's ministry went to the farms and performed the eradication. "The majority of the farmers accepted it, and of course there was compensation. They lost no money. There were no financial consequences for the farmers." The seed company was ordered to pay most of the tab because Hungarian authorities determined that the farmers, who did not intend to plant GMO seeds, were victims. The government provided the rest of the compensation. He says the contamination of the seed was an accident.

I can't help but notice that Bognár is a well-fed fellow; he's stocky. I ask him if he eats GMO food. "Personally I don't want to eat it," he says, letting out a Santa Clausian belly laugh. He finds it funny that our conversation shifted from the details of Hungarian agriculture policy to his own diet. "From my point of view I don't think science knows what will happen if we eat or feed the animals GMOs. I can believe that there's no problem, but I can't see any evidence that there's no problem." He laughs again. "Of course I can't see any evidence for consequences. So who knows?" Better, he says, to just avoid the GMOs—out of concern for his own health and that of the Hungarian landscape.

"Are you a folk hero for standing up to Monsanto?" I ask. It was Monsanto seed shipments—shipments that were supposed to be GMO-free—that were tainted. "You became famous." Bognár's name was flashed around organic news outlets worldwide because he was the responsible official.

His demeanor is modest. "No, I don't think so. I just did my job. In our point of view it was clearly defined by law. We just did what we had to do." Monsanto, by definition, is not considered evil in Hungary—its non-GMO corn seed is embraced by farmers.

I want to engage Bognár as my organic label quest continues because just as GMOs polluted the conventional corn seed, so can traditional conventional products (and GMOs) pollute organics. Hungarian inspectors happened to catch the GMO shipment. But they don't check—can't check—every load of corn seed coming into the country. Perhaps the Rural Development Ministry's radical slash-and-burn response to finding the GMO seed acted as a deterrent—scaring away bad guys or influencing legitimate traders to take greater care. Perhaps similar theatrics are in order for the organic world. I ask Bognár why I should believe the organic label.

"That's a good question," he says. (I tighten—as I've mentioned, this is always an unsettling start.) "It's always a question: How the consumer can believe the label? The major problem is the lack of information available to the consumer. The food producer knows everything about his or her product. The authority," the Rural Development Ministry, "knows a lot about the product." The food chain is monitored, but not—of course—100 percent of all groceries; that would be an impossible logistical task. "The consumer only knows what the label contains. It should contain enough information for the consumer to rely on the food. I think the consumer can believe the label if they get enough information: what is organic, why is the product organic." Greater consumer awareness is needed, he says, so if we wonder what we're eating, we easily can trace it and travel back from fork to farm. But, Bognár insists, in Hungary food producers and grocers are obligated by law to inform curious consumers where the nuts and beans they sell originate.

His words are reassuring, but—notwithstanding the harsh image of burning Monsanto cornstalks—the Hungarian government Bognár serves is no progressive paragon. His prime minister, Viktor Orban, has been warned repeatedly by the European Union to reverse constitutional changes Orban pushed through the parliament that limit the independence of the judiciary, infringe on free speech, criminalize homelessness, and define family as a married man and woman along with their children.

"Does anybody do it?" I ask. "Has anybody demanded to know the sources of their dinner?"

"I don't know," he says, and he looks amused at the idea of chasing goulash and paprika and Tokay back to their sources. Ministry spot checks include traceback checks. "Our officials go to the food business operators and one of the first questions is, 'Please show us the traceability system.'"

I ask Bognár what he eats. His physique reminds me of one of my Hungarian cousins, a fellow who stuffs himself with the national diet of meats cooked in lard and plenty of noodles and scoops full of sour cream topped off with rich pastries and shot after shot of pálinka. "Will you be eating an organic dinner?"

I'm greeted with another laugh. "I don't think so! I believe that it is healthier, but I don't have time to be aware of the organic label."

"It's expensive," I offer as an escape.

But he rejects that concern. "For me, it's not the question of cost, it's the question of time. In Hungary now, if you want organic, you can find the organic corner."

"But it is a corner."

"Yes, it is a corner."

I found that corner in a down-market Spar in Győr. The market was in a depressing strip mall a few blocks from downtown Győr, a border city just inside Hungary on the Austrian frontier. A lonesome table in the produce section was littered with wilted this and bruised that, understandably ignored by shoppers, and not just because of the ugly factor. A kilo of *bio* onions was four times the price of the regular one; organic apples cost double what the conventional ones brought. Looking at those sad, overpriced onions was a stark reminder that organic food is no priority for the average Hungarian's diet and remains out of reach for most Magyar pocketbooks.

A few months later another GMO crop was destroyed, this one sugar beets valued by their owners as a million dollars' worth, yanked out of Oregon soil by what the FBI termed "economic sabotage." Organic farms share fertile valleys around Ashland with land used by the agribusiness company Syngenta. Along with a long list of other products, Syngenta grows GMO beets for seed. It is an international concern, and far from organic. "Insecticides, fungicides and herbicides protect crops from insects, diseases and competition from weeds," it informs potential customers.[93] The organic growers in the neighborhood fear cross-pollination and the polluting of their harvest with GMOs.

For several months Syngenta representatives and local organic farmers met, trying to create some sort of plan for coexistence. Just before the attack on the beets, Syngenta representatives quit the talks. Days later the company's GMO sugar beets were dead, drying in the hot July sun. Police told the local newspaper they figured "local activists" did the job. Organic crops near the Syngenta fields were destroyed the month before the beets were uprooted. Steve Fry's chard and beets are certified organic. Worries about infestation with GMO pollen led him to plow under rows of both. "GMO doesn't care if it gets a little bit of golden chard in their beet," Fry said, explaining why he killed his beets and chard himself. "We have zero tolerance for GMOs."[94]

Armed rent-a-cops in the L.A. Whole Foods. Burning GMO corn on the Hungarian plains. Clandestine warfare waged by organic and GMO growers in bucolic southern Oregon farmlands. The organic food industry is a long way gone from its peace-and-love, tie-dye, and have-a-nice-day days.

Chapter Fifteen

Sic Transit Italy

It is dawn on a cloudless late spring day in Italy, and I am sitting on the balcony of my apartment in Via Piana, looking down onto the Liri River valley at the sprawling city of Sora. A couple of hours farther west is Rome, where I landed the day before yesterday. To the east in the soaring Apennines (the mountain range where Natural Directions claims it forages) is Abruzzo National Park. I'm here, far off the packed Italian tourist trails, for an interlude on a family organic farm. Italy worried its neighbors in 2011 when over twenty-five hundred tons of beans, corn, and wheat showed up in its supply chains, food that was labeled organic yet turned out to be conventional. Certifiers and traders were arrested by the Verona fiscal police and ended up behind bars, "where people who do these things go," announced AssoBio, an Italian organic food producers organization. "Obviously the crime leaves the sector with a bad taste," proclaimed AssoBio, apparently without intending the pun. "The hunger for easy money of seven outlaws compromises the image, the hard work and passion of the other 47,658 companies that make the Italian organic an excellence that all the world envies."[95]

Despite the successful investigation and prosecution, the case added to Italy's sullied reputation as a haven for corrupt business practices and made organic foodstuffs from Italy further suspect. Typical is a news item from the *Times of Malta* in 2013 that tells a tale of soybeans, corn, and wheat labeled organic and seized by Italian customs, en route from Malta via Italy to other points in Europe. The problem, according to investigators cited by the paper: The load of Ukraine-grown beans and grain was adulterated with GMOs.[96] Another case was reported by the Berlin newspaper *Taz:* a criminal gang counterfeiting organic certificates and laundering conventional food through Italy into other European marketplaces. *Taz* correspondents Michael Braun and Jost Maurin reported that in the spring of 2013 Italian police seized fifteen hundred tons of corn and thirty tons of soybeans from the Ukraine and Moldova, labeled organic by a Moldovan certifier—corn and beans that landed in the Italian port of Pesaro—via Malta. Italian prosecutor Silvia Cecchi told the reporters her office was investigating a couple of dozen suspects, including Moldovan representatives of an Italian organic certification outfit. Cecchi said that other organic fraudsters relabeled products in Italy, but that the gang she caught "stamped 'organic' in Moldova, certified it right on site, then exported it and brought it to market." Such criminal sophistication makes discovering and stopping fraud extraordinarily problematic. Or, as Paolo Carne Molla, the president of the Italian organic food producers, processors, and distributors organization Federbio, told the paper, "We don't know who we can trust to talk to."[97]

And I'm supposed to trust the global trade in groceries that line the shelves of local supermarkets?

After I talk with Cecchi, the background I receive about the mislabeled imports only exacerbates my skepticism regarding imported "organic" food. The scam she's investigating, she tells me, is not just a onetime event in Pesaro. She's convinced the crooks were operating in other Italian cities—Cagliari, Larino, Campobasso, and Ravenna—importing conventional goods labeled organic. She sees links past Europe, a conspiracy connected with India and Brazil for sourcing tainted goods from Asia and South America destined to be relabeled organic. The tonnage initially reported is eclipsed by the new numbers she offers.

"The amounts are even higher," she says, making calculations while answering my query. "We seized more like 3,040 tons of corn, but this is just from one shipment. We also have other shipments of notable size. There are several thousand tons." The number of shipments investigated by her office suggests tofu- and tortilla-eaters across Europe who were adhering to an organic diet were dosed with conventional soybeans and corn—and worse. "We found dozens and dozens of shipments, and each of these had their own toxicity. One contained genetically modified foods. Others contained pesticides and other worrisome substances naturally prohibited in the sale of organic goods but also even in conventional goods." Prosecutor Cecchi expresses both disgust and concern. "These are alarming conditions. There is a basic scam in the exchange of these goods, and then there is another part of the investigation that deals with the contaminating substances found in these shipments. Therefore we had to hunt them down." The alleged crimes include both falsifying organic certificates and falsifying quality analyses.

Cecchi does not confirm that her office is investigating some two dozen suspects, because the case is open and the investigation is ongoing. She does tell me that she is accusing the suspects of wrongdoing characterized as transnational crimes. Transnational crimes are, by Italian definition, felonies—the extra charges for crossing borders are severe like those for crimes that become federal cases when they're committed across US state lines. If she does obtain guilty verdicts at trial (or if the suspects acknowledge guilt), she hopes to seize their profits. But her further hopes are even more ambitious. She wants to reach beyond Italy's borders and confiscate tainted goods en route to Italy. She hopes to punish the middleman and impede the illegal trade at its source. Meanwhile, as the investigation continues and she plots how to cooperate with her counterparts around the world, spreading the word about food scams is her priority.

"The proper reaction to this is to inform the public—the consumers—about this kind of fraud." Concerned and aware consumers, she says, would "block the market on which the criminals are selling" because they would not buy the tainted food. "Close these companies!" is her call. "Confiscate the products!" And lock up the perpetrators. With penalties that include prison time for the felonious "transnational crime," she sees guilty verdicts that could result in a minimum of five years behind bars and as much as ten years.

The international scope of the conspiracy is important for her to emphasize. It's not just Moldova, she says again, listing countries where she says fraudulent organic labels were affixed to foodstuffs destined for Italy and throughout Europe. It's a long list that she ticks off: Serbia, Romania, Ukraine, India, Brazil, Montenegro, and Slovenia. "These crimes were committed on a very wide global scale." Even *pura vida* Costa Rica is on her rap sheet. With goods hopscotching around the world, it's relatively easy for smugglers to mislabel and relabel food to hide its origin. That tactic can obscure the names of places with suspect reputations and instead show off products so that they seem to come from locales known for high quality. Malta, charges the prosecutor, is notorious as a lax stopover for the label-changing scam.

Italian companies are players in the conspiracy she describes, companies that created subsidiaries in Third World countries to falsely certify products as organic. "They did this in order to jump the barriers and avoid the inspection of the products." One way that they went about jumping these barriers and many of the regulations that have to do with customs was to associate themselves with a European Union country—for example, Malta—where there is a lower standard for inspections. It wasn't just Moldova, "it was this geographic distribution of associations that faked being organic producers. These associations were working with Italian companies in order to avoid the inspections during export or import."

But Cecchi didn't just uncover faked or counterfeit organic certification documents. She charges that those under investigation also engaged in fraudulent analysis of the food products being traded across international borders into Italy. "We found a correlation between those who were verifying the analysis and those who were being verified. They were all working together." The prosecutor is exercised about exactly what stinks about organic certification when the certifiers are paid by those they certify. There is an incentive to be sloppy—or worse—when your bills are paid by the guy you're inspecting. Unless an independent investigator like Cecchi gets suspicious or lucky, there's precious little oversight of the worldwide organic business and plenty of opportunity for mutual back-scratching.

Just as was the case with Lajos Bognár, I wonder if Cecchi herself eats organic food. And if so, does she shy away from organic food produced in the Third World? She figures all those imports are risky. "The real problem is that transporting these goods such a long distance can cause issues, like germination, mold, or growing mushrooms. Organic food should therefore come from the country in which it will be sold. I believe that the products that come from India and Brazil are all at risk—even if they meet the regulations—always at risk of contamination." But she's happy to offer further opinions now that I've asked about her personal proclivities. "Organic products should be produced as close to where they will be consumed as possible. This also makes the food more connected to the natural cycle of life and digestion. When I talk about organic products, I don't mean just a product that hasn't been treated with chemicals; that's the minimum. I mean that the concept behind organic food is that it was grown in nature, fighting to live, using its own biochemicals as weapons, we can say, in order to survive. This kind of product is so much healthier for the ingestion of the consumer as well as for nature.

These kinds of foods are filled with vitamins and minerals that are good for humans, as well as natural antibodies."

Cecchi reminds me of the prosecutor back home in Eugene, Scott Bradford, who put Harold Chase in federal prison. Bradford and Cecchi are organic aficionados, fighting for both the public good and what they themselves eat. They both exert the substantive powers of their respective offices to fight criminals out to make big bucks in bogus food.

After the sobering exchange with Cecchi, I again take advantage of the refuge I find at the organic farm, I need a respite from the news that *bio* on the label could just mean GMO. The farm is an oasis far removed from the bad news I'm collecting.

Italian Organic Farm Idyll

Roosters wake me up early on the farm, along with a myriad of competing tunes from songbirds; it's a nice alternative to the garbage trucks that did the same job in Vienna. The red tile roofs of neighboring white stucco houses line the hillsides, houses spotted around intimate olive orchards and plots of vegetables. A goatherd meanders home with her flock. I'm in a utopian space, the envy of colleagues I left back in the workaday world. When I told a usually nonviolent city friend about my farm interlude, he sent back a message of not-well-disguised envy: "I'll have to say that the last paragraph of your note is one that stirred feelings of—well, let's just say deep burning hatred. Organic farm between Rome and Naples? Yeah, maybe you'd like a good punch in the face!"

He's right to be jealous.

Sheila and I are at a property called Italy Farm Stay, where the evenings are just as idyllic as the mornings. Proprietor Antonello Siragusa welcomes us to dinner, and we sit down at a long communal table for a glass of organic red wine, made by Antonello's father, Giuseppe (his mother, Maria, is chief cook). After working as a waiter in

San Francisco, Antonello returned to the family homestead convinced he knew what would attract the tourist trade: organic food amid the peace and quiet of what looks like a travel poster for idyllic Italy.

"The wine is delicious," I tell Giuseppe.

He smiles. "*Biologico,*" he tells me, "*sin solfiti.*" No sulfites.

Dinner is served by Linda; she came to the farm as an organic tourist, trading work for room and board. Before we know her relationship to Antonello ("She's my wife," and the mother of their two daughters), Sheila asks her how long she's been on the farm.

"Four years." Linda smiles, too.

"And how long will you stay?" Sheila asks.

"Forever." Her answer comes in a soft and satisfied voice, through a slight Dutch accent. Ensconced as we are in what immediately feels to us like a rural paradise, it was easy to appreciate her decision even without factoring in the family ties. We eat penne with tomato sauce, big fresh anchovies in garlic and olive oil, tomatoes with chopped onions, lentils, and a lettuce salad. All washed down with Giuseppe's organic wine, first red and then white. That night is the festival of San Antonio di Padova in the next village up the road, Forcella. We're exhausted, but Antonello convinces us join the party. We dance to rollicking and romantic Italian pop tunes that a band called I Sottotono plays on a stage next to the church in the little piazza. No gringos but us. We buy two wine tickets at what we think is two euros a glass and receive two *bottles* of local (unlabeled) quite delicious wine. Paradise. As we open the second bottle of wine, I picture tearing up our return airline tickets and agreeing then and there to move to Italy.

The next day, to escape the heat and humidity at the farm, we crank up the air-conditioning in the rented Ford and head into Abruzzo

National Park. High in the mountains we settle in for a late lunch of local trout at a trattoria in the village of Villetta Barrea next to the lake named Barrea. As we're in Italy, we of course order wine. The surprise comes when we look at the label. It's local and announces in a bold typeface: *Ottenuto da uve cultivate in Agricoltura Biologica.* Even though it's just a house white, it's made from organically grown grapes.

Dinner is again at the communal table on Italy Farm Stay. Antonello (we were immediately on a first-name basis) is a clever marketer. He says he came up with the name so that when a traveler is searching the Internet for opportunities to stay on an Italian farm, his business will prevail. It works. That's exactly how I found him.

"Before I got the certification for my farm," he recalls, "I thought that *bio* was like growing vegetables without the use of any chemicals or pesticides whatsoever." He speaks English with precision and with a Hollywood-Italian accent: not quite Chico Marx, more romantic sounding—along the lines of Marcello Mastroianni. "But after the certification I realized that you're actually allowed to use some chemicals, just certain categories that are not too strong and maybe in less quantity. This is what the certification is about."

The ICEA certifies Italy Farm Stay—the *Instituto per la Certificazione Etica e Ambientale,* the same outfit that certified my white wine at Lake Barrea. ICEA boasts "13,000 controlled companies, 300 inspectors, 20 offices in Italy and 10 abroad." The institute is proud of its cooperation with the Verona police in the 2011 fraud case that's contributed to Italy's sour reputation regarding the veracity of its organic foodstuffs. The ICEA president that year, Nino Paparella, says that the Verona exposé is proof certifications works. "Bad apples cannot throw mud on the entire system, consisting of thousands of farmers, technicians and inspectors who work every day with professionalism and honesty. In this framework, they too become victims."[98]

Looking out over the quiet of his farmstead, Antonello Siragusa is not impressed. "They come every year," he says about the ICEA certifiers, "but it's a little bit strange because you pay this organization to check you. It's a system for this reason that might not work so well."

How refreshing it is to hear him echo my escalating disgust with the incestuous certification process. With a wry smile he offers a harsh example of the flawed process, one that highlights its ridiculousness. "It's like you have to pay the police to arrest you. And if you pay them, they might not want to arrest you." The certifiers come to the farm, he says, and mostly just ask him questions and check his paperwork, "and not the substantial aspects. But in my case I think they might not be so strict because I don't sell anything." It's hard to imagine why there would be such a double standard, especially since Antonello serves the farm's fruits and vegetables to paying customers—in essence selling the produce.

"Maybe they're not even strict in that case," he muses.

Antonello says ICEA inspectors rarely trek around Italy Farm Stay. "The first time they walked a little bit here." Antonello points from the farmhouse porch where we're sitting in the shade to the garden in front of us. "The farm goes down to the creek. They didn't check the whole farm." Credibility for an organic farm depends on the farmer. "It's your moral obligation rather than the farm being scrutinized." He was raised with an organic food philosophy, he tells me. "My father grew food for us. The food that we grow is also for my daughters and it's for me. These principles belong to us."

That attitude is vast fields distant from organic factory farming, and government subsidies for organic acreage add complexities. Some farmers, Antonello is convinced, get into organics not because they believe it is a morally responsible act, but because of available subsidies and because the niche is growing. "It might be like a mere business, a best business. In that case because you pay the people who check your farm for certification, maybe the certification process doesn't work so well."

"You're suspicious of the process?" I ask.

"Yes," he responds with no hesitation, "because you pay them to inspect you and there is competition between certifiers. They don't want to give you problems. They want to make it easy so that you stay with them and not go to the competition." Certifiers with reputations for fielding strict inspectors, he theorizes, are apt to lose business to those who conduct superficial walkabouts such as the one he observed at Italy Farm Stay.

Antonello pays about four hundred dollars a year for his organic certification, an investment he thinks pays off because of its marketing value for the tourist trade he seeks. But as a business decision it required no analysis beyond the fact that the government subsidizes his operations about four hundred dollars a year because it is organic. And he does apply some of the allowable pesticides to his grapes. "We use stuff that's not strong, basically natural stuff."

He says either the farm is planted with crops that don't need treatment or the crops are located in places on his acreage where the pests don't frequent. Olives are an example. He identifies a fly that preys on olives growing near his farm, a fly that leaves his fruit alone, fruit thriving on trees planted along a hillside. Perhaps the breezes through the gullies shoo the flies off. He says he does not use chemical fertilizers for his olives even though that means his yields suffer. "We get approximately half of what the other people get. But we don't mind because it's only for ourselves. We prefer to plant more trees rather than use chemical fertilizer that also costs money." The money spent on fertilizer, he says, can outweigh the value of the extra yield. "People get greedy. They want to get more and more from one tree. Therefore they use chemical fertilizer."

Antonello's clients like figs, and the fig trees require no help. His voice rises and falls with the music of his accent, music accentuated by the vowels he adds as if the words were Italian. "Figs-a are very perishable and they don't have a big market. The people who come here happen to like-a them, so we grow them. And also, they're a good tree for the shade." He says when he initially studied English he made an attempt to eliminate his accent. But when he discovered that it was considered charming, he quit trying to sound American. "Pomegranates don't need anything. Persimmons don't need anything. Plums don't need anything. The fruits that don't give us any problems, we grow them. The fruits that give us problems, we don't grow them." He laughs. The farm follows the same basic strategy for vegetables. No more potatoes, for example. Giuseppe was killing potato-eating bugs every day by hand. "It's lots of work. It's not practical."

When Antonello goes into Sora to shop for what he doesn't raise on the farm, he says he favors what's marked organic but looks at the label with caustic eyes. "When I go to a restaurant, I don't drink wine because they use sulfites, even when the label says organic." Later I check the label again on the wine I brought home from the Lake Barrea restaurant. Sure enough: *contiene solfiti*. "They say, 'wine from organic grapes.' The chemicals they use give me a headache. Some people are not sensitive, but I am. Maybe because I am used to eating organic food," he offers as self-analysis. "I'm a delicate flower." He displays, I learn fast, what usually is a bizarre (and often charming) sense of humor. The first night, when we asked what was for dinner, he told us it was a local specialty: braised goat testicles. "I would prefer to eat everything that is organic, but I'm not so strict, so fanatical. I don't think it's good to be fanatical."

Antonello Siragusa may not be a fanatic, but his experiences with the organic food bureaucracy ensure that he's a skeptic. "If I see on the label the same certifying organization I'm with," he says, flashing a wide grin, "I think, 'How strict are they going to be when they check the farm?' since they are not so strict with me. Will they be strict when they inspect a farm that is selling? Maybe they use a different policy. I don't know."

Pointing a Finger Back at Northern Europe

All roads may lead to Rome, but try finding an address in that sprawling city with no GPS and no map and no roaming connection to the iPad. Sheila and I are on the Autostrata as the late spring temperature climbs toward one hundred and the iPad goes dark. We take what looks like a promising exit and head through the apartment blocks on the outskirts, following the flow of traffic, encouraged that we are indeed heading for the city center as the architecture changes from 1960s utilitarian to the ornate of a century before. We are further encouraged by a Roman ruin here and a Roman ruin there, pretty thrilled when we pass the railroad station, and convinced we can get specific directions from the concierge when I spot a grand-looking building aptly labeled with a fading sign that reads GRAND HOTEL.

I double-park (it's Rome; everybody double-parks) and feel as if I look like a player in a 1960s Italian movie as I walk through the suffocating heat to the hotel. I am wearing a white linen suit and very dark wire-rimmed glasses, and on my head is the Panama hat I bought in Costa Rica for the trip out to Ernie Carman's coffee *finca*. (I had the suit custom made by Luigi, a tailor in Cairo who told me that he had been forced to leave his hometown. I harbored thoughts of intrigue—spies maybe, or the Mafia—until I wore it for a few weeks; he was likely chased from Italy because of his sloppy craftsmanship.) The Grand Hotel is now the opulent St. Regis, and when I show the concierge the address for the farm lobby Coldiretti, he points at an adjacent street, saying I will find the place just a few blocks from the hotel. Who needs a map, a GPS, or an iPad? I've stumbled across Rome like a steely in a pinball machine and landed at my appointment. *Buona fortuna!*

Stefano Masini is a professor of food law at the University of Rome Tor Vergata and heads the Environment Sector at Coldiretti, a nationwide advocacy group for Italian farmers. He's convinced that inadequate food-labeling laws in Italy contribute to fraud in the organic food business. His office is on the top floor of a villa, in a complex hidden behind high walls on the Via XXIV Maggio. The grounds are lush, featuring a lawn and towering palm trees, and offer welcome relief from the hectic Rome streetscape. Even on this steamy day—I am bathed in my own sweat—Masini's tie is knotted tight. A lone duck illustrates the Greenpeace calendar on his office wall. Through the windows the rooftops of Rome stretch off to distant hills.

I query him about why Coldiretti is lobbying the Italian government for stricter food-label laws. "Do you remember mad cow disease?" he asks me. Of course I do. (His question reminds me of a joke from that era: A woman goes into a shop in Yorkshire, points at a side of beef, and says to the butcher, "I just want enough to make me slightly eccentric.")

Because of the devastating nature of bovine spongiform encephalopathy, Masini says, it became obligatory in Italy for producers to identify the origin of meat products. Since that time other foods have been added to the list of those whose origin must be stated on the package: fish, olive oil, honey, and all fruit. But if food is processed—say, a spaghetti sauce made from tomatoes, olive oil, mushrooms, garlic, and onions—and processed in Italy, a legal label can identify it as an Italian product without bothering to note that all those components came from Africa, Asia, and South America. It is an obfuscating—if not outright dangerous—loophole in the law.

Masini wants the Italian government to mandate that labels inform consumers not just what's in a can or jar but also where it all originates—and not just for food safety factors. "If you import from Asia, where teenagers work," he says, "you engage in unfair competition with Italian farmers," not to mention the inhumane costs of child labor. Environmental costs are on his list, when food is imported into Italy from countries where pollution controls are minimal and minimally enforced. These human costs of our fancy food too often fail to enter our "you are what you eat" debates. "The food business must respect consumer will. Only products with thorough and honest labeling should be sold. Choosing one product or another must be a conscious decision." International agribusiness, he says, lobbies against such detailed labeling, although if a product is identified as organic with the EU seal and it contains just one farmed ingredient, the locale of the farm is required to be listed under the EU logo.

"Italy is different from other countries because our food is special," Masini says; he offers automobiles as an example. Car showrooms worldwide do not try to hide the pedigree of a Maserati or a Ferrari. That the brands of sought-after cars are identified with Italian design and craftsmanship is a selling point. The same is true with food—organic and otherwise. If a label says "Product of Italy," it conjures a sought-after taste, style, and quality that increase its perceived value. That stock-in-trade is compromised if ingredients sourced elsewhere are hidden behind a "Made in Italy" label, which brings to mind Panera, the chain eatery that changed its name from the St. Louis Bread Company. "Italy has a landscape, a culture and history that's valuable for marketing." And for abusing. Masini says Coldiretti keeps track of some fifteen thousand crimes committed annually in the food industries, including organic fakery and fraud.

Italian food is, of course, special the world over; that's hard to argue with. But Italy suffers another reputation in the food business, the sullied reputation. I tell Masini about the charges I heard in Austria: Italy is a nice place for a holiday, but the organic controls are slippery. His response is immediate and tribal. "I don't trust German products," he says, dismissing his fellow European Union farmers to the north as he cites the dioxin scandal that roiled the German egg industry in 2011. Dioxin in chicken feed spread into organic eggs.[99] Two years later the validity of German organic eggs was questioned again when government prosecutors claimed companies were calling their chickens free range when they were, in fact, cooped up in pens.[100] At that time the German consumer protection minister, Ilse Aigner, said if the charges were true it was a "massive fraud against consumers."

"The Germans behaved badly," Masini says with disgust, "because at the beginning of the scandal they said it was Spain's fault, and then they blamed the Italians." Such finger-pointing, he tells me, violates the philosophy that Europe is one big happy family. "Italian food products are the safest in Europe because of our controls."

Maybe so. Italian food certainly tastes *delizioso*. But what about those porous borders? Italy seems a bridge from lawless lands into the rest of Europe. Masini says it's not just Italy where bogus food slides into Europe. "Rotterdam port is a place where food is coming into Europe mislabeled and the quality control is poor. Our problem is Europe-wide." But we tend to embrace our own. "Food is culture and every country has its own culture. Europeans don't tend to mix up their cultures. We promote our own cultures."

I break journalistic character for a moment and whisper across the desk to Stefano Masini, "I like Italian food more than I like Austrian food." So do most of my Austrian friends, I imagine.

Chapter Sixteen

MY GROCER AGREES: WE DON'T KNOW BEANS ABOUT OUR BEANS

It's a sunny Sunday morning in Eugene, and I'm back in America after the long flight from Italy, home at the south end of the Willamette Valley, just that hour-long drive from farmer MacCormack's bean fields. My breakfast routine is a bowl of oatmeal and a cup of green tea. The oatmeal (Natural Directions!) sits in the cupboard and—since I am immersed in food labels these days—I glance at the bottle of Spectrum Naturals sunflower oil jammed against the oatmeal box. "USDA Organic," shouts the label, along with "expeller-pressed organic high-heat sunflower oil." QAI is listed as the certifier. Ingredients? "100% mechanically (expeller) pressed naturally refined high oleic organic sunflower oil." And from where is it sourced? The label offers that information, too: Product of USA, Switzerland, and/or Argentina. In other words, you—Mrs. and Mr. Customer—have no idea where it comes from, and neither Hain Celestial (the conglomerate that owns Spectrum) nor QAI offer any clues beyond the one, two, or combination of three continents.

Fed and with a green tea–level caffeine buzz, I meander across my sleepy college town to Market of Choice, where I bought the can of Bolivian black beans that conspired with the Kazakh walnuts to start this organic trek. The family-owned chain operates several stores in Oregon from its Eugene headquarters. The corporate offices are

Silicon Valley chic—the look is business casual, as is Rick Wright's. The company's president and CEO ushers me into the conference room; its high ceilings and glass walls suggest transparency in an office suite accessible only to those who know the doors' keypad codes. A sprawling, V-shaped, laminated hardwood meeting table fills the room—a room equipped for teleconferencing or sales presentations via the flat-screen monitor that dominates the back wall. Wright's blue jeans and sports shirt—the top button undone—match the decor, as does his faux-hawk hairstyle. He reaches for a pearl-flake coaster to protect the shiny table from his black coffee, and he waits for my first question.

Before I left home, Sheila and I figured that about 85 to 90 percent of our grocery dollars are spent at Market of Choice. I report that news to Wright. "Excellent," he says, offering a faint smile. I'm looking for common denominators because I do not want this to be an adversarial meeting. So I tell him another story. A caller to my local Eugene talk-radio show tarred me with what the caller intended as an insult. Winco is a Pacific Northwest discount grocer. "You don't sound like a Winco kind of guy," the caller spat at me, alluding to what he perceived as my elitist, leftist attitudes. "You sound like a Market of Choice guy." The reference elicits another faint smile from Wright. "Perfect," he says.

When I turn the conversation toward organic food and how he defines it, he offers his broader marketing philosophy. "We think of groceries as groceries. We blend it all together on our shelves, products our customers want."

"Because somebody might want a tofu hot dog with French's mustard, right?" I'm thinking of my own family's proclivities for mixing and matching.

"Absolutely," he agrees, "and somebody may end up buying tofu hot dogs who didn't necessarily want tofu but bought them and then thought, 'These are better than I thought.'"

"Or they might want tofu hot dogs because they don't want meat but they don't care if the tofu is organic."

"You're right," he says. "There are tons of differences in consumer shopping habits."

Back in the mid-1990s Market of Choice began stocking products labeled organic, a few years before the USDA established the federal organic standards. In those days Wright and his staff looked to Oregon Tilth for guidance about organic definitions and for guarantees that products met those definitions. Oregon Tilth and other similar outfits offered certification to their standards, standards that often exceeded those established in 2000 by the USDA. Eugene shoppers helped Wright figure out how to stock his stores; he calls his customers among the most sophisticated clientele anywhere regarding organic food.

"They're probably the most educated consumers I've come across in the whole country. Eugene and this area were the home of natural foods; it was the start of it." It certainly was one of the hotbeds of that *Whole Earth Catalog*–era back-to-the-land resurgence: Eugene, Berkeley, Ann Arbor, Boston, and Austin—home of that original Whole Foods store. "The craze kind of started here. They already know what they want," he says about his customers. "Stores around universities, where most of our stores are located, serve a super-educated consumer." That creates a distinct challenge for the grocer. "We absolutely have to deliver what we promise." One of those promises is that much of the food he stocks meets USDA organic standards.

Before the federal government standardized the legal-for-the-US definition of organic, Wright's crews double-checked the organic claims of his suppliers with independent audits, and they never found discrepancies. No longer do they send their own hired hands out into the field. "With the USDA National Organic Program established as the law of the land, we basically have to trust that the certifiers are doing their jobs." But he worries that with the organic market expanding so rapidly nationwide, "there probably is a lot more opportunity for fraud than there used to be. Back in the day, there was only a handful of people growing organic," he says about Oregon agriculture. "Now the large farms have taken over, and a lot of the large manufacturers are manufacturing products that they're calling organic." I'm thinking about Coca-Cola and Odwalla again, General Mills and Muir Glen. The spiking volume alone, Wright figures, creates opportunities for slippage in organic standards, if not outright fraud. "Anytime the market gets larger," he says, "there's a lot more opportunity for fraud to happen. You know the Grain Millers situation," he says, referring to Harold Chase, and as we talk Chase is still in federal prison, just a few miles up Interstate 5 from Eugene.

Now that Market of Choice relies on the National Organic Program to guarantee that products on the shelves marked with the USDA Organic seal are organic, Rick Wright is less than sanguine that the companies in business to certify products as organic are paid by the producers they certify. "They pay the person who comes to tell them they're doing their job right." He shakes his head at the opportunities for conflicts of interest.

"That smacks of potential trouble," I offer.

"Yes," he agrees. "Yes it does."

"Especially when there are many certifiers in competition for the business," I say.

"Exactly."

At this point in our chat I reach into my satchel and bring out the can of Natural Directions black beans marked "Product of Bolivia" that came from my neighborhood Market of Choice.

Wright looks at the familiar package design. Market of Choice, he tells me, is not a large enough chain to rationalize its own private label. As a member of the Unified Grocers cooperative, Market of Choice can take advantage of the group's buying power, and he chooses to stock the Natural Directions brand. That doesn't mean

Wright is thrilled to line his shelves with their products. "We've had many discussions with Natural Directions about where they're sourcing products. They had organic products coming from China and from Russia, from a number of places around the world, because there are only a few places to go in the US that are certified to provide an organic product in a can." It's an issue of volume. Natural Directions requires large quantities of black beans and other canned goods in order to satisfy the demand from shoppers.

I'm showing off the bean can, careful to keep it from marring the fancy conference room table.

"Where's it from?" asks Wright.

With the palm of my hand I hide the lid where the source is printed in blue ink. "Want to guess?"

"It's probably Russia," he proposes, and quickly adds, "I don't know."

"Bolivia," I say, and recount my doubts about the likelihood the beans could pass muster as Eugene-friendly organic. "How am I supposed to give this any credence?"

"Exactly," answers Wright. I'm surprised. He offers zero defense of Natural Directions and its beans. On the contrary, he joins me, equally mystified. "I agree. It's surprising how many of the national brands are still sourced from overseas. It's amazing."

I'm almost caught off-guard at his agreeableness. "So you, too, question the veracity of the claim on this label: organic and Product of Bolivia?"

"I would question it, but Natural Directions claims they have the processes in place to absolutely guarantee that it is an organic product."

Time to spill more beans. I tell Wright about Natural Directions and its certifier QAI denying my request to visit the bean fields in Bolivia. I talk about my colleague, the Bolivian journalist Peter McFarren, and his insistence that there is no organic black bean export business of consequence from Bolivia to the United States.

I recount my exchange with one of the two USDA-certified organic black bean traders in Bolivia, who told me that his company is not exporting black beans to the United States this year—the other is incommunicado. I explain that I've filed a formal complaint with the National Organic Program, and that the USDA agreed to launch an official investigation into the origin of the Natural Directions beans. And I invite him—if I can find a field allegedly growing organic beans in Bolivia—to join me on a road trip to South America.

"You're my point man, Rick. I bought this can from you. How do I find out where these beans came from?"

His answer is succinct. "That's a very good question." *Uh-oh,* I think, my journalist's alert going off. But again Wright surprises me. He tells me that he's made demands of Natural Directions about their sources. "I said to them, 'We've got to know where this stuff is coming from.' Their basic answer was, 'Yes, we're working on the process.' I asked the same question you're asking: 'How are we going to guarantee that a product that says organic on it is organic?' Not just because it shows off the USDA stamp, because I don't know if that has much credence anymore. You hire somebody to look at your documents, and if the documents look accurate, you put the USDA label on it. It's just a bunch of paperwork. It's all a bunch of paperwork that goes to the USDA, and the USDA says these are organic. Like we found out right here in the Willamette Valley," he says about Harold Chase and his corn, "you can make something look organic that's not." He pauses to ruminate about the origin of my beans. "Yeah, I'd be very interested to find out myself how Natural Directions can tell me that they can guarantee that those black beans are organic."

"I'm working on it," I retort.

"Maybe I can help," he shoots back.

A fellow traveler! After months of being told the contents of the food I'm buying and eating are none of my business, I've found a coconspirator in my Eugene backyard.

"Just so you know," Wright adds, making it clear that he's important to the Natural Directions ledger sheet, "I probably sell half of all the product Natural Directions manufactures." And the black beans are one of the company's bestsellers.

"Then they better listen to you."

"You would think so."

Perhaps I'll be traipsing through Bolivian bean fields despite the ludicrous secrets kept by the big players of the organic food business.

"I would hope that Natural Directions is doing their job and the beans are organic," Wright says as we agree to work together to trace my beans back to their home, "because it would be very damaging to Natural Directions if they weren't."

Meanwhile, I can't help but wonder what's in the larder at Wright's house.

"We're mixed up," Wright says about what fills his family's fridge and kitchen cabinets. "We're everything from vegans to meat eaters to people who want organic to people who eat Oreos." He laughs. "My house is a typical Market of Choice shopping basket; it's got a mixture of everything." Not that the Oreo eater in the Wright household must be mutually exclusive from the organic fanatic. Nabisco once marketed Oreos that the company claimed were made with organic flour and sugar (alongside Ritz crackers, Wheat Thins, and Chips Ahoy! that also contained some organic ingredients).[101]

There's an appealing footnote to the Market of Choice role in this story. What initially drew my attention to the can of Natural Directions Bolivian beans was Sheila's concern about BPA in cans. Since her first inquiry, the potential health hazards of BPA have spread throughout the popular culture. For example, the syndicated newspaper column "Dr. Oz/Dr. Roizen" (written by the TV doctor

Mehmet Oz and the chief medical officer of the Cleveland Clinic Wellness Institute, Dr. Mike Roizen) devoted an article to the chemical. "Avoid BPA," they advised, calling it a "hormone-disrupting chemical." They cited studies linking it to infertility, prostate cancer, and obesity. "If you're pregnant or have young children," advised the MDs, "avoid foods packaged in plastics, and any container with the recycle code No. 7 on the bottom." And this admonition: "Dodge receipts. If you touch one, wash your hands soon—and always before touching a child. If BPA from receipts goes from your hands to food, you get a dose 1,000 times greater than from BPA cans."[102]

The other day Sheila noted a message on a receipt at the bottom of a bag of groceries from Market of Choice. We bought a pint of organic blueberries that day ($4.99), a bag of Guiltless Gourmet corn chips (they're baked, not fried, but not organic and set us back $2.99), two tubes of Tom's toothpaste (we sure are tempted by those old *Whole Earth Catalog*-type brands even though Tom's is now owned by Colgate-Palmolive), and a bag of organic carrots ($1.99). The message at the bottom of the receipt read, "We use Greenleaf Paper BPA-FREE thermal receipts."

Eureka?

A couple of weeks after my encounter with Rick Wright, my mobile phone rings on a sleepy summer Monday morning.

"Hello, Peter?"

"Yes." I don't recognize the incoming number.

"Rick Wright." Dramatic pause. "I have a farm."

"Let's go to Bolivia!" I tell him, channeling Butch Cassidy talking to the Sundance Kid. I ask for details.

Wright explains that he contacted Natural Directions and talked with a representative at the company whom he knows from previous business dealings. Nothing like being a valued customer for getting attention—his Market of Choice equals lots of dollars for the brand. "They buy it from a bean processor." Wright is looking at his computer as he conveys the breaking news to me. "They don't buy it directly from the farm." But the online trail leads him from the processor to the farm to the certifier. And the farm listed is Bolivian Shoji's, the same operation in Santa Cruz that ignored my earlier attempt to connect with it. The local certifier comes up on Wright's screen as we talk: Biolatina, with offices in La Paz.

The message from Natural Directions addresses the question that has puzzled me from the beginning of this quest: Why buy beans from Bolivia to sell in Oregon when beans grow in the Willamette Valley? "Our supplier is committed to purchasing all the beans from a U.S.A. source first," explained the Natural Directions contact. "They only buy outside of the U.S.A. as needed if the crop supply is depleted or at a substantial cost variance. The last several years have been difficult seasons for black beans in terms of supply quantities."

After almost of year of chasing my beans, it is finally time to get my hands dirty.

I check fares and schedules from Eugene to Santa Cruz de la Sierra.

Finding the Bean Field

Armed with the confirmation from Natural Directions that my black beans are indeed from Bolivian Shoji, I try again to make contact with the processor and distributor. Their website, an e-mail address, and a telephone number take only a few Google clicks to find. Trouble is that the website is dead, the telephone number doesn't ring through, and still another e-mail message to Bolivian Shoji goes unanswered.

Frustrated, I look out the window of my office at the University of Oregon and decide to crowdsource my colleagues. Out there across the campus are some of the best minds in academia, doing fieldwork worldwide. I spread the word along the grapevine that I'm looking for Bolivia experts. A few days later I hear from Derrick Hindery, a geography professor who engaged in extensive fieldwork in Bolivia, work that included developing close ties with NGOs that work with organic farmers! "I'd be very happy to help," he writes, citing his extensive academic and familial contacts in Santa Cruz, where Bolivian Shoji supposedly is headquartered. "Derrick," I write back, "I feel like I've hit the jackpot receiving your note."

The jackpot it is. After some creative detective work fueled by Hindery's familiarity with Bolivia, he manages to make contact with the bean producer in question. When we meet on campus, we trade Bolivia stories. I tell him about traveling with DEA officers into the Amazon basin, supposedly to arrest cocaine traffickers, and about the crowd that yelled, "Kill the Yankees!" and "String them up!" His story is much better: the romantic tale of meeting his wife in Bolivia at a conference dealing with environmental concerns, a meeting that was held in Santa Cruz. After the drug and love stories, we talk beans.

Hindery tells me he searched the Internet for contact numbers, just as I did. "Most of the phone numbers that were listed for Bolivian Shoji were the ones that you presumably tried." But Hindery is familiar with standard Bolivian phone numbers. He tells me he noticed that the number I've been calling is one digit short. A tenacious researcher, he pushed his search for the bean producer deep into Google's memory. He skimmed through more than a hundred results, looking for a phone number that was slightly different from the one I dialed, a phone number with the typical series of digits he was used to punching when contacting his colleagues in Bolivia. After a few clicks he found a number that matched the Bolivian norm. Minutes later he was talking to a fellow named Hiroshi at Bolivian Shoji in Santa Cruz.

"He was nice. He probably was a little suspicious. I summarized your interest in organic agriculture." Hindery was told that Bolivian Shoji does indeed produce organic black beans and buys the beans from mom-and-pop farmers like the coca growers I visited on my last trip to Bolivia, farmers with just a few acres and farmers suffering such a severe drought that this year there's not enough yield to export.

Their plots are in Charagua in the Chaco region, an enormous plain reaching from Bolivia into Argentina, Paraguay, and Brazil. Hindery told Hiroshi that I want to travel to Bolivia and visit the company's bean fields. Hiroshi said to call back tomorrow and talk to the boss.

"It sounds to me that it could be legitimate," Hindery says, noting my enthusiasm about the possibility of finding the source of my beans. "There are small farmers that do use pesticides," he concedes, speaking from his experience in the fields. "But a lot of them just don't have the means to purchase them." What a concept: organic by default due to a lack of funds to buy the 'cides.

When I call back the phone line is scratchy and the call brief. "Send an e-mail with details," Tetsuo Kochi at Bolivian Shoji says. A few days later Hindery connects me with Miguel Angel Crespo at Probioma, an organization in Santa Cruz that helps small landowners develop sustainable agriculture. Crespo (it's always reassuring to work with a fellow named Angel) offers to connect me with farmers in the Chaco growing organic black beans, and he says he'll help orchestrate a meeting with Bolivian Shoji. That's all I need to hear; I book my flights to Bolivia.

Meanwhile, I check in with the USDA to determine how the official investigation into my complaint is progressing. "I am still investigating the matter," Tammie Wilburn, the caseworker assigned to my beans and nuts writes from Washington. "It is NOP policy to not discuss the details of an open investigation, but I will promptly notify you of our findings upon case closure." Fair enough. I pack my bags for the Bolivian Chaco.

Just before I leave for Bolivia, in search of beans this time instead of cocaine, I make a stop across campus from my office and look in at the Schnitzer Museum to check out the Alberto Korda exhibit.

The bean fields I seek are not far from Che's last stand, and Korda's iconic photograph of *Comandante* Guevara is on display, the one in which he's looking off into the distance in 1960, the one reproduced on posters and T-shirts in greater numbers—according to the show's curator—than any other image save Mona Lisa's. It's titled *Guerrillero Heroico*. Seven years later Che was shot dead in La Higuera by first one and then several US-trained Bolivian soldiers. "I was surprised by his look," said Korda later about that famous faraway gaze, which combines ideally in the picture with the beret and its star, the rugged face and flowing hair.

Another Korda photograph in the gallery shows Che driving a sugarcane-cutting machine. Korda said Che asked him that day if he had ever cut sugarcane. When the photographer said no, Che told another worker, "Alfonso, find a machete for *compañero* journalist." The words feel like a fitting send-off as I head for Bolivia—of all places—looking for the source of my QAI-certified, USDA Organic can of Natural Directions black beans.

En Route to Santa Cruz de la Sierra

Bumped up to *clase ejecutiva*, I'm in seat 1F on Copa Airlines flight 125. A royal-blue tablecloth is spread out on my tray table, decorated by a plate of warm cashews and almonds along with a tasty glass of Chilean Riberas Cabernet Sauvignon Gran Reserva (with balsamic notes, the menu promises). Nonstop from Panama to Bolivia, but the total trip is four hops from Eugene via San Francisco and Houston, then on to Panama City and Santa Cruz. By the time I get to my downtown hotel, I'll have been traveling over twenty-four hours.

My body is packed with antityphoid this and antimalaria that; my suitcase is packed with DEET and mosquito netting, Permanone and Benadryl. There's yellow fever in the neighborhood (I've had my shot), along with dengue and that nasty Chagas disease, spread by the triatomine bugs (nicknamed kissing bugs and assassin bugs) that tend to drop off of rustic ceilings, find your nice warm skin, bite it, and defecate. When you scratch at the irritating place where Señor Bug used you for his toilet, you spread the Chagas parasite-laced feces into your blood, and years later the disease may cause a stroke or an aneurysm or make it difficult to swallow.[103] Don't scratch that itch.

As we fly over Colombia toward the equator, I check out the US State Department warnings about Bolivia. The list is long. "Roadblocks are common," cautions State, and "may occur without warning and have stranded travelers for several days." Hence for road trips, "take extra food, water and warm clothing." Between Santa Cruz and Cochabamba "violence and civil unrest, primarily associated with anti-narcotics activities, periodically create a risk for travelers. Confrontations between residents and government authorities over coca eradication have resulted in the use of tear gas and stronger force to quell disturbances. Pro-coca groups have expressed anti-U.S. sentiments," a warning that reminds me of the Amazon mob yelling, "Kill the Yankees!" at me on my last trip to Bolivia. But the Chaco is in the opposite direction from Santa Cruz. Nonetheless, watch out for "express kidnappings," says State, "incidents in which tourists are robbed and forced to withdraw money from ATMs." The modus operandi is nasty: "Typically the victim enters a taxi driven by a criminal and then an additional person or two gets in the vehicle. The victim is robbed and driven to an ATM where he or she is forced to provide PINs for debit and credit card withdrawals." Watch out for "false police," warns State, "persons using police uniforms, identification and even buildings modified to resemble police stations."

Finally, says State, guard against "choke and rob" assaults. "Victims report being choked from behind until they lost consciousness and later awoke to find all their possessions gone." (I sip my wine and wonder how I would go about untangling myself from garrotes at ATMs.) Don't travel alone is the safety and security advice offered, particularly when you're out wandering late at night and/or drunk. Pretty good advice for New York and San Francisco, too—and even sleepy Eugene. I order another Riberas Gran Reserva and settle into my cushy leather chair, watching the sun set through the thunderheads of a lightning storm over South America—cartoonlike bolts of primal electricity flashing at thirty thousand feet.

Chapter Seventeen

MY BEANS GO HOME

The next night I wander over to the city's main square, the Plaza 24 de Septiembre, across the street from my hotel, and it is jumping: couples kissing and hugging; kiddies chasing each other; boys break dancing to boom-box noise, showing off head spinning and airborne somersaults. "*Vino para mi, vino para ti,*" sings a strolling band dressed in black capes with red sashes, castanets clacking and guitars strumming. Shoeshine stands compete with wandering coffee salesmen pushing carts jammed with pitchers of strong coffee and steaming milk—the salesmen wearing stark white jackets and caps like milkmen wore for their 1950s delivery rounds. The plaza is framed with colonnaded colonials painted as white as the coffee peddlers' uniforms. Bells in the spotlit brick cathedral announce each quarter hour with a few lilting dings. A larger-than-life statue of Colonel Ignacio Warnes—a hero of the fight for independence from Spain—looms over the festive scene, the colonel's unsheathed sword pointed majestically forward, ready to protect the organic bean fields out in the Chaco, I allow myself to fantasize. Caricature artists are on duty along with balloon sellers. Carts lined with sticky candied apples and pushed by expressionless peddlers cruise the crowd. Palm fronds drift in the temperate breeze. A telescope is pointed at the bright full moon, and for a coin the astronomer-on-duty offers a look and an adage: "Both the heavens and the earth are God's work." At the Café Irlandes on the balcony overlooking that storybook Latin

American plaza scene, dinner is a perfectly grilled trout from Lake Titicaca washed down with an unidentified Bolivian red table wine that competes quite favorably with the airline Riberas Cabernet.

My first Santa Cruz meeting is with Fernando Gonzáles, the general manager of the bean, quinoa, and sesame seed producer Gramma. I'm taking advantage of all my contacts to secure an appointment at Bolivian Shoji, but in the midst of that hectic work I want to take advantage of being in the neighborhood to meet with the manager at Gramma—the company was in the organic bean business but ceased such operations after a brief test, and I want to know why. Gramma's offices are a twenty-minute taxi trip from the plaza, a ride in a crumbling Toyota with cracked side-view mirrors, through the city's vast chaotic and dusty sprawl—squeegee men wiping windshields and stooped grandmothers selling sugarcane juice are on the job at each red light. A block down a dirt road from the traffic-filled boulevard of jumbled commerce I've been jammed on is Gramma's headquarters, a manicured oasis of offices and warehouse space. Gramma's contract farmers in the Chaco grew organic black beans that the company processed and exported, an endeavor that ended after a few years.

"The black bean is the noblest bean," Gonzáles tells me as we sit at his office desk. "It resists drought and disease." For a few years in the early 2000s, Gramma was selling its organic beans into the European market. But the organic crop yields were less than what was harvested from fields treated with pesticides and herbicides. The result: The company was making no extra money for all the extra trouble, plus it feared the untreated beans were susceptible to fungus attacks during the long trip from South America to the Old World. Gramma, Gonzáles says, shut down its organic bean experiment without ever approaching the North American market with them. My beans weren't his. Check with Bolivian Shoji, he advises. They're in the organic black bean business. Talk with Tetsuo Kochi.

"Delicate" is the word agronomist Gonzáles chooses to describe organic agriculture. "One has to have good faith in the people involved." He fears that if an organic farmer faces losing his crop to an infestation of pests, he'll be tempted to stop the insects with pesticides.

The next day I finally reach Tetsuo Kochi by telephone at his office, and he invites me to come check out the Bolivian Shoji plant that afternoon. It's located in a sprawling industrial park far from the plaza, a district where the streets have no names and the buildings have no numbers. My taxi driver gets lost, which is understandable considering the directions we are working with: "At the Virgin of Cotoca statue, pass over a bridge and go one hundred meters. Turn right when you see the Kulzis sign and go another two hundred meters." We hail a guard at a warehouse gate near the Kulzis sign and she provides more specific directions. The cab bounces along a rutted dirt road and we round a corner to find a sign for Bolivian Shoji. After chasing my beans for over a year, no question I feel some bizarre sense of accomplishment as we pull off the road and into the company's compound. A fierce wind keeps the Santa Cruz flag on full display at Shoji's front gate; in just a few days Santa Cruz celebrates 203 years of independence from Spain, and the department's flags fly throughout the city (Santa Cruz is one of Bolivia's nine constituent departments, or states). A tractor-trailer is in the yard about to be filled, I learn later, with beans destined for Israel. Shoji ships worldwide. The guard at the gatehouse points me toward the offices above the warehouse.

Kochi greets me with a wide smile and with what I interpret as thoughtful curiosity as I recount my bean quest. He's topped with a shock of white hair that looks out of place on his youthful unlined face. On the wall behind his desk is a world map, and tacked to it is a calendar courtesy of the Maersk shipping line. This month's illustration is the Golden Gate Bridge. It's comforting to see a touch of home so far from it.

There's a look on Kochi's face that suggests he's wondering what the heck I am doing in his office. As I finish telling him about my research from my pantry back to the beans' place of birth, I ask if his company trades in organic black beans.

"*Muy pocos*" is his to-the-point answer. Very little. Only about 5 percent of Bolivian Shoji's annual bean output is certified organic.

He explains that there is little financial incentive for him to deal with organic beans because the price differential between the conventional beans and the organic ones is only about 10 percent. "That's good for the small farmer," he says about his organic suppliers, "but for a big processor it complicates production." Kochi must make sure his workers efficiently segregate the organic and conventional beans.

Kochi confirms that the black beans he exports grow on plots of just a few acres cultivated by indigenous family farmers deep in the Chaco region. Large agriculture operations, he says, express little interest in the organic sector, both because of the rigors required to meet international organic standards and because of the extra work. "Organic farmers weed only by hand. Conventional farmers can kill weeds with Monsanto *glifosato*," he says, using the Spanish word for glyphosate, the chemical well known in North America as Roundup.

"But isn't the *glifosato* dangerous?" I interrupt; it is a gentle query since the vast majority of his company's output is conventional and hence laden with 'cides.

"That will be seen in the future" is his philosophical response.

"If there's only a nominal price difference and since working the land without *glifosato* is difficult, why do these farmers grow organic beans?" I ask.

Just these few minutes into our conversation, I am excited. I'm feeling pretty confident I'm going to meet the farmer who grew my beans. As he further describes his suppliers, I begin to get a picture of the simple heritage of my Bolivian black beans. The Chaco farmers do almost all of their work by hand. Consequentially, if they can get even a slightly better price for organic beans, it is worth their while. In addition, there is little history of 'cide use by these family farmers. And no nearby farmers crop dust, so there is no danger of overspray onto the organic fields.

"The Chaco indigenous small farmers don't know chemical products," says Kochi. "We tell the farmers that this zone is organic and that they cannot use chemicals." There is no conflict about that prohibition. "They're not accustomed to using chemicals."

Working the land to earn money is not a part of the Chaco bean farmers' cultural heritage, Kochi tells me—from his perspective as a merchant and an immigrant to Bolivia from Okinawa (there is a consequential population of Japanese immigrants and Bolivians of Japanese ancestry thriving in Santa Cruz's agriculture sector). "With a few acres they're happy because there are fish in the river and there is meat in the mountains. At home they grow some corn, yucca, and rice. They have enough for their family. For centuries they never worked."

Never worked? They're fishing and hunting. They're cultivating enough corn, yucca, and rice to feed themselves. That's not work? But Kochi means work to accumulate wealth, of course. And he's proud to be an agent of change. "They're learning," he says.

It's time for show-and-tell. I reach into my satchel and pull out the can labeled Natural Directions Organic Black Beans that—over a year ago—started this trek. I hand it to Kochi and point out the blue lettering on the top of the can that reads "Product of Bolivia."

"Are these your beans?" I ask.

He studies the label, intrigued by the American packaging.

"Could be," he says. "We sell to a broker, and we don't know where the product goes." He rolls the can around in his hand. "Could be ours," he says. "Probably is ours." I agree. Bolivian Shoji and Alimentos Naturales Latco are the only organic bean exporters certified to sell organic black beans into the US market, and Latco told me that lately it has not been sending beans north. Kochi's "probably ours" is good enough for me.

Remembering how protective QAI and Natural Directions were about the provenance of my can of beans, I summon my most diplomatic Spanish and ask Kochi if it's possible to pay a visit to the organic farmers who supply him with black beans.

"It's possible," he says, "but it's very far from here."

Far? I've come over six thousand miles to find and talk with these bean farmers. What are a few more miles at this point in my journey? "It's necessary for me to speak with the farmers and to see their operations in order to successfully complete my research," I say.

Kochi has been leaning back in his office swivel chair, accommodating my questions and suffering me as if I am an unwanted interruption to weather until my inquiries cease. But when I explain that I don't care how far I must travel, I need to connect with the source of the beans, his attitude changes. He grabs his telephone, punches in a number, and commands, "I've got a gentleman from the United States here who needs to see the organic black bean farms." He talks logistics with his employee on the other end of the line and looks back at me. "It's a seven-hour trip," he says.

I give him a thumbs-up and ask for advice on how to get to the bean fields. Rent a car? Take the bus? Can I get there by train? Kochi dismisses such thoughts, telling me it's impossible for me to make the trip alone. I would never find the farms. And without an introduction, he implies, I shouldn't expect the farmers would talk with me even if I could find them. He smiles and tells me to be ready at four in the afternoon the day after tomorrow because he's assigning one of his men to take me the 175 or so miles to Charagua in a company four-wheel-drive truck. I do a quick calculation and wonder: seven hours to negotiate 175 miles? I can do that on I-5 in half that time with most of the traffic passing me.

Kochi shows off his teeming warehouse to me as we continue to talk beans. Big sacks stacked upon sacks of beans—sixty to seventy kilos of beans in each. Towering machines clean beans from the fields. Women in white smocks, hairnets, and face masks stand at a broad table piled with a seemingly endless supply of beans and finish the cleaning job. A chain of sweating men carries the bags filled with beans bound for Israel to the waiting truck, only one heavy bag each.

I head back to the hotel, ready for my road trip to Charagua in a comfortable Shoji truck, pleased I'm not on the overnight bus to the wilds of the Chaco.

Southbound on Bolivia Route 9

Charagua is the border market town where the Bolivian army stopped advancing Paraguayan troops during the Chaco War in the early 1930s. Before it's time to depart for the remote area, I walk down to the Hipermaxi to buy some supplies for the road. Bottled water (with a Coca-Cola Bolivia label suggesting *viviendo positivamente,* living positively), a big bag of peanuts (oven roasted with no oil and no salt), and a bar of Para Ti brand dark chocolate (57 percent cacao) from Bolivia's capital, Sucre. Wandering around the supermarket's aisles I stumble on a bizarre example of globalization. The mostly English-language label catches my eye: All Natural Casa Fiesta Whole Black Beans. I turn the can around to read the fine print: Bruce Foods Corporation/General Offices: New Iberia, LA/Product of USA. "Casa Fiesta is a full line of authentic Mexican prepared foods and ingredients sold in supermarkets in over 100 countries worldwide," proclaims Bruce Foods with understandable pride.[104] Crazy. While Bolivians are shipping black beans to me in Oregon, my Cajun friends in Louisiana are sending gringo beans south to Bolivia. Why? Maybe Bruce Foods figures there's cachet among south-of-the-border consumers for all things Yankee. But there's no indication that Casa Fiesta's beans are particularly popular—they're stacked deep on the supermarket's shelf.

It's the first full day of Southern Hemisphere spring as I journey out of Santa Cruz in a brand-new Nissan pickup with Yelio Prado, Shoji's liaison with the indigenous farmers who manage to cultivate the dry Chaco. Prado is a jolly and relaxed fellow who seems perfectly happy to head south as the day wanes. He confirms that we'll be on the road for about seven hours.

"Seven hours for a few hundred kilometers?"

"We need to drive calmly and watch for animals on the road," he says. Fair enough. A calm Third World drive sounds good to me; preferable to the daredevil high-speed tiny Toyota taxi rides in Tunisia that made me nauseated or terrified or both. But as we leave the urban sprawl and hit desolate countryside, we're rolling along at a decent pace. I figure we can make Charagua in half the estimated time, just after dark. Ha. After a couple hours driving south on Route 9, we cross the Rio Grande at Abapó, where we fill the truck with gas (at about two bucks a gallon—Bolivia is an oil producer). As we continue onward I lean back in my seat, resigned to a long ride.

Prado has turned the Nissan off the Route 9 two-lane blacktop, and we are moseying down a rutted dirt road, up hillocks and down into gullies, fording some streams and crossing over others on one-lane wooden bridges. At the crawling rate we're traveling, I figure we'll be lucky to make Charagua by midnight. As we meander along, Prado picks up his phone and checks in with one of Bolivian Shoji's contracted farmers. He asks if we can stop off and talk beans. It's clear from listening to Prado's side of the conversation that the farmer he calls Pedro is surprised by the last-minute request, but then acquiesces to the impromptu nighttime visit.

"There is no bean crop this year because it's been so dry," Prado says, confirming the news I heard while still in Oregon. "There's been no rain." And the farmers who sell organic beans to Shoji do not irrigate their land. Prado is an agronomist who specializes in organic agriculture. He says that Biolatina, the certifying company Shoji uses, comes to the Chaco once a year to check the farms and the company's documents. He shows me a sheaf of papers that lists each of the farmers, indicates the amount of acreage cultivated, and asserts that no 'cides are used—pesticides, herbicides, fungicides. We drive on as the day turns to night, the truck's headlights picking out looming dirt and rock obstacles, treacherous ditches, and bridge approaches. We see a pickup dark, quiet, and still—a truck that missed a bridge. We stop and shine a flashlight into what we see is an empty cab.

My Beans Meet Their Maker

The kilometers and hours click by slowly. We encounter only a couple of cars and buses—one of the buses left empty in the middle of the road. Without warning Prado stops the truck, shuts off the engine and headlights. The night is pitch black. He points over to the left, and I see a single light in the distance.

"That's Pedro's house," he says, "one of our farmers. He'll talk to you."

I grab my camera and follow Prado across the road into the dark to meet Pedro Carayuri. He greets us sitting at a long table in front of the simple adobe where he lives with his wife, daughter, and three sons. A small propane tank fuels the light I had seen from the road. Next to the house is the outdoor kitchen where his wife cooks over an open fire. Their earthen oven is in the backyard. The air is brisk. Except for our voices and the sporadic barks of faraway dogs, the night is refreshingly silent. Carayuri—probably in his forties—is wearing a knit cap and a blue windbreaker adorned with white stitching that calls out "La Paz, Bolivia." We shake hands and I explain my mission. He looks somewhat bemused by my intrusion at his remote homestead, but he agrees to entertain my questions.

"Are the beans you grow organic?" I ask.

He offers a warm smile and confirms that his produce is 100 percent organic.

"And what is the difference between an organic bean and a conventional bean?" I want to make sure our definitions match.

"The difference is that the organic bean is grown with no chemical products," he tells me. "Conventional beans are grown with whatever chemicals are necessary to combat what might plague them. But for organic production no chemicals are added and they're produced naturally."

I ask him about his motivation. Why does he grow organic black beans? "Is it for the extra money? Is it for health reasons—your own as you work the land and that of those who eat your beans? Is it out of concern for the environment?"

"Our world is invaded by chemical products," he tells me in a slow and quiet but passionate tone of voice. Organic food is good for those who eat it, he says, and although farming without 'cides means he risks catastrophic crop losses, his goal is to "produce a healthy product free of contamination. We opt for organic for the good health of our customers and to reach a good price with our products without damaging the environment."

"How difficult is it for you to grow the beans without resorting to chemical help?" I ask.

"It's not so difficult. But it needs some dedication, some work and nothing more." The black bean is hearty, he says, not susceptible to crop-devastating pests. "What's important is to keep the fields free of weeds." And that herbicide-free weeding is done with hand tools.

As we talk Carayuri smiles more and acts less skeptical about my late-night visit and barrage of questions. He talks about the tranquility of his lifestyle, far from the hustle of cities. Oranges and papayas grow on his few dry acres. And he acts particularly pleased with his beans when I explain that I'm pretty convinced I bought a can full of them at a market in Oregon.

"I'm proud our product is arriving in the United States," he says.

"And why should the Americans buying your beans in Oregon be confident that they are, in fact, organic?" I ask. "Is there anything further you can say to offer them some sense of security when they buy beans from your farm, beans grown six thousand miles from their dinner plate?"

"Good," he says about the challenge, happy to promote his product. He reiterates that he uses no chemicals and then explains how Biolatina inspectors document his work. Finally, with a sly smile, he invites me to stick around for the entire cultivation cycle—from planting to harvest. "You could watch it all, and as a journalist you would be able to report what you actually see in the fields. This is the guarantee we have," he says about his seductive invitation, "that we use zero chemicals. The consumers of our beans can trust the guarantee that we produce them with natural organic methods."

Carayuri and farmers who work land adjacent to his made the transition to organic farming in 2006, after their land was certified as free from the chemicals that were used on it in years past. Prior to that time Carayuri used 'cides on his fields. The Bolivian Shoji promise of a better price helped convince him to make the change. Lounging in hammocks as we talk are two of Carayuri's fellow farmers. "We want to send our greetings to the American friends who buy our beans," he says.

I thank him for his time and for growing the beans. "I think it's important that we know the origin of what's on our dinner plates," I say, "and that we get a sense of the land and people who produce the food we eat." I'm looking at the real cost of the inexpensive beans lined up on my supermarket shelves: dirt roads, no electricity, rationed potable water, and only one old tractor for all the farmers in the neighborhood.

Carayuri is a leader of the Guaraní indigenous community in the countryside near Charagua. In addition to his farming duties he teaches at the primary school. From his calm yet engaged demeanor I imagine he must be a potent mentor for the local schoolchildren. He has a further message for the Americans who eat his beans. Tell them, he says, "about the poor condition of our homes and roads. We don't have potable water and electricity. We need to have the necessities to live well and to live better."

In that sentence, offered in a quiet but firm voice, Carayuri conflates two at times contradictory Bolivian ambitions. Indigenous traditions revolve around the concept of *Pachamama*, Mother Earth, and hold that living in concert with *Pachamama* allows one the satisfaction of *vivir bien,* living well. *Vivir bien* usually is seen by its proponents in contrast to the capitalist and modern goal of *vivir mejor,* living better.[105]

"There is a great difference," Carayuri tells me, "between this place and where you live. If there is an opportunity with your support," he says about those of us eating his beans, "to help us regarding the lights, water, and dirt roads, we would very much appreciate it."

There we sit next to each other at his basic plank table, two guys named Pedro and Peter. We're prime examples of the schisms separating the First and Third Worlds at the same time as we're prime examples of the opportunities and wastes of globalization. I find out later that Carayuri earns the cash equivalent of some two or three thousand dollars a year, about the same amount my trip to Bolivia cost. I'm carrying a can filled with the beans he grew, beans I bought for less than two bucks some six thousand miles from his farm even though the same type of bean is grown in my Willamette Valley. How much more would (or should) we Market of Choice shoppers pay for these beans if a surcharge would provide him with a paved road and safe drinking water and would bring electricity to his *casita*? Or is it an environmental obscenity that fuel is wasted bringing those beans north when we can grow our own in fertile Oregon?

I am moved by the intimacy of the moment and my comparative wealth. "We Americans should pay more for your beans," I say.

Carayuri is not assuaged. "You Americans could donate something that would be of value to all of us farmers." The Charagua Guaraní community shares its one tractor, plowing the fields just down the road from Carayuri's place, acreage where—when adequate rain falls—he and his neighbors cultivate the black beans.

I thank him for the meeting and reiterate that I am convinced it is important for us to be aware of the history of our food from the farm to the fork.

"Thank you for your visit," he responds, and then he adds, "although I never expected it." I am, in fact, an uninvited guest. But I reflect on how our warm formality makes us sound like the diplomats we are, representing divergent and codependent interests. As we're saying our good-byes, I remember I have a gift for him. I hand him a baggie of the black beans I bought from Harry MacCormack at his Willamette Valley Sunbow Farm in Corvallis.

"These were grown on a farm near my house," I explain to Carayuri, deep in the Chaco night. "They're organic."

He graciously accepts them and somberly proclaims, "I am going to sow these black beans that you brought from the United States." I'm both thrilled and humbled. I've managed to trace my beans back to their source. But it's not what I expected. I've encountered the harsh reality of their origin. The Sunbow Farm beans I gave my new farmer friend are no tractor. They're not water, lights, or a road. But at least I brought something valued from my home to his.

On to Charagua

Yelio Prado and I climb back in the truck. He starts the engine and we head on toward Charagua. It's late, nearly midnight. After just a few kilometers Prado is yawning. I offer to drive but he shakes his head no. After a few more yawns he stops the Nissan and flicks on the dome light. He reaches between the seats and pulls out a plastic bag stuffed with leaves.

"Coca," he says. "You want to try some?"

The coca leaf is not, of course, the famous white powder; the alkaloid for that infamous drug is extracted from the leaf. Legal coca leaf and coca leaf–based products—various elixirs and teas—are sold throughout Bolivia. Coca leaf tea is what was served to me at the US embassy in La Paz. The Spanish conquistadors noted that indigenous people they encountered in the Andes venerated the leaf and chewed it. The result: a quick cure for drowsiness and not much interest in dinner. Prado was tired and we neglected to stop for a meal back at Abapó.

"You want some?" he asks again, showing me how he takes the approximately inch-long oval-shaped leaves, bends them in half, and masticates them with the molars on one side of his mouth. "You don't chew it like you're going to eat it," he says. "You mash it." He stuffs more into his mouth, building a wad of leaves in his cheek.

Here I am, exhausted and hungry in the middle of the night and in the middle of nowhere. I've found my black bean grower. My guide is offering me a participatory ethnographic opportunity. Of course I want some.

I follow his instructions leaf-by-leaf until I, too, pack a wad of the greenery in my cheek. Out comes another plastic sack, a little one filled with a white powder. Prado takes the tip of a coca leaf, loads it with a dose of the powder, and adds it to the mix of saliva and coca in his mouth. He directs me to do the same.

"What's that stuff?" I ask.

"Not cocaine!" he laughs at me.

The white stuff is bicarbonate of soda. It helps free the alkaloids—the psychoactive ingredients—in the coca leaves.

Prado switches off the dome light and starts the engine, and we continue on toward Charagua, chewing coca.

"You feel anything?" Prado asks.

Yes, as a matter of fact, I do. I feel a relaxed sense of well-being: calm and tranquil with—at the same time—a seemingly heightened awareness of outside influences and inner thoughts. I sense a removal from the moment while conscious of being in the moment. How much of this is caused by chewing the coca and how much by suggestion combined with lack of sleep and food, I sure don't know. But one thing is for certain: I'm no longer tired or hungry. Nor am I much concerned about when we'll get to the hotel in Charagua. And I notice that our road chatter—we've been talking with each other since we left Santa Cruz—has ceased. We're alone in our thoughts, thoughts decorated by the stark Chaco landscape that's lit bright for us by the Nissan's passing headlamps.

"Is this coca organic?" I interrupt the comfortable silence in the truck cab, always the journalist.

"No," says my guide, "but there is organic coca."

Epilogue

After tracking my black beans to Bolivia, I felt relatively sanguine about their origin. They probably were shipped north by my amigo at Bolivian Shoji, Tetsuo Kochi, and I'm convinced he bought them from the Guaraní and Tarijeño farmers I met in the Chaco, or their neighbors. And after visiting the Guaraní farmlands, I figure they are as organic as Harry MacCormack's Sunbow Farm in the Willamette Valley (although they sure could use some of our Oregon rain).

Given that the organic walnut trail went cold with Kazakhstan corruption, I remained quite convinced that it was highly unlikely those Trader Joe's walnuts were organic—unless my imaginary friend Nigel existed.

Just as this book was going to press, I received word from the USDA that the National Organic Program investigation into my complaint about the Trader Joe's walnuts reaped results. The notice came in a letter from the NOP's Compliance and Enforcement division. Matthew Michael, the director of the division, wrote:

> *Your complaint alleged that Trader Joe's organically labeled walnuts identified Kazakhstan as the country of origin, although there is no evidence of organic walnut cultivation in the Province [sic] of Kazakhstan.*

Your complaint also disclosed an email exchange from a Trader Joe's representative stating that Trader Joe's sourced walnuts from Kazakhstan. In response to your complaint, Trader Joe's certifying agent, Quality Assurance International, conducted a trace back of Trader Joe's walnut sourcing and suppliers. QAI found no evidence that Trader Joe's sources walnuts from Kazakhstan.

QAI found no evidence that Trader Joe's sources walnuts from Kazakhstan. That the official government investigation concurred with my conclusion definitely was satisfying and vindicating. Of course I'd prefer that Trader Joe's label its products with honesty. But given what I learned during my organic quest, I was not surprised by the USDA's official findings. What was a surprise were the concluding lines of the letter.

The chief investigator added, "In regard to the email exchange from [the] Trader Joe's representative, QAI determined that the employee misspoke and incorrectly stated that Trader Joe's sourced walnuts from Kazakhstan."

Wait a minute! It was not just one errant employee. The Trader Joe's–labeled bags stacked on shelves in Trader Joe's stores identified the nuts as organic and from Kazakhstan. The Trader Joe's brand, representing the entire company and its credibility, lied to me and to all its customers and attempted to cover up the lie with another lie about only sourcing nuts from Kazakhstan when it exhausted supplies in California. After those egregious lies the company refused to answer further questions.

"The case is hereby closed," announced the USDA. "Thank you for bringing this matter to our attention. We appreciate your support of the NOP and the USDA."

Not so fast. Of course I fired a letter back to Matthew Michael, thanking him for the investigation but adding, "I do want to pose a few crucial follow-up questions and ask you to clarify a few points that I believe are especially germane to this case. I do not believe the case can be considered closed as yet. Most important," I wrote, "is your conclusion that QAI found no evidence that Trader Joe's sources walnuts from Kazakhstan. But the next sentence of your letter says, 'QAI determined that the [Trader Joe's] employee misspoke and incorrectly stated that Trader Joe's sourced walnuts from Kazakhstan.'"

Yes, I agreed, the Trader Joe's employee stated the walnuts were organic and that they were sourced from Kazakhstan. "However," my letter to the USDA continued, "he/she so stated not verbally (when perhaps a slip of the tongue is understandable) but in a written email message in response to my query."

Which brought me to the second important point of my follow-up letter: "What occurred here cannot simply be blamed on an employee error in response to my inquiry—whether that response was oral or written. The Trader Joe's brand bag was labeled 'organic' and 'product of Kazakhstan.' Hence the error or fraud here is systemic and not limited to one rogue employee."

I asked that the case not be closed until more investigation addressed several obvious and unanswered questions:

- Why is Trader Joe's labeling walnuts as organic and from Kazakhstan when there are no organic walnuts grown commercially in Kazakhstan?

- Are walnuts sold by Trader Joe's in bags labeled as organic and from Kazakhstan in fact organic and not from Kazakhstan? If so, where are they grown and processed?

- How did QAI determine that Trader Joe's does not sell walnuts from Kazakhstan? Did Trader Joe's admit the error or fraud to QAI, or did QAI determine the error or fraud on its own? What was QAI's trackback process?

- How is it that QAI, since the certification company certified the walnuts as organic and sourced from Kazakhstan, did not determine that there is no organic sector in Kazakhstan prior to my complaint? Does that fact indicate a consequential flaw in their certification process?

- Did the USDA contact Trader Joe's after making its determination? If so, what was Trader Joe's response to the finding that they are selling a product that is grossly misleading because it is mislabeled?

- What are the ramifications of this error or fraud for QAI and Trader Joe's? What does the USDA NOP intend to do with this knowledge vis-à-vis QAI and Trader Joe's? Is there a fine or a letter added to their files or any other punishment? Will the USDA force Trader Joe's to inform its customers of the error or fraud and to change the packaging that identifies the contents as organic walnuts from Kazakhstan?

It is completely unacceptable for the USDA to blame an unnamed errant employee for what obviously is a corporate compliance crisis at Trader Joe's and an institutional breakdown of the USDA National Organic Program. "Is you is or is you ain't my baby," sings Louis Jordan and so many others, and that's how we ought to approach our grocery cart: Is this is or is this ain't organic?

At press time I was still waiting for answers from the USDA while contemplating those billions of dollars in "organic" food trade and that handful of overworked USDA inspectors.

And I cannot help but wonder: Were I not writing a book about the credibility of organic food labeling, and were I not exercising the credentials of an investigative journalist and a university research professor in my request that the USDA investigate the provenance of the walnuts, would the National Organic Program have opened this case? When I first expressed doubt about the credibility of the Trader Joe's label, I was told that just my doubt was not enough to initiate action. It was not until I shared the detailed results of research my staff and I developed that the investigation was launched.

This quest started with the simple goal of establishing if the foreign-born beans and nuts I bought in Oregon were, in fact, organic. I end it with a troubling conclusion. Of course the news here is not just my beans and nuts; that bag and can are indicative of gross flaws plaguing organic commerce. Among the most egregious are the following:

- There is a grotesque lack of business transparency in the international organic food industry.
- There are inherent conflicts of interest when the farmers and the food processors inspected and certified as organic pay the inspection and certification operators for their services.
- Official certificates guaranteeing a product is organic are too easily forged, which is just one example of how susceptible the multibillion-dollar organic food sector is to criminal fraud.
- Farms and food production concerns engaged with both conventional and organic crops and products too easily can commingle the two, thus tainting the organic foodstuffs.
- It's all but impossible to ascertain the quality and purity of a product containing one type of ingredient—apples in apple

juice, for example—from multiple sources, especially when those sources span the globe.

- The globalized organic food industry suffers from inconsistencies in the world's trade and food purity regulations and from lapses in the enforcement of those regulations.

Soul and trust make organic food commerce credible. I trust Tetsuo Kochi, and there's no question in my mind that Pedro Carayuri's soul is indelibly connected with his land and beans. But we cannot travel around the world to taste-test all our dinners.

The Wild Organic West is ripe with opportunities for hustlers. Labels distract, mislead, and lie. Grow your own. Know your farmer. Or belly up to the organic lunch counter and the organic grocery store with your wallet stuffed with banknotes and your fingers crossed for good luck.

Acknowledgments

What were known back in the 1950s—often pejoratively—as health foods have been part of my diet since my childhood days in Madison, Wisconsin. There was a health food store near Capitol Square that my family frequented. Neither my sister nor I can remember the name of it; she thinks it was on State Street; I think it was a few blocks down Washington Street from long-gone Manchester's department store. Funny what we remember vividly and what we don't. I can still sing the Manchester's radio jingle: "Manchester's East and Manchester's on the Square / You'll do all your family shopping there / At Manchester's East and Manchester's on the Square." What I do remember about the Madison health food store is enjoying fresh carrot juice there and my mother buying Joyva brand sesame seed candy bars for us while I was looking at the bizarre pictures (to me) on the cans of Loma Linda brand fake meat.

My diet was different than that of most of my mates at Highlands Mendota Beach School. I would eye their white bread and baloney sandwiches with a certain amount of envy. My lunches were more apt to be whole wheat bread spread with cream cheese and dotted by walnuts. I would get no takers when I tried to trade. I don't recall any talk at home about the food being organic, but most of it was old-fashioned nutritious: Brown rice was a staple, as were fresh fruits and vegetables (when the harsh Wisconsin winters allowed). Soda pop and most processed foods were frowned upon, if not forbidden. I can remember puzzling over the famous Carl Rose *New Yorker* cartoon of a mother and daughter at the dinner table, with its caption by E. B.

White. "It's broccoli, dear," says the mother, and the child's notorious response is, "I say it's spinach and I say the hell with it." I liked the fresh reply, but I didn't understand what was wrong with the spinach.

When the family moved to California, this Wonder Bread–free diet only improved. We bought king salmon fresh off the boats on the Sausalito docks and traveled on Saturday mornings to the San Francisco farmers' market, back in those days when the urban opportunities to skip the supermarket middlemen were rare. The health food store required a trip across the Bay Bridge to Oakland where, out on MacArthur Boulevard, the Food Mill was stocked with a vast array of what was still considered health food in the 1960s. The store dates to 1933, calls itself "Oakland's original health food store," and in this era of Whole Foods marching across America, stays in business with the motto "Shop, learn—be healthy."

Except for a brief rebellious flirtation, stuffing myself with the entire contents of boxes containing a wide variety of Nabisco cookies (what was the attraction?) and too many Egg McMuffins for breakfasts and Big Macs for dinners (I did want fries with that), my diet has been heavily influenced by those early health food years. Thanks go to my parents for instilling in me an awareness of healthy food and its value, along with a palate that developed early and acquired a taste for treats like buttermilk, brussels sprouts, and, course, broccoli.

In addition to her artistry at turning our daily meals into gourmet treats, my wife, Sheila, is merciless with her red pencil as first editor of my work. She diligently guards our kitchen against invasive 'cides, unnecessary additives and preservatives, and against Frankenfoods while working hard to keep what we eat fresh and local. Her food activism—on the global political front and in our home—was the obvious catalyst for this book.

Invaluable research assistance came from University of Oregon graduate teaching fellows and journalists Charles Deitz and Thomas Schmidt, along with Thomas Weber, the founder of *Biorama* magazine. Last-minute fact-checking was handled with aplomb by UO graduate teaching fellow Willemien Calitz. My colleague and friend Daniela Kraus, the managing director of the Forum Journalismus und Medien (FJUM) in Vienna, opened her Austrian Rolodex to me. It's always a comfort to work with someone who knows everybody in town, and with Daniela Kraus and Thomas Schmidt riding shotgun as I cruised across Österreich, I never was more than one of their iPhone calls away from my next source. Further critical research and contact help came from journalist Gunther Müller at FJUM and my neighbor in Vienna, journalist Joe Barth. Star students in my Vienna-based interview techniques course—Darcy Walker, Adam Vaughn, and Victor Flores—shared data they collected on a news-gathering foray in Hungary.

Thanks to Jaclyn Weintraub at the Brewha Tranquil Mountain Retreat in Costa Rica for the introduction to her coffee-growing neighbor. My Spanish tutor, Victor Reyes, double-checked the Costa Rica interviews (while criticizing my grammar, as usual). Further Spanish *ayuda* was provided by Elda Saavedra in Bolivia. Help with translating my Austrian interviews (speaking of grammar), came from the aforementioned Thomas Schmidt and Vienna-based journalist Georg Eckelsberger. Monica Baronchelli at Coldiretti in Rome and Brandi Freeman, graduate teaching fellow in the Romance Languages department at the University of Oregon, translated the Italian. My gracious host at the farm in Pescosolido, Antonello Siragusa, took over the questioning duties for a crucial interview in Italy. (Here's an important lesson: Yelling in Spanish is no substitute for learning Italian.) An olive oil toast to food writer Nancy Harmon-Jenkins for introducing me to Abdelmajid Mahjoub in Tunisia.

My friend and journalism colleague Terry Phillips, fresh off the campaign trail after running for Congress, saved me from a trip to Bakersfield, where he conducted a needed interview. It's always nice to avoid, as Mick Jagger sang, "driving home early Sunday morning through Bakersfield." Phillips, along with my friend the poet André Spears, helped me navigate some needed French language mysteries from Tunisia. My friend since kindergarten, the scientist-at-large Tom Steinberg, graciously read through the manuscript, making sure I kept my 'cides and other food facts straight (although any errors—in the science, the French, or otherwise—are, of course, my own).

My *¡Eureka!* trip to Bolivia was fueled by a serendipitous introduction to my University of Oregon colleague Derrick Hindery, an international studies and geography professor. As luck would have it, one of Hindery's specialties is Bolivia's role in the globalized economy. His book *From Enron to Evo: Pipeline Politics, Global Environmentalism, and Indigenous Rights in Bolivia* kept me company and informed me on the long flight to South America, and he shared his network of sources in Santa Cruz de la Sierra selflessly. *Gracias, compañero.*

Our legendary dean at the university's School of Journalism and Communication, Tim Gleason, was a steadfast supporter of this project (as he has been of all my journalism work since I joined the faculty), including the gallivanting across continents that the book's research necessitated.

It's customary to thank sources who cooperate with research ventures like the quest chronicled here. Of course I appreciate the time and energy key players in the organic food subculture generously provided during the reporting phase of the project. Most of them appear as characters in the story, so there is no need to name them here. But I also want to thank the counterproductive closed-door misanthropic policies of Trader Joe's, Natural Directions, and QAI. Were their public relations agents more agile and sophisticated, my curiosity about the origins of the beans and nuts tracked in these pages perhaps would have been satiated before I realized how problematic it is to decode the truths absent from our food labels. Joseph Pulitzer was correct when he reminded us back in 1903,

"There is not a crime, there is not a dodge, there is not a trick, there is not a swindle, there is not a vice which does not live by secrecy."

It's probably time to explain the genesis of Nigel, because he does bridge my Kazakh fantasies and my Bolivian realities. When I traveled through Bolivia reporting on cocaine, I took the railroad from La Paz to Cochabamba, a fabulous ride that peaked a couple of miles high through the Andes. Swaths of pink flamingos colored a broad lake as the *ferrobus*—a two-car train—rattled down the eastside slopes. I shared a car with an Englishman whom I nicknamed Nigel. Nigel acted with grand Victorian style the part of the stereotypical eccentric British world traveler. His stuffed rucksack, scraggly beard, and clipped accent were the perfect complements to his matter-of-fact announcement of his upcoming itinerary. "After we arrive in Cochabamba," he told me, "I'm off to Santa Cruz to connect with the Death Train on to Brazil." Why is it called the Death Train? Theories abound. Is it because of the notoriously vicious malaria-carrying mosquitoes on board? Or is it because the train was used to carry yellow fever victims off to a mortal quarantine? Did the train get its name because stowaways riding on the roofs of the cars fell asleep on the long journey and slipped off to die trackside? Or is it just because the ride is notorious for being slow, delayed, and excruciatingly uncomfortable—so bad that en route passengers become suicidal? No matter. Nigel personified for me the chance that there could have been an organic walnut orchard in Kazakhstan. After surviving the Death Train and his wanderings for years around South America, he returned home, I allowed myself to imagine, surprised by an unexpected inheritance. Finding Mother England too tame after his years abroad, he pocketed the windfall and decamped for the southern reaches of Kazakhstan, which is famous for its wild walnuts. There he established his modest orchard, I could daydream, living out a quiet life selling his organic crop to Trader Joe's.

My publisher Globe Pequot Press continues to do a fine production job with my books. A special note of appreciation goes to the *Organic* editor, Jon Sternfeld. While this book was still just an idea, he expressed enthusiasm for its quest, convinced that—as the 1923 beef ad in that Connecticut newspaper insisted—we are what we eat. Hence we bloody well ought to know what it is we're swallowing. "This is how we're feeding our family," Sternfeld said about the organic food in his household, "and we're not a Berkeley commune." A toast of organic champagne (of course it exists! A comfortable bubbly is made with organic grapes by Korbel just north of my old California hometown, and is certified by CCOF) to my agent Michelle Tessler and her Tessler Literary Agency for finding the correct house for *Organic*.

I am privileged to hold the James Wallace Chair in Journalism at the University of Oregon, endowed by the *U.S. News & World Report* foreign correspondent and Oregon alumnus James Wallace and his wife, Haya. His datelines ranged from Moscow to Peking to Saigon, from Havana (Fidel Castro reportedly expelled him from Cuba for his reporting) to capitals throughout Latin America. Unfortunately I never had the opportunity to meet Wallace, but from everything I've learned about him, I wager we would have enjoyed each other's company—especially sitting at a saloon in Almaty or La Paz, nursing Bols gin and tonics, trading tales about being on the road in search of the next story.

NOTES

1. "Consumer Demand Drives Growth in the Organic Food Sector," USDA Economic Research Service, www.ers.usda.gov/data-products /chart-gallery/detail.aspx?chartId=35003&ref=collection#.UcRSmq UWPFI.

2. Beth Kowitt, "Inside the Secret World of Trader Joe's," *Fortune,* August 23, 2010.

3. Mark Gardiner, *Build a Brand Like Trader Joe's* (Self-published, 2013), 107–108.

4. Stephen Castle and Douglas Dalby, "Horse Meat in Food Stirs a Furor in the British Isles," *New York Times,* February 9, 2013.

5. "Aldi Confirms up to 100% Horsemeat in Beef Products," *The Guardian,* February 9, 2013.

6. "More Than Mere Fraud," *El País,* March 2, 2013 (English edition with the *International Herald Tribune*).

7. "Statutes of Autonomy of Catalonia 2006," www.gencat.cat/general itat/eng/estatut/titol_preliminar.htm.

8. "About the OCA: Who We Are and What We're Doing," www .organicconsumers.org/aboutus.cfm.

9. "Who We Are," Organic Trade Association, www.ota.com/about/ accomplishments.html.

10. Stewart Brand, ed., *The Next Whole Earth Catalog* (Sausalito, CA: Point, 1980), 75.

11. Brand, ed., *The Next Whole Earth Catalog,* 72.

12. Kimberly Kindy and Lyndsey Layton, "Integrity of Federal 'Organic' Label Questioned," *Washington Post,* July 3, 2009.

13. "Borat Spoof Kazakhstan Anthem Played by Mistake," *Telegraph*, March 23, 2012, www.telegraph.co.uk/news/newsvideo/weird newsvideo/9163577/Borat-spoof-Kazakhstan-anthem-played-by-mistake.html.

14. Alex Marshall, "Please Rise for the National Rap Song," *International Herald Tribune,* November 30, 2012.

15. Vance Packard, *The Hidden Persuaders* (Brooklyn: Ig Publishing, 2007), 35.

16. You can read the entire list of what may be in your "organic" food at this US government website: www.ecfr.gov/cgi-bin/text-idx?c=ecfr &SID=9874504b6f1025eb0e6b67cadf9d3b40&rgn=div6&view=text &node=7:3.1.1.9.32.7&idno=7.

17. "Carrageenan: How a 'Natural' Food Additive is Making Us Sick," www.cornucopia.org/carrageenan-2013.

18. "National Organic Program; Sunset Review (2013)," *Federal Register,* April 30, 2013, www.federalregister.gov/articles/2013/ 05/03/2013-10556/national-organic-program-nop-sunset-review -2013.

19. Cornucopia Institute, *The Organic Watergate—White Paper,* www.cornucopia.org/USDA/OrganicWatergateWhitePaper.pdf.

20. Stephanie Strom, "Has 'Organic' Been Oversized? To Purists, Big Companies Are Co-opting an Industry," *New York Times,* July 8, 2012.

21. "About Eden: Integrity," www.edenfoods.com/about/integrity.php.

22. Steven DuBois, "Organic Apples to Be Antibiotic-free," Associated Press dispatch, April 13, 2013.

23. Ken Picard, "Crop Watcher: International Food Certifier Joe Smillie Aims to Mainstream Organics," *Seven Days* (Burlington, VT), November 11, 2010.

24. "Agriculture South Building, Washington DC," www.gsa.gov/ portal/ext/html/site/hb/category/25431/actionParameter/explore ByBuilding/buildingId/676.

25. "Atlantic Salmon," NOAA Fisheries FishWatch, www.fishwatch .gov/seafood_profiles/species/salmon/species_pages/atlantic_ salmon.htm.

26. Stefan Gehrer interview with Nikolaus Berlakovich on ORF TV, Vienna, Austria, May 3, 2013.

27. Nate Cavalieri, *Costa Rica* (Melbourne: Lonely Planet Publications, 2012), 121.

28. "Fraudulent Organic Certificates," National Organic Program, www.ams.usda.gov/AMSv1.0/ams.fetchTemplateData.do?template= TemplateN&navID=NOPFraudulentCertificates&topNav=&leftNav =NationalOrganicProgram&page=NOPFraudulentCertificates&des cription=NOP%20Fraudulent%20Certificates&acct=nopgeninfo.

29. Tomás Andréu, "Country Tops Farm Chemical Use List," *Latinamerica Press,* September 1, 2011, http://lapress.org/articles .asp?art=6449.

30. Pete Majerle, "First Sewage-Treatment Plant to be Built in San José," *Tico Times,* January 31, 2011, www.ticotimes.net/2011/01/31/ first-sewage-treatment-plant-to-be-built-in-san-jose.

31. "Participatory Guarantee Systems," www.ifoam.org/en/value-chain/ participatory-guarantee-systems-pgs.

32. Hannah J. Ryan, "Labeling Not Easy for Organic Food Vendors," *Tico Times,* August 3, 2012, www.ticotimes.net/2012/08/03/labelling -not-easy-for-organic-food-vendors.

33. "Frequently Asked Questions," Certified Naturally Grown, www .naturallygrown.org/about-cng/frequently-asked-questions.

34. Mary Esch, "Farmers Rejecting Organic Label: Fearing Federal Fines for Minor Violations, More Growers Turn to 'Naturally Grown,'" Associated Press dispatch, August 18, 2013.

35. Stephanie Clifford and Quentin Hardy, "Attention Shoppers: Stores Are Tracking Your Cell," *New York Times,* July 14, 2013.

36. Jaclyn Trop, "A Black Box for Car Crashes," *New York Times,* July 22, 2013.

37. Richard A. Oppel Jr., "Taping of Farm Cruelty Is Becoming the Crime," *New York Times,* April 6, 2013.

38. Peter Laufer, *No Animals Were Harmed: The Controversial Line between Entertainment and Abuse* (Guilford, CT: Lyons Press, 2012), 197.

39. "Welcome to the Agricultural Marketing Service," www.ams .usda.gov/AMSv1.0.

40. Robert Sobel, "Coolidge and American Business," www.calvin -coolidge.org/coolidge-and-american-business.html.

41. "What Is Orthorexia?" www.orthorexia.com.

42. John Paull, "Biodynamic Agriculture: The Journey from Koberwitz to the World, 1924–1938," *Journal of Organic Systems* 6, no. 1 (2011), www.organic-systems.org/journal/Vol_6(1)/pdf/6(1)-Paull-pp27-41.pdf.

43. Wolf D. Storl, *Culture and Horticulture: The Classic Guide to Biodynamic and Organic Gardening* (Berkeley, CA: North Atlantic Books, 2013), 35.

44. "Demeter FAQs," http://demeter-usa.org/about-demeter/demeter -faq.asp.

45. "Social Justice Labeling from Seed to Table," Food Agricultural Justice Project, http://agriculturaljusticeproject.org/?page_id=13.

46. Fair Trade USA homepage, http://fairtradeusa.org.

47. "Product Verification," Non-GMO Project, www.nongmoproject .org/product-verification.

48. "About Animal Welfare Approved (AWA)," www.animal welfareapproved.org/about.

49. Certified Humane homepage, www.certifiedhumane.org/index .php?page=overview.

50. "About Us," American Grassfed, www.americangrassfed.org/ about-us.

51. Fran McManus, "What's In a Name?" *Edible Buffalo,* Summer 2013. McManus's story provides a representative list of various certifiers.

52. Helga Willer, Julia Lernoud, and Diana Schaack, "The European Market for Organic Food 2011," Paper presented at the BioFach Congress, Nuremberg, Germany, February 2013, http://orgprints.org/22345/19/willer-2013-session-european-market.pdf.

53. "Italian Police Uncover Organic Food Fraud," Xinhua news service, July 20, 2013, http://news.xinhuanet.com/english/world/2013-07/20/c_125037496.htm.

54. "North American Olive Oil Association Introduces Olive Oil Seal Program," www.naooa.org/sealprogram.

55. "International Olive Council Mission Statement," www.internationaloliveoil.org/estaticos/view/100-mission-statement.

56. Stephanie Armour, John Lippert, and Michael Smith, "Food Sickens Millions as Company-Paid Checks Find It Safe," Bloomberg, October 11, 2012. Powell's full study is available here: http://krex.k-state.edu/dspace/bitstream/handle/2097/15431/PowellFood Control2013.pdf?sequence=3.

57. Meg Carter, "With Fraud on the Rise, Do You Know the Real Origin of Your Food?" The Independent, February 10, 2011.

58. Sabrina Tavernise, "FDA Says Importers Must Audit Food Safety," New York Times, July 26, 2013, www.nytimes.com/2013/07/27/health/fda-proposes-rules-to-ensure-safety-of-imported-food.html?_r=0.

59. "FDA Takes Step to Help Insure the Safety of Imported Food," FDA press release, July 26, 2013, www.fda.gov/NewsEvents/Newsroom/PressAnnouncements/ucm362610.htm.

60. General Mills neglected to incorporate the second apostrophe when it abbreviated "and."

61. Janney and McKendrick v. General Mills, http://cspinet.org/new/pdf/complaint_nature_valley.pdf.

62. Mike Esterl, "Some Food Companies Ditch 'Natural' Label," Wall Street Journal, November 6, 2013.

63. Stephanie Strom, "Major Grocer to Label Foods with Gene-Modified Content," New York Times, March 9, 2013.

64. "GMA Leadership," www.gmaonline.org/about/board-councils -committees/gma-leadership.

65. Michael Pollan, *Food Rules: An Eater's Manual* (New York: Penguin Books, 2009), 9.

66. Kyle Steenland, Tony Fletcher, and David A. Savitz, "Epidemiologic Evidence on the Health Effects of Perfluorooctanoic Acid (PFOA)," *Environmental Health Perspectives* 118, no. 8 (August 2010), www .ncbi.nlm.nih.gov/pmc/articles/PMC2920088.

67. Holland Taylor, "Is Popcorn Giving You Heart Disease?" *Prevention,* May 12, 2013.

68. David Lazarus, "Carcinogen Worries Stick to Food Packaging," *Los Angeles Times,* July 30, 2008.

69. "Basic Information," EPA, www.epa.gov/oppt/pfoa/pubs/pfoainfo .html.

70. Michael Russell, "Labels Often Tell a Fish Story," *The Oregonian,* February 22, 2013.

71. "Seafood Fraud: Overview," Oceana, http://oceana.org/en/ our-work/promote-responsible-fishing/seafood-fraud/overview.

72. William W. Watson, "Trust, but Verify: Reagan, Gorbachev, and the INF Treaty," *The Hilltop Review,* Western Washington University, Fall 2011, 38.

73. Christopher Pala, "Tough Job? Try Reporting on Corruption in Kazakhstan," Inter Press Service, October 26, 2012.

74. "Kazakh Journalist in Surgery after Being Shot, Stabbed," Committee to Protect Journalists news alert, April 19, 2012, http://cpj .org/2012/04/kazakh-journalist-in-surgery-after-being-shot-stab.php.

75. "Kazakhstan: Journalist Badly Beaten," Human Rights Watch, August 22, 2013, www.hrw.org/news/2013/08/22/kazakhstan -journalist-badly-beaten.

76. "Court Issues Warrant for Two Months' Arrest of Zhanaozen Ex-Mayor," Interfax-Kazakhstan News Agency, February 9, 2012, www .interfax.kz/?lang=eng&int_id=expert_opinions&news_id=820.

77. Rayhan Demytrie and Shodiyor Eshaev, "Abuse Claims Sweep Kazakh Oil Riot Trial," BBC News, May 15, 2012, www.bbc.co.uk/news/world-asia-18055249.

78. "Kazakhstan: General Information, Political Climate," Business Anti-Corruption Portal, www.business-anti-corruption.com/country -profiles/europe-central-asia/kazakhstan/show-all.aspx.

79. "Kazakhstan Will Wage Uncompromising War on Corruption—Nazarbayev," Interfax-Kazakhstan News Agency, September 1, 2011, www.interfax.kz/?lang=eng&int_id=expert_opinions&news_id=513.

80. "Corruption by Country/Territory," Transparency International, www.transparency.org/country.

81. Central Asia Invest: Projects Funded under the Call for Proposals 2007–2008, EuropeAid Cooperation Office, http://ec.europa.eu/europeaid/ infopoint/publications/europeaid/documents/199a_en.pdf.

82. "Discover Kazakhstan: Agricultural Sector," www.kazakhembus .com/page/agricultural-sector.

83. Maral Zhantaykyzy, "Almaty's Tram Café Is Favourite Ride for Romance," Astana Times, February 20, 2013.

84. Worldwide Opportunities on Organic Farms Kazakhstan homepage, www.wwoofkazakhstan.org/home.

85. "Experiences of Pierre, France," WWOOF Kazakhstan, www .wwoofkazakhstan.org/about/news/news/experiences-of-pierre -france/?cHash=df76597281.

86. Jamil Anderlini, "Chinese Police Smell a Rat after 'Mutton' Sickness," Financial Times, May 4/5, 2013.

87. "Bolivia," The World Factbook, Central Intelligence Agency, https:// www.cia.gov/library/publications/the-world-factbook/geos/bl.html.

88. "Former Governor Tom McCall's Message to Visitors," Oregon Public Broadcasting, March 19, 2013, www.opb.org/artsandlife/ article/former-governor-tom-mccall-message-visitors.

89. Lizzie Melby Jespersen, Organic Certification in Selected European Countries: Control Fees and Size of the Sector, CERTCOST

report, July 2, 2011, www.certcost.org/Lib/CERTCOST/Deliverable/ D13_D8.pdf.

90. "About Us," Latco International, www.latcointernational.com/ paginas/About.htm.

91. Matt Stevens, "Venice's New Bloom," *Los Angeles Times,* December 11, 2012, http://articles.latimes.com/2012/dec/11/local/la -me-rose-avenue-20121211.

92. Café Gratitude homepage, http://cafegratitudevenice.com/about.

93. "Choices on the Farm," Syngenta, www.syngenta.com/global/ corporate/en/grow-more-from-less/caseStudy1/Pages/choices-on- the-farm.aspx.

94. Kimberly A. C. Wilson, "GMO Beet Crops Sow Anger," *Oregonian,* July 16, 2013.

95. "An Organic Fraud in Italy," AssoBio, www.federbio.it/files/587 .pdf.

96. "Italian Police Suspect Fake E European Organic Food Was Imported through Malta," *Times of Malta,* April 15, 2013, www.times ofmalta.com/articles/view/20130415/local/italian-police-suspect- fake-e-european-organic-food-was-imported-through-malta.465583.

97. Michael Braun and Jost Maurin, "War Against the Biofälscher," *Taz,* May 20, 2013, www.taz.de/Italien-und-Lebensmittelbetrueger/ !116553.

98. "Operation 'Puss in Boots,'" Ethical and Environmental Certification Institute, December 8, 2011, http://old.icea.info/ tabid/57/articleType/ArticleView/articleId/484/Default.aspx.

99. Siobhán Dowling, "The World from Berlin: Germany's Food Contamination Scandal Widens," *Spiegel,* January 5, 2011, www .spiegel.de/international/germany/the-world-from-berlin-germany- s-food-contamination-scandal-widens-a-737952.html.

100. Hannah Fuchs, "What Makes an Egg Organic?" Deutsche Welle, February 2, 2013, www.dw.de/what-makes-an-egg-organic/ a-16628236.

101. "Nabisco Goes Organic with Traditional Cookies, Crackers," McClatchy-Tribune Information Services, April 1, 2007, www .jsonline.com/features/food/29228384.html.

102. Mehmet Oz and Mike Roizen, "Avoid BPA for Safety," *Register-Guard* (Eugene, OR), July 13, 2013.

103. "Triatomine Bug FAQs," Centers for Disease Control and Prevention, www.cdc.gov/parasites/chagas/gen_info/vectors.

104. "Casa Fiesta," Bruce Foods, www.brucefoods.com/casa-fiesta .html.

105. Derrick Hindery, *From Enron to Evo: Pipeline Politics, Global Environmentalism, and Indigenous Rights in Bolivia* (Tucson: University of Arizona Press, 2013), 2.

INDEX

About the Author

Peter Laufer, PhD, is the author of more than a dozen books that deal with social and political issues—from borders and identity to human relationships with other animals—including *The Dangerous World of Butterflies: The Startling Subculture of Criminals, Collectors, and Conservationists*; *The Elusive State of Jefferson: A Journey through the 51st State*; *Mission Rejected: U.S. Soldiers Who Say No to Iraq*; *Wetback Nation: The Case for Opening the Mexican-American Border*; and *Slow News: A Manifesto for the Critical News Consumer*. He is the James Wallace Chair Professor in Journalism at the University of Oregon School of Journalism and Communication. More about his books, documentary films, and broadcasts, which have won the George Polk, Robert F. Kennedy, Edward R. Murrow, and other awards, can be found at peterlaufer.com.